The Ultimate New York City Tr[avel Guide]
(2025 Edition)

Everything You Need to Know – Top Attractions, Where to Eat, Best Places to Visit & Local Tips

Grace Bennett

Grace Bennett

Copyright Notice

No part of this book may be reproduced, written, electronic, recorded, or photocopied without written permission from the publisher or author.

The exception would be in the case of brief quotations embodied in critical articles or reviews and pages where permission is specifically granted by the publisher or author.

Although every precaution has been taken to verify the accuracy of the information contained herein, the author and publisher assume no responsibility for any errors or omissions. No liability is assumed for damages that may result from the use of the information contained within.

All Rights Reserved ©2025

The Ultimate New York City Travel Guide (2025 Edition)

TABLE OF CONTENTS

INTRODUCTION — 9

- Quick Facts About New York City — 10
- Why Visit New York? — 11
- History of New York — 13
- New York's Geography and Climate — 15
- Best Time to Visit New York — 16

CHAPTER 1: PLANNING YOUR TRIP TO NEW YORK CITY — 19

- Currency and Banking in New York — 19
- Entry Requirements and Travel Documentation — 21
- Budgeting for Your New York Trip — 22
- Travel Insurance Considerations — 24
- What to Pack for New York — 26

CHAPTER 2: GETTING TO NEW YORK CITY — 31

- By Air: Major Airports — 31
- By Train: Regional and International Rail Connections — 33
- By Car: Road Travel Tips and Routes — 35
- By Ferry: Arrival from Neighboring Countries — 37

CHAPTER 3: TOP CITIES IN NEW YORK CITY — 41

- Jersey City, New Jersey — 41
- Hoboken, New Jersey — 43
- Yonkers, New York — 45
- Tarrytown, New York — 47
- Sleepy Hollow, New York — 50
- Beacon, New York — 52
- Cold Spring, New York — 54

CHAPTER 4: WHERE TO STAY IN NEW YORK CITY — 57

- Luxury Hotels — 57
- Top 5 Luxury Hotels — 57
- Mid-Range Hotels — 68
- Top 5 Mid-Range Hotels — 68

BUDGET ACCOMMODATION	**80**
TOP 5 BUDGET ACCOMMODATION	80
BOUTIQUE HOTELS	**91**
TOP 5 BOUTIQUE HOTELS	91
BUSINESS HOTEL	**104**
TOP 5 BUSINESS HOTEL	104

CHAPTER 5: TOP ATTRACTIONS IN NEW YORK CITY — 119

STATUE OF LIBERTY AND ELLIS ISLAND	119
CENTRAL PARK	121
TIMES SQUARE	123
EMPIRE STATE BUILDING	125
BROADWAY AND THE THEATER DISTRICT	127
METROPOLITAN MUSEUM OF ART (THE MET)	129
BROOKLYN BRIDGE	131
MEMORIAL AND MUSEUM	133
9/11 ROCKEFELLER CENTER AND TOP OF THE ROCK OBSERVATION DECK	135
THE HIGH LINE	137
MUSEUM OF MODERN ART (MOMA)	139
ONE WORLD OBSERVATORY	141
FIFTH AVENUE SHOPPING	143
CHINATOWN	145
ST. PATRICK'S CATHEDRAL	147

CHAPTER 6: GETTING AROUND NEW YORK CITY — 149

SUBWAY	149
BUSES	150
TAXIS AND RIDESHARES (UBER, LYFT)	151
WALKING	152
BIKING (CITI BIKE)	153
FERRIES	155
DRIVING AND CAR RENTALS	156
TRAINS (COMMUTER RAIL)	158
TRAINS (COMMUTER RAIL) ☐	160

CHAPTER 7: SHOPPING IN NEW YORK CITY — 163

FIFTH AVENUE AND LUXURY SHOPPING	163
SOHO: BOUTIQUE SHOPS AND HIGH FASHION	164
WILLIAMSBURG: VINTAGE AND INDIE STORES	166
CHELSEA FLEA MARKETS	167

SHOPPING MALLS AND DEPARTMENT STORES	**169**

CHAPTER 8: NEW YORK'S FOOD AND NIGHTLIFE — 171

MUST-TRY DISHES IN NEW YORK	**171**
STREET FOOD AND FOOD TRUCKS	**181**
BEST RESTAURANTS IN NYC	**183**
BROADWAY SHOWS AND OFF-BROADWAY PRODUCTIONS	**185**
MUSIC VENUES: JAZZ CLUBS, CONCERT HALLS, AND NIGHTCLUBS	**187**
COMEDY CLUBS: THE STAND, COMEDY CELLAR, AND MORE	**189**

CHAPTER 9: PARKS AND OUTDOOR ACTIVITIES IN NEW YORK CITY — 191

EXPLORING CENTRAL PARK	**191**
PROSPECT PARK AND BROOKLYN GREEN SPACES	**193**
RIVERSIDE PARK AND THE HUDSON RIVER	**195**
THE HIGH LINE AND ELEVATED URBAN PARKS	**197**
BIKING IN NYC: BEST ROUTES AND BIKE RENTALS	**199**
BEACHES NEAR NEW YORK CITY	**201**

CHAPTER 10: DAY TRIPS AND EXCURSIONS — 205

LONG ISLAND: BEACHES AND VINEYARDS	**205**
THE HAMPTONS: LUXURY GETAWAY	**208**
HUDSON VALLEY AND CATSKILLS	**211**
BEAR MOUNTAIN STATE PARK	**213**
PHILADELPHIA	**215**
WASHINGTON, D.C.	**218**
NIAGARA FALLS	**221**

CHAPTER 11: SEASONAL EVENTS AND FESTIVALS IN NEW YORK — 225

NEW YEAR'S EVE IN TIMES SQUARE	**225**
MACY'S THANKSGIVING DAY PARADE	**227**
NEW YORK FASHION WEEK	**229**
PRIDE WEEK AND PARADE	**231**
VILLAGE HALLOWEEN PARADE	**233**
HOLIDAY MARKETS AND ICE SKATING RINKS	**236**

CHAPTER 12: MUSEUMS AND ART GALLERIES — 239

METROPOLITAN **M**USEUM OF **A**RT — 239
MUSEUM OF **M**ODERN **A**RT (M**O**MA) — 242
AMERICAN **M**USEUM OF **N**ATURAL **H**ISTORY — 244
GUGGENHEIM **M**USEUM — 246
WHITNEY **M**USEUM OF **A**MERICAN **A**RT — 248

CHAPTER 13: 5 DAY NEW YORK CITY ITINERARY — 251

DAY 1: **I**CONIC **M**ANHATTAN & **M**IDTOWN — 251
DAY 2: **C**ENTRAL **P**ARK, **M**USEUMS, AND **F**IFTH **A**VENUE — 254
DAY 3: **L**OWER **M**ANHATTAN & **B**ROOKLYN — 257
DAY 4: **M**USEUMS AND **N**EIGHBORHOODS — 260
DAY 5: **D**AY **T**RIP OR **R**ELAX — 263

CHAPTER 14: PRACTICAL TRAVEL INFORMATION — 267

LANGUAGE **T**IPS AND **U**SEFUL **P**HRASES — 267
HEALTH AND **S**AFETY **T**IPS — 269
EMERGENCY **C**ONTACTS AND **S**ERVICES — 271
INTERNET AND **C**ONNECTIVITY — 273
ACCESSIBILITY IN **N**EW **Y**ORK **C**ITY — 274

CHAPTER 15: TRAVEL TIPS AND FINAL THOUGHTS — 277

FREQUENTLY **A**SKED **Q**UESTIONS — 277
TIPS FOR **F**IRST-**T**IME **V**ISITORS — 279
TIPS FOR **S**OLO **T**RAVELERS — 281
HOW TO **A**VOID **T**OURIST **T**RAPS — 283
WHAT TO **D**O IN **C**ASE OF **E**MERGENCIES — 285
USEFUL **T**RAVEL **A**PPS — 287

The Ultimate New York City Travel Guide (2025 Edition)

Grace Bennett

The Ultimate New York City Travel Guide (2025 Edition)

INTRODUCTION

Are you overwhelmed by the sheer size and energy of New York City? Not sure where to start or what you absolutely can't miss? Worried about navigating the busy streets, finding the best food, or choosing the right neighborhood to stay in? Are you concerned about the best ways to move around, avoid tourist traps, or experience the city like a local? Confused about the right time to visit or what festivals you can't miss? Wondering how to balance your budget while still seeing top attractions? What about dealing with airport chaos, complex subway systems, or securing entry tickets to popular sites? And how do you plan for the unexpected in a city that never sleeps?

Welcome to **The Ultimate New York City Travel Guide (2025 Edition)**—your one-stop resource to answer all these questions and more. Whether you're a first-time visitor, a seasoned traveler, or even someone just looking for fresh experiences in the Big Apple, this guide is designed to help you navigate the city with ease, confidence, and excitement.

We'll walk you through every step of planning your adventure, from entry requirements to budgeting and packing tips, so you'll arrive prepared. Once you're in the city, our chapters on accommodation, transportation, and top attractions will ensure you experience New York at its finest—whether you're seeking luxury or traveling on a budget.

Looking for insider tips? We've got you covered! From hidden gems in iconic neighborhoods to local advice on the best food trucks, nightlife, and shopping spots, this guide will help you experience New York like a true local. Plus, our 5-day itinerary will take the stress out of planning, ensuring you make the most of your time in this bustling metropolis.

Filled with practical travel information, seasonal event highlights, day trip suggestions, and even tips for solo travelers, this guidebook is your ultimate companion to discovering New York's rich culture, world-class landmarks, and unique charm.

Let us help you craft the trip of a lifetime, uncovering the very best of New York City in 2025!

Quick Facts About New York City

New York City, often referred to as "The Big Apple" or simply "NYC," is one of the most iconic cities in the world, known for its vibrant culture, towering skyscrapers, and fast-paced lifestyle. Here are some essential quick facts that capture the essence of this bustling metropolis:

Population:
NYC is the most populous city in the United States, with a population of over 8.8 million people spread across its five boroughs: Manhattan, Brooklyn, Queens, The Bronx, and Staten Island. This immense diversity makes it one of the most culturally and ethnically varied cities in the world, with more than 800 languages spoken.

Area:
The city covers approximately 302.6 square miles (784 km²), making it large but incredibly dense. Manhattan, the city's heart, spans just 22.7 square miles, yet is home to over 1.6 million people.

The Five Boroughs:
NYC is made up of five distinct boroughs, each with its unique character:

The Ultimate New York City Travel Guide (2025 Edition)

Manhattan: The cultural, financial, and entertainment core of the city, home to Times Square, Central Park, Wall Street, and Broadway.

Brooklyn: Known for its artistic vibe, hip neighborhoods, and landmarks like the Brooklyn Bridge and Coney Island.

Queens: The largest borough by area and one of the most diverse, with vibrant cultural enclaves and landmarks like Flushing Meadows and Citi Field.

The Bronx: The birthplace of hip-hop and home to Yankee Stadium and the Bronx Zoo.

Staten Island: A more suburban borough accessible by ferry, known for its parks and nature reserves.

History:
Originally founded as New Amsterdam by Dutch settlers in 1624, the city was later renamed New York in 1664 when the British took control. It has since grown into a global financial and cultural capital.

Economy:
NYC is a global financial hub, home to Wall Street, the New York Stock Exchange (NYSE), and many Fortune 500 companies. Key industries include finance, media, technology, fashion, and tourism. The city's GDP is one of the highest in the world, and it plays a pivotal role in international business.

Tourism:
New York City attracts over 60 million visitors annually. Tourists flock to its world-famous landmarks like the Statue of Liberty, Empire State Building, Times Square, and Central Park. Broadway shows, museums, and culinary experiences add to its global appeal.

Transportation:
NYC has an extensive public transportation system, including subways, buses, taxis, and ferries. The Metropolitan Transportation Authority (MTA) operates one of the largest and busiest subway systems in the world, with 472 stations and over 1.7 billion annual riders. The city also has three major airports: John F. Kennedy International (JFK), LaGuardia (LGA), and Newark Liberty International (EWR).

Iconic Skyline:
The New York City skyline is world-renowned, featuring some of the tallest and most famous buildings, including the One World Trade Center, the Empire State Building, and the Chrysler Building. Its skyline is a testament to the city's architectural history and innovation.

Culture:
NYC is a global center for art, music, theater, and fashion. From the galleries of the Metropolitan Museum of Art and MoMA to the performances on Broadway and the thriving street art scene, the city's cultural offerings are vast. NYC also hosts world-class events like New York Fashion Week, the Tribeca Film Festival, and the Macy's Thanksgiving Day Parade.

Sports:
New York is home to some of the most famous sports teams in the world, including the New York Yankees (MLB), the New York Mets (MLB), the New York Knicks (NBA), the Brooklyn Nets (NBA), and the New York Rangers (NHL). The city's sports culture is a significant part of its identity, and games are major events for locals and tourists alike.

Climate:

New York City has a humid subtropical climate, with cold winters and hot, humid summers. Winters can see temperatures drop below freezing with occasional snowstorms, while summers are often marked by temperatures exceeding 90°F (32°C).

Why Visit New York?

1. Iconic Landmarks

New York City is home to some of the most recognizable landmarks in the world. From the towering **Statue of Liberty** to the historic **Empire State Building** and the dazzling lights of **Times Square**, NYC's landmarks are must-see sights. Climb to the top of the **One World Observatory** or visit **Rockefeller Center** for panoramic views of the city's skyline, or take a stroll across the **Brooklyn Bridge** for unforgettable views of Manhattan.

2. Cultural and Artistic Hub

NYC is a cultural capital, boasting world-class museums, galleries, and theaters. Art lovers can explore the **Metropolitan Museum of Art (The Met)**, the **Museum of Modern Art (MoMA)**, and the **Guggenheim Museum**, which showcase masterpieces from across the globe. Broadway fans can catch an award-winning show, while off-Broadway productions offer unique and intimate theater experiences.

3. Diverse Food Scene

The culinary diversity in New York is unparalleled. From Michelin-starred restaurants to mouthwatering street food, you can sample dishes from every corner of the globe. Whether you're craving New York-style pizza, a bagel with lox, or something from a food truck, NYC offers endless choices. Areas like **Chinatown**, **Little Italy**, and **Koreatown** provide authentic international flavors, while local favorites like pastrami sandwiches and hot dogs are easy to find.

4. Shopping Paradise

New York is a haven for shoppers. **Fifth Avenue** is the epitome of luxury shopping, lined with high-end stores like Gucci, Prada, and Tiffany & Co. But there's also **SoHo**, known for trendy boutiques, and **Williamsburg** in Brooklyn, offering vintage shops and indie designers. Whether you're looking for designer clothes, unique vintage finds, or just some souvenirs, NYC is a shopper's dream.

5. Vibrant Nightlife

New York truly earns its nickname "The City That Never Sleeps." From swanky rooftop bars with breathtaking views to legendary jazz clubs in Harlem, there's something for every kind of night owl. The nightlife scene includes everything from speakeasy-style cocktail bars to world-class nightclubs, live music venues, and comedy clubs like **Comedy Cellar**, ensuring that your evenings in the city are just as exciting as your days.

6. Rich History

New York City has a fascinating history, from its days as a Dutch colony (New Amsterdam) to its role as the gateway for millions of immigrants arriving through **Ellis Island**. Historical sites like **The 9/11 Memorial and Museum** honor the city's past, while neighborhoods like **Harlem** and **Greenwich Village** reflect NYC's contribution to the arts, music, and social movements.

7. Parks and Outdoor Spaces

Despite its urban reputation, New York City offers stunning green spaces. **Central Park** is a must-visit for its walking trails, lakes, and iconic spots like Bethesda Terrace and the Bow Bridge. Beyond Central Park, there's **Prospect Park** in Brooklyn, the **High Line** (a unique elevated park), and waterfront parks like **Riverside Park** along the Hudson River, where you can relax and enjoy the outdoors.

8. Events and Festivals

New York hosts countless events and festivals throughout the year. From the world-famous **New Year's Eve in Times Square** and the **Macy's Thanksgiving Day Parade**, to cultural celebrations like **Pride Week** and the **Village Halloween Parade**, the city is always buzzing with activities. For fashion lovers, **New York Fashion Week** is a highlight, while foodies can enjoy restaurant weeks and food festivals all year long.

9. Unmatched Energy and Vibe

New York's energy is like nowhere else. The fast pace, the diversity of people, the mix of cultures, and the constant flow of activity make it a city that feels alive 24/7. Every corner of the city tells a story, and no two days are ever the same. Whether you're sipping coffee in a quiet café in **Greenwich Village** or watching the hustle and bustle in **Times Square**, the energy is contagious.

10. Gateway to Nearby Destinations

New York's location also makes it a perfect hub for day trips. Take a quick train ride to scenic destinations like the **Hudson Valley**, **Bear Mountain**, or **The Hamptons** for a relaxing getaway. You can even plan day trips to nearby cities like **Philadelphia** and **Washington, D.C.**, which are just a few hours away by train.

History of New York

1. Early Inhabitants and Native Tribes

Before European explorers arrived, the region we now call New York was inhabited by Native American tribes, primarily the **Lenape**. The Lenape lived in the areas surrounding present-day New York Harbor, engaging in farming, fishing, and trading. Their extensive trade networks and knowledge of the land played an important role in the city's early development.

2. The Dutch and New Amsterdam (1609–1664)

In 1609, English explorer **Henry Hudson**, sailing under the Dutch East India Company, arrived in the area that would become New York Harbor. The Dutch soon recognized the potential of the region for trade and in 1624 established a colony called **New Netherland**. A year later, the settlement of **New Amsterdam** was founded on the southern tip of Manhattan Island, where it quickly grew as a trading post due to its strategic location.

New Amsterdam became a bustling port under the Dutch, who built the city's first street grid, which included **Wall Street**, originally a defensive wall to protect the settlement. Dutch influence still echoes in New York today, seen in place names like **Brooklyn** (from Breuckelen) and **Harlem** (from Haarlem).

3. British Control and the Birth of New York (1664–1776)

In 1664, the British seized control of New Amsterdam without a fight and renamed it **New York** in honor of the Duke of York, later King James II. Under British rule, the city grew rapidly, becoming a vital port for trade between Europe, the Caribbean, and the American colonies.

By the mid-18th century, New York had become a thriving commercial center. However, tensions between the American colonies and the British government began to rise, culminating in the **American Revolution**. New York was a critical battleground during the war, with the **Battle of Long Island** in 1776 marking one of the largest battles of the war. The city was occupied by British forces for much of the Revolutionary War.

4. Post-Revolution and Growth (1776–1860)

After the war, in 1783, New York emerged as an important symbol of American independence. It briefly served as the first capital of the United States from 1789 to 1790, and George Washington was inaugurated as the nation's first president in **Federal Hall** on Wall Street.

Throughout the 19th century, New York became a major center of immigration and commerce. The opening of the **Erie Canal** in 1825 transformed the city into a gateway for goods moving between the Atlantic Ocean and the American interior. This also positioned New York as a financial powerhouse. Waves of immigrants, primarily from Ireland, Germany, and later Italy and Eastern Europe, arrived through **Ellis Island** starting in the 1800s, shaping the city's cultural diversity. By 1860, New York was the largest city in the United States.

5. The Civil War and Reconstruction Era (1861–1890)

During the Civil War (1861–1865), New York's economy boomed, largely due to its role in supplying the Union army with goods and financial support. However, the city was also home to significant opposition to the war, most notably in the form of the **New York City Draft Riots** of 1863, which resulted in violent clashes, destruction, and deaths.

The Ultimate New York City Travel Guide (2025 Edition)

In the post-war era, New York entered a period of tremendous growth. Industrialization transformed the city into a manufacturing hub, while Wall Street emerged as the center of American finance. The construction of iconic bridges like the **Brooklyn Bridge** (completed in 1883) further solidified New York's status as a modern metropolis.

6. The Gilded Age and Immigration Boom (1890–1920)

The late 19th and early 20th centuries saw New York City emerge as the cultural and financial capital of the United States. This period, known as the **Gilded Age**, was marked by the rise of powerful business magnates like **John D. Rockefeller** and **J.P. Morgan**, whose wealth was reflected in the city's grand buildings and lavish lifestyles.

At the same time, the city experienced a massive influx of immigrants from Europe. By the early 20th century, New York's population had exploded, and neighborhoods like the **Lower East Side** became densely populated immigrant communities. In 1904, the city opened its first subway line, which helped connect the expanding boroughs.

7. The Roaring Twenties and the Great Depression (1920–1940)

The 1920s were a time of prosperity and cultural vibrancy in New York. The **Harlem Renaissance** flourished during this time, with Harlem becoming a cultural center for African-American literature, music, and art. Jazz clubs, speakeasies, and the theater scene in **Broadway** also thrived.

However, the prosperity of the 1920s came to a halt with the **Great Depression** in 1929. The **stock market crash** on Wall Street plunged the nation into economic hardship, and New York was deeply affected. Unemployment and poverty soared, but under the leadership of Mayor **Fiorello La Guardia**, the city began to recover, largely through public works projects that provided jobs and infrastructure improvements.

8. Post-War Boom and Modern Era (1940–2000)

After World War II, New York City entered a period of immense growth and development. The construction of massive infrastructure projects, like bridges, highways, and housing complexes, transformed the city. It also became the headquarters for the newly formed **United Nations** in 1952, solidifying its status as a global city.

In the 1970s, New York faced economic challenges, including high crime rates and a fiscal crisis. However, the city rebounded in the 1980s and 1990s with a surge in real estate, finance, and tourism. Iconic developments like **Times Square's revitalization** and the rise of Wall Street as a global financial hub cemented its resurgence.

9. 9/11 and Resilience (2001–Present)

On September 11, 2001, New York City experienced one of the darkest days in its history when the **World Trade Center** towers were attacked, killing nearly 3,000 people. The event deeply impacted the city and the world, but New York displayed incredible resilience. The site was eventually rebuilt, with the **One World Trade Center** rising as a symbol of strength and renewal. The **9/11 Memorial and Museum** now stands as a tribute to the lives lost and the city's perseverance.

In recent decades, New York has continued to grow and evolve. It remains a cultural, financial, and technological leader, attracting millions of visitors and new residents each year. Today, it is known for its diversity, world-class museums, thriving arts scene, and status as a global city that shapes culture, finance, and innovation on an international scale.

Grace Bennett

The Ultimate New York City Travel Guide (2025 Edition)

New York's Geography and Climate

Geography

Location and Boroughs: New York City is located in the northeastern United States, in the state of New York. It lies at the confluence of the Hudson River and the East River, on the Atlantic coast. The city is made up of five boroughs:

Manhattan: The central borough, home to the iconic skyline and many of the city's most famous landmarks.

Brooklyn: Located to the south and east of Manhattan, known for its cultural diversity, neighborhoods, and attractions like Coney Island.

Queens: Situated to the east of Manhattan, it's the largest borough by area and known for its multicultural communities and major airports.

The Bronx: Located to the north of Manhattan, it's known for its rich history and institutions like Yankee Stadium and the Bronx Zoo.

Staten Island: The southernmost borough, connected to Manhattan by the Staten Island Ferry, known for its suburban feel and natural parks.

Islands and Waterfronts: New York City is situated on several islands. Manhattan Island is the most famous, but the city also encompasses parts of Long Island, which includes Brooklyn and Queens. The city's waterfronts along the Hudson River, East River, and Harlem River provide stunning views and are integral to its layout.

Parks and Green Spaces: Despite its urban density, New York City boasts a significant amount of green space. **Central Park**, a sprawling 843-acre park in Manhattan, is one of the city's most famous landmarks. Other notable green spaces include **Prospect Park** in Brooklyn, **Flushing Meadows-Corona Park** in Queens, and the **High Line**, an elevated park built on a former railway track.

Natural Features: The city's geography includes a mix of natural and urban features. The **Harlem River** and the **East River** separate Manhattan from the Bronx and Queens, respectively, while the **Hudson River** lies to the west of Manhattan. The city also has several smaller waterways and lakes, which contribute to its diverse landscape.

Climate

New York City experiences a humid subtropical climate with distinct seasons, characterized by:

Winter (December to February): Winters in NYC are cold, with average temperatures ranging from the mid-30s to low 40s Fahrenheit (1-5°C). Snow is common, though snowfall amounts can vary. Snowstorms can occasionally bring heavy accumulations, but winters are generally manageable with cold winds and occasional ice.

Spring (March to May): Spring is a pleasant time to visit New York, with temperatures gradually warming up. Average temperatures range from the 40s to 70s Fahrenheit (4-25°C). The city's parks and gardens come alive with blooming flowers and greenery, making it a great time for outdoor activities and sightseeing.

Summer (June to August): Summers in New York are hot and humid, with temperatures often reaching into the 80s and 90s Fahrenheit (27-35°C). Humidity levels can make the heat feel more intense. The city's waterfronts and parks offer respite, and outdoor events and festivals are abundant. Be prepared for occasional thunderstorms, which are common in the summer months.

Fall (September to November): Fall is one of the most beautiful times in NYC, with temperatures cooling down and the humidity dropping. Average temperatures range from the 50s to 70s Fahrenheit (10-25°C). The city's trees change color, offering stunning autumn foliage in parks like Central Park. Fall is also a busy time for events and cultural activities.

Overall Climate Considerations: NYC's climate can be unpredictable, with sudden weather changes and occasional extremes. It's wise to check the forecast before traveling and pack accordingly. The city is also affected by urban heat island effects, meaning temperatures can be slightly higher in the city compared to surrounding areas.

Best Time to Visit New York

Spring (March to May)

Pros:

Pleasant Weather: Spring brings mild temperatures and blooming flowers. Daytime highs generally range from the 50s to 70s Fahrenheit (10-25°C), making it a comfortable time to explore the city.

Less Crowded: Compared to summer, spring sees fewer tourists, so you can enjoy attractions with shorter lines and less crowded streets.

Cultural Events: Spring features a variety of events, including outdoor festivals, concerts, and the famous **New York International Auto Show**.

Cons:

Unpredictable Weather: Spring weather can be unpredictable, with occasional rain showers and fluctuating temperatures. Packing layers and a rain jacket is advisable.

Summer (June to August)

Pros:

Outdoor Activities: Summer is perfect for enjoying outdoor activities like picnics in Central Park, rooftop bars, and outdoor concerts. The city hosts numerous street festivals, parades, and events.

Extended Daylight: Longer days mean more daylight hours to explore the city's attractions and neighborhoods.

Beach Access: You can take day trips to nearby beaches like Coney Island or Rockaway Beach to escape the urban heat.

Cons:

Heat and Humidity: Summer temperatures often exceed 80°F (27°C), with high humidity making it feel hotter. It's important to stay hydrated and take breaks from the heat.

Crowds and Higher Prices: Summer is peak tourist season, so expect larger crowds at popular attractions and higher hotel rates. Book accommodations and tickets in advance.

The Ultimate New York City Travel Guide (2025 Edition)

The Ultimate New York City Travel Guide (2025 Edition)

Fall (September to November)

Pros:

Beautiful Scenery: Fall offers stunning foliage in parks and neighborhoods, particularly in Central Park and Prospect Park. The cooler temperatures, ranging from the 50s to 70s Fahrenheit (10-25°C), are ideal for sightseeing.

Festivals and Events: Fall is packed with events like the **New York Film Festival**, **Broadway Week**, and Halloween festivities, including the famous **Village Halloween Parade**.

Comfortable Weather: The weather is generally crisp and comfortable, with less humidity and moderate temperatures.

Cons:

Early Chills: Late fall can bring cooler temperatures and occasional rain. Be prepared for variable weather, especially if traveling in November.

Winter (December to February)

Pros:

Holiday Magic: Winter, particularly December, is a magical time with holiday decorations, ice skating rinks, and events like the **Macy's Thanksgiving Day Parade** and **New Year's Eve in Times Square**.

Reduced Crowds: After the holiday season, the city is less crowded, and you can enjoy attractions with shorter lines and lower hotel rates.

Festive Atmosphere: The city is beautifully decorated for the holidays, and you can experience festive events, Broadway shows, and cozy indoor activities.

Cons:

Cold Weather: Winter temperatures can drop below freezing, with occasional snow and ice. Be prepared for cold weather with appropriate clothing and footwear.

Limited Outdoor Activities: Some outdoor attractions and activities may be less enjoyable or unavailable due to the cold weather.

Summary

Spring: Ideal for mild weather, fewer crowds, and cultural events.

Summer: Great for outdoor activities, festivals, and beach access, but expect heat and higher prices.

Fall: Offers beautiful foliage, comfortable weather, and a range of events, with cooler temperatures and fewer tourists.

Winter: Perfect for experiencing holiday magic and reduced crowds, but be ready for cold weather and potential snow.

The Ultimate New York City Travel Guide (2025 Edition)

Chapter 1: Planning Your Trip to New York City

Currency and Banking in New York

Currency

Currency Used:

U.S. Dollar (USD): The official currency of New York City is the United States Dollar. Bills come in denominations of $1, $5, $10, $20, $50, and $100. Coins include pennies (1 cent), nickels (5 cents), dimes (10 cents), quarters (25 cents), and dollar coins (less common).

Currency Exchange:

Airport and Hotel Services: Currency exchange services are available at major airports, like John F. Kennedy International (JFK) and LaGuardia Airport (LGA), as well as many hotels. However, exchange rates at these locations may not be as favorable as those at dedicated currency exchange offices.

Currency Exchange Offices: Numerous currency exchange offices are scattered throughout the city, particularly in tourist areas like Times Square and Midtown. These offices often offer competitive rates and can be a convenient option.

Banks: Many banks provide currency exchange services, though they may require an account or charge a fee. Major banks include JPMorgan Chase, Bank of America, and Citibank.

ATMs:

Availability: ATMs are widely available throughout New York City, including at banks, convenience stores, and popular tourist spots. They provide a convenient way to withdraw cash using a credit or debit card.

Fees: Be aware of potential fees associated with using ATMs, such as withdrawal fees from your home bank and additional charges from the ATM operator. It's a good idea to check with your bank about international fees and use ATMs that are part of your bank's network, if possible.

Banking

Bank Branches:

Major Banks: New York City is home to many major banks with branches throughout the city. These include JPMorgan Chase, Bank of America, Citibank, and Wells Fargo. Bank branches offer services such as cash withdrawals, deposits, and account management.

Hours of Operation: Most bank branches are open Monday to Friday, from around 9 AM to 5 PM. Some branches in busy areas or near airports may offer extended hours.

Opening a Bank Account:

Requirements: If you plan to stay in NYC for an extended period and need to open a bank account, you'll typically need a valid passport, proof of address, and possibly a visa or other identification documents. Some banks also require an initial deposit.

Types of Accounts: You can open various types of accounts, including checking accounts for daily transactions and savings accounts for earning interest.

Credit and Debit Cards:

Widely Accepted: Major credit and debit cards (Visa, MasterCard, American Express, Discover) are widely accepted throughout New York City, including at hotels, restaurants, shops, and attractions.

Chip Technology: Most places use chip-enabled card readers, so ensure your card has a chip for added security.

Cashless Transactions:

Mobile Payments: Mobile payment options like Apple Pay, Google Pay, and Samsung Pay are increasingly popular and accepted at many retailers, restaurants, and public transit options in NYC.

Tipping: While many transactions can be cashless, it's a good idea to carry some cash for tipping service workers like taxi drivers, doormen, and restaurant servers.

Budgeting and Financial Planning

Costs:

General Costs: New York City is known for its high cost of living. Budgeting for accommodations, dining, transportation, and attractions is crucial. Expect to pay a premium for food, lodging, and entertainment in tourist-heavy areas.

Taxes and Tips: Sales tax in NYC is 8.875%, which will be added to most purchases. Tipping is customary in restaurants (typically 15-20% of the bill), taxis, and other service industries.

Banking Apps and Tools:

Mobile Banking: Consider using banking apps to manage your finances, check account balances, and track expenses. Many banks offer mobile apps that provide real-time information and allow you to transfer funds or pay bills.

Emergency Funds:

Access to Funds: Keep a backup plan for accessing funds in case of emergencies. This might include carrying an additional credit card or having emergency contact numbers for your bank.

Entry Requirements and Travel Documentation

1. Passport Requirements

Validity: Ensure your passport is valid for at least six months beyond your planned departure date from the United States. This is a standard requirement for international travelers.

Condition: Your passport should be in good condition, with no damage or missing pages.

2. Visa Requirements

Visa Waiver Program (VWP): Citizens from countries that are part of the Visa Waiver Program (VWP) can enter the United States for tourism or business stays of up to 90 days without a visa. These travelers must apply for an **Electronic System for Travel Authorization (ESTA)** before their trip.

Application: ESTA applications can be completed online at the official ESTA website. Approval typically takes minutes, but it's advisable to apply well in advance of your travel.

Fee: There is a small fee for the ESTA application.

Visa Required: Travelers from countries not included in the VWP will need to obtain a visa for entry into the U.S.

Types of Visas: Common visa types for tourism include the **B-2 Tourist Visa**. You can apply for a visa at a U.S. embassy or consulate in your home country.

Application Process: The application process involves filling out the DS-160 form, paying a visa fee, and attending an interview at a U.S. consulate or embassy.

3. Customs Declarations

Arrival in the U.S.: Upon arrival in New York, you will need to complete a **Customs Declaration Form**, which is usually provided during your flight. This form asks about items you are bringing into the country, including any goods, gifts, or currency over $10,000.

Duty-Free Allowances: Be aware of duty-free allowances for items such as alcohol, tobacco, and gifts. Exceeding these limits may result in additional duties or taxes.

4. Health and Vaccinations

General Health Requirements: As of now, the U.S. does not require specific vaccinations for entry. However, travelers should be up-to-date on routine vaccinations.

COVID-19: Check current COVID-19 regulations and requirements before travel. As policies can change, review the latest guidelines on the official U.S. government or CDC websites for any testing or vaccination requirements.

5. Insurance

Travel Insurance: While not a requirement, travel insurance is highly recommended. It can cover unexpected events such as trip cancellations, medical emergencies, or lost luggage. Check with your insurance provider to ensure coverage is valid in the U.S.

6. Important Documents

Travel Itinerary: Keep a copy of your travel itinerary, including flight details and accommodation bookings.

Proof of Funds: Have proof of sufficient funds for your stay, such as bank statements or a credit card.

Emergency Contacts: Carry emergency contact information, including the local U.S. embassy or consulate in case you need assistance.

7. Customs and Border Protection

Customs Inspection: U.S. Customs and Border Protection (CBP) officers will inspect your documents and may ask questions about your trip and your stay in the U.S. Answer their questions truthfully and clearly.

Biometrics: Travelers may be subject to biometric screening, including fingerprinting and photographs, as part of the entry process.

8. Special Considerations

Minors Traveling Alone: If a minor is traveling alone or with someone who is not their parent or legal guardian, additional documentation may be required, such as a notarized letter of consent from the parent(s) or guardian(s).

Traveling with Pets: If you're bringing pets into the U.S., be aware of specific regulations and documentation required for their entry.

Budgeting for Your New York Trip

1. Accommodation

Luxury Hotels: $300 - $600+ per night. Options include high-end hotels like The Peninsula or The Ritz-Carlton.

Mid-Range Hotels: $150 - $300 per night. Examples are Hilton Garden Inn or Holiday Inn.

Budget Accommodation: $100 - $150 per night. Consider budget chains or basic hotels.

Hostels and Shared Spaces: $50 - $100 per night. Hostels and shared accommodations can be more affordable.

Vacation Rentals: $100 - $300 per night. Platforms like Airbnb and Vrbo offer a range of options.

2. Dining

Fine Dining: $100 - $300 per person. Experience world-class restaurants like Eleven Madison Park or Per Se.

Mid-Range Restaurants: $30 - $70 per person. Enjoy diverse cuisines in places like Joe's Pizza or The Smith.

Casual Dining: $10 - $30 per person. Includes diners, fast-casual eateries, and street food.

Street Food and Food Trucks: $5 - $15 per meal. Options include food trucks and vendors offering everything from hot dogs to ethnic cuisine.

3. Transportation

Subway and Buses: $2.75 per ride. Consider purchasing a MetroCard for unlimited rides if using public transit frequently.

Taxis and Rideshares: $10 - $30 per ride, depending on distance. Rideshare apps like Uber and Lyft are available.

Car Rentals: $50 - $100 per day, plus parking fees. Parking in Manhattan can be expensive and challenging.

Biking: $12 - $15 per day for a Citi Bike rental. Bike-sharing programs are a convenient option for short trips.

Ferries: $2.75 per ride. Ferries can provide scenic and efficient travel to places like Staten Island.

4. Attractions and Entertainment

Broadway Shows: $100 - $200+ per ticket. Prices vary based on the show and seat location. Consider discount ticket services like TKTS for lower prices.

Museums and Attractions: $20 - $40 per ticket. Museums like The Met or MoMA have varying admission fees, and some offer suggested donations or free entry days.

Tours: $30 - $100 per person. City tours, boat cruises, and guided experiences can be a great way to explore.

5. Shopping

Luxury Shopping: Varies widely. High-end stores on Fifth Avenue or SoHo can be expensive.

Mid-Range Shopping: $50 - $200 per item. Includes department stores like Macy's and more affordable boutiques.

Souvenirs and Gifts: $5 - $50. Tourist shops and markets offer a range of items from keychains to art.

6. Miscellaneous Expenses

Tips: 15% - 20% of your bill in restaurants, bars, and taxis. It's customary to tip service workers.

Internet and Connectivity: $0 - $10 per day. Many public places offer free Wi-Fi. Consider a local SIM card or international plan for mobile data.

Emergency Funds: Always have some extra money set aside for unexpected expenses or emergencies.

7. Sample Daily Budget

Luxury Traveler: $600 - $1,000+ per day. Includes high-end accommodation, fine dining, premium attractions, and shopping.

Mid-Range Traveler: $300 - $600 per day. Features moderate accommodation, dining, and activities.

Budget Traveler: $150 - $300 per day. Covers budget accommodation, casual dining, and free or low-cost activities.

8. Tips for Saving Money

City Passes: Consider purchasing a city pass or attraction bundle for discounted entry to multiple attractions.

Free Attractions: Take advantage of free or low-cost activities like walking tours, parks, and public events.

Discounts and Deals: Look for deals on tickets, dining, and attractions through apps and websites.

Travel Insurance Considerations

1. Types of Travel Insurance

Trip Cancellation Insurance:

Coverage: Reimburses you for prepaid, non-refundable trip expenses if you have to cancel your trip due to covered reasons like illness, a family emergency, or other unforeseen events.

Consideration: Useful if you've booked non-refundable flights, hotels, or tours and want protection against cancellations.

Travel Medical Insurance:

Coverage: Provides coverage for medical expenses incurred while traveling, including doctor visits, hospital stays, and prescription medications. It can also cover emergency medical evacuation if needed.

Consideration: Essential if your health insurance doesn't provide coverage abroad or if you want additional protection for medical emergencies.

Emergency Medical Evacuation Insurance:

Coverage: Covers the cost of transportation to the nearest adequate medical facility or back to your home country if necessary due to a medical emergency.

Consideration: Important for destinations where medical facilities may be limited or if you want extra peace of mind.

Baggage and Personal Belongings Insurance:

Coverage: Reimburses you for lost, stolen, or damaged luggage and personal items, including delays in baggage arrival.

Consideration: Useful if you're traveling with valuable items or if you want coverage in case your luggage is delayed or lost.

Travel Delay Insurance:

Coverage: Provides compensation for additional expenses incurred due to travel delays, such as accommodation, meals, and transportation.

Consideration: Beneficial if you're concerned about flight delays, cancellations, or other disruptions.

Accidental Death and Dismemberment Insurance:

Coverage: Provides benefits in the event of accidental death or severe injury resulting in dismemberment while traveling.

Consideration: Offers an additional layer of protection in the unfortunate event of a serious accident.

2. Key Factors to Consider

Coverage Limits:

Understand the Limits: Review the policy's coverage limits for different types of claims, including medical expenses, trip cancellations, and baggage loss. Ensure the limits are adequate for your needs.

Exclusions:

Read the Fine Print: Be aware of common exclusions, such as pre-existing medical conditions, high-risk activities (e.g., extreme sports), or certain types of travel (e.g., cruises). Make sure you understand what is not covered.

Pre-Existing Conditions:

Waivers: Some policies offer waivers for pre-existing medical conditions if purchased within a certain timeframe after booking your trip. If you have pre-existing conditions, check if this applies to your policy.

Policy Cost:

Compare Quotes: Travel insurance costs vary based on coverage levels, trip duration, age, and other factors. Compare quotes from different providers to find a policy that offers the right coverage at a reasonable price.

Policy Provider:

Reputation and Reviews: Choose a reputable insurance provider with positive reviews and good customer service. Look for companies that are well-regarded in the travel insurance industry.

Emergency Assistance:

24/7 Support: Ensure the policy includes access to 24/7 emergency assistance services. This can be crucial if you need help navigating a medical emergency or other issues while abroad.

3. How to Purchase Travel Insurance

Research Providers:

Online Comparison Tools: Use online comparison tools to compare different travel insurance policies and providers. Websites like Squaremouth, TravelInsurance.com, and InsureMyTrip can help with this process.

Purchase Timing:

Early Purchase: Purchase travel insurance as soon as you book your trip to maximize coverage benefits, especially for trip cancellation and pre-existing condition waivers.

Policy Review:

Read Carefully: Thoroughly review the terms and conditions of the policy before purchasing. Ensure you understand the coverage, exclusions, and claims process.

Keep Documentation:

Save Records: Keep a copy of your insurance policy, emergency contact numbers, and any related documents with you during your trip. Store these in a secure location.

4. Filing a Claim

Document Everything:

Record Details: Keep detailed records of any incidents or expenses related to your claim. This includes receipts, medical reports, and correspondence with service providers.

Contact Your Insurer:

Notify Promptly: Contact your insurance provider as soon as possible after an incident occurs. Follow their instructions for filing a claim and submit all required documentation.

Follow Up:

Track Progress: Follow up with your insurer to ensure your claim is processed and resolved in a timely manner.

What to Pack for New York

1. Clothing

Comfortable Walking Shoes:

Reason: New York is a city best explored on foot, so bring comfortable walking shoes or sneakers. Choose pairs that are supportive and well-broken-in.

Consider: If you plan to walk a lot, opt for shoes with good cushioning and arch support.

Weather-Appropriate Clothing:

Spring (March-May): Light layers, a medium-weight jacket, and a mix of long-sleeve shirts and lighter clothing. Temperatures can vary, so be prepared for both cool and mild weather.

Summer (June-August): Lightweight, breathable fabrics, sunglasses, and a hat. Temperatures can soar, so pack shorts, T-shirts, and comfortable shoes.

Fall (September-November): Layers, including a warm jacket, sweaters, and long pants. The weather can range from warm to chilly, so be prepared for temperature fluctuations.

Winter (December-February): Warm clothing, including a heavy coat, thermal layers, gloves, a hat, and a scarf. New York winters can be cold and windy.

Smart Casual Attire:

Reason: NYC is known for its fashion-forward culture, so having a few smart-casual outfits is useful for dining out or attending theater performances.

Consider: Pack dressier items like blouses, slacks, or a casual dress for more upscale dining or events.

Workout Clothes:

Reason: If you plan to use hotel gyms or explore the city by bike, pack appropriate workout gear.

Consider: Moisture-wicking fabrics and comfortable athletic wear.

Umbrella:

Reason: Rain is common in NYC throughout the year. A compact, durable umbrella can be a lifesaver on rainy days.

Consider: A sturdy, wind-resistant umbrella is ideal.

2. Accessories

Sunglasses:

Reason: Protect your eyes from the sun while exploring the city. New York can be quite sunny, especially in summer.

Consider: Polarized lenses can reduce glare and improve visibility.

Hat and Gloves:

Reason: Essential for winter travel or if you're sensitive to the cold.

Consider: Opt for warm, insulating materials if traveling in colder months.

Scarf:

Reason: Adds warmth in the winter and can be a stylish accessory in any season.

Consider: A versatile scarf can complement various outfits.

3. Essentials

Passport and ID:

Reason: Necessary for identification, especially if traveling internationally or checking into hotels.

Consider: Keep copies in a separate location from the originals.

Travel Documents:

Reason: Include flight tickets, hotel reservations, and any necessary visas or travel authorizations.

Consider: Digital copies can be useful as backups.

Credit Cards and Cash:

Reason: Most places in NYC accept credit cards, but having some cash on hand is useful for small purchases or tips.

Consider: Carry a small amount of cash for convenience.

Portable Charger:

Reason: Keep your phone and other electronic devices charged throughout the day.

Consider: A power bank with a high capacity can be helpful.

The Ultimate New York City Travel Guide (2025 Edition)

The Ultimate New York City Travel Guide (2025 Edition)

Reusable Water Bottle:

Reason: Staying hydrated while walking around the city is important. Many public spaces offer water refill stations.

Consider: A sturdy, leak-proof bottle is ideal.

4. Personal Items

Toiletries:

Reason: Bring essential items like toothbrush, toothpaste, shampoo, conditioner, and any medications you need.

Consider: Travel-sized containers to comply with airline regulations and save space.

Medications:

Reason: Include any prescription medications and basic over-the-counter remedies for common ailments.

Consider: Keep medications in their original packaging and carry a copy of your prescription if needed.

Sunglasses:

Reason: To protect your eyes from UV rays and reduce glare.

Consider: Pack a case to prevent scratches.

5. Tech and Gadgets

Smartphone and Charger:

Reason: Essential for navigation, communication, and capturing memories.

Consider: Download maps and essential apps before your trip.

Camera:

Reason: For capturing high-quality photos of your trip.

Consider: A compact, portable camera can be a good option if you want to avoid using your phone for photos.

Laptop or Tablet:

Reason: Useful for work or entertainment during downtime.

Consider: Pack a lightweight, protective case.

6. Miscellaneous

Travel Guide or Map:

Reason: Useful for navigating the city and discovering attractions.

Consider: Digital guides and maps are often available on smartphones.

Daypack or Tote Bag:

Reason: Handy for carrying daily essentials like water, snacks, and souvenirs.

Consider: A lightweight, foldable bag can be convenient.

Grace Bennett

Chapter 2: Getting to New York City

By Air: Major Airports

1. John F. Kennedy International Airport (JFK)

Location: Located in the Queens borough of New York City, about 15 miles (24 kilometers) from Manhattan.

Airlines: JFK is the primary international gateway to New York City and serves as a hub for several major airlines, including American Airlines, Delta Air Lines, and JetBlue Airways.

Facilities: The airport offers a wide range of amenities, including lounges, dining options, shopping, and car rental services. JFK has six passenger terminals (Terminals 1-8), each with its own features and services.

Transportation to Manhattan:

AirTrain: The AirTrain JFK connects all terminals to the New York City subway system at Jamaica and Howard Beach stations. From there, you can take the subway to various parts of Manhattan.

Taxi: Yellow cabs are available at designated taxi stands outside the terminals. Fares to Manhattan are metered, and there's a flat fee of $70 plus tolls and tip.

Ride-Sharing: Services like Uber and Lyft operate at JFK. Follow signs to the ride-sharing pick-up areas.

Airport Shuttle: Shared shuttle services are available, offering door-to-door service to various locations in Manhattan.

2. LaGuardia Airport (LGA)

Location: Situated in the Queens borough, about 8 miles (13 kilometers) from Midtown Manhattan.

Airlines: LGA primarily handles domestic flights, though it also offers some international services. Major carriers include American Airlines, Delta Air Lines, and United Airlines.

Facilities: LaGuardia has four terminals (A, B, C, and D) with a variety of food options, shopping, and car rental services. Terminal B is the largest and recently underwent a significant renovation.

Transportation to Manhattan:

Bus: Several city buses connect LGA to the subway system, including the Q70 Limited and the M60 Select Bus Service. The Q70 provides a direct connection to the Jackson Heights-Roosevelt Avenue subway station, while the M60 goes to the Astoria Boulevard subway station.

Taxi: Taxis are available at designated pick-up areas. Fares to Manhattan are metered and generally less expensive than from JFK.

Ride-Sharing: Uber and Lyft services are available. Pick-up locations are specified at the airport.

Airport Shuttle: Shared shuttle services offer transportation to various Manhattan destinations.

3. Newark Liberty International Airport (EWR)

Location: Located in Newark, New Jersey, approximately 16 miles (26 kilometers) from Midtown Manhattan.

Airlines: EWR serves both domestic and international flights, with major airlines including United Airlines, American Airlines, and Delta Air Lines.

Facilities: The airport features three terminals (A, B, and C) with dining, shopping, lounges, and car rental services. Terminal C is primarily used by United Airlines.

Transportation to Manhattan:

AirTrain: The AirTrain Newark connects the airport to the Newark Liberty International Airport train station, where you can catch a New Jersey Transit or Amtrak train to Penn Station in Manhattan.

Taxi: Taxis are available at the designated pick-up areas outside each terminal. Fares to Manhattan are metered and usually higher due to the distance.

Ride-Sharing: Uber and Lyft are available. Follow signs to the designated ride-sharing pick-up areas.

Airport Shuttle: Shared shuttle services and private car services offer transportation to various Manhattan locations.

General Tips for Air Travel to NYC

Booking: Book flights well in advance to secure the best fares and preferred travel times. Consider flying into the airport most convenient to your itinerary and accommodation.

Arrival: Arrive at the airport at least 2-3 hours before your flight for domestic and 3-4 hours for international flights to account for check-in, security, and potential delays.

Luggage: Be aware of baggage policies and fees for your airline. Each airport has luggage storage options if you need to drop off bags before heading into the city.

Customs and Immigration: If flying internationally, allow extra time for customs and immigration processing upon arrival. Follow airport signage for international arrivals.

By Train: Regional and International Rail Connections

1. Amtrak

Overview: Amtrak is the primary provider of intercity passenger rail service in the U.S., connecting New York City with major cities across the country.

Penn Station: Amtrak services arrive and depart from Penn Station, located in Midtown Manhattan, making it a central and convenient location for travelers.

Popular Routes:

Northeast Corridor: Connects New York with Boston, Providence, and New Haven. High-speed Acela Express and Northeast Regional trains serve this route.

Empire Service: Links New York with Albany, Syracuse, and Buffalo, offering scenic views of the Hudson River Valley and upstate New York.

Cardinal: Runs between New York and Chicago, passing through cities like Washington, D.C., and Cincinnati.

Lake Shore Limited: Connects New York with Chicago via Cleveland and Buffalo.

2. Long Island Rail Road (LIRR)

Overview: The Long Island Rail Road is a commuter rail network connecting Long Island with Manhattan.

Penn Station: LIRR trains also operate from Penn Station, making it easy to transfer between Amtrak and LIRR services.

Popular Routes:

Port Jefferson Branch: Connects to the North Shore of Long Island, including towns like Port Jefferson and Huntington.

Babylon Branch: Serves the South Shore, including towns like Babylon and Patchogue.

Ronkonkoma Branch: Provides access to central Long Island, including Ronkonkoma and Smithtown.

3. New Jersey Transit

Overview: New Jersey Transit (NJ Transit) operates commuter trains connecting New Jersey with New York City.

Penn Station: NJ Transit trains also arrive at Penn Station, allowing for easy access to Manhattan.

Popular Routes:

North Jersey Coast Line: Connects towns along the New Jersey coast, such as Hoboken and Long Branch.

Raritan Valley Line: Links New Jersey towns like Newark and Bridgewater with Manhattan.

Morris & Essex Lines: Provides service to towns in northern New Jersey, including Montclair and Morristown.

4. Metro-North Railroad

Overview: Metro-North Railroad connects New York City with the northern suburbs of New York and parts of Connecticut.

Grand Central Terminal: Metro-North trains depart from Grand Central Terminal, located in Midtown Manhattan.

Popular Routes:

Hudson Line: Travels along the Hudson River, connecting NYC with towns like Yonkers and Poughkeepsie.

Harlem Line: Connects NYC with communities in the northern suburbs, such as White Plains and Brewster.

New Haven Line: Provides service to Connecticut cities like Stamford and New Haven.

5. International Rail Connections

Amtrak's Maple Leaf:

Overview: This Amtrak service operates between New York City and Toronto, Canada, passing through cities like Buffalo and Niagara Falls.

Arrival: The train arrives at Penn Station in Manhattan.

Via Rail (Canada):

Overview: While not a direct service to New York City, Via Rail provides connections to the Maple Leaf service for international travelers coming from other Canadian destinations.

6. Tips for Train Travel to NYC

Booking Tickets: Book tickets in advance to secure the best fares and preferred travel times. Tickets can be purchased online, at ticket offices, or through mobile apps.

Travel Time: Plan your trip based on the travel time from your departure city to NYC. High-speed trains like Acela Express have faster travel times compared to regional services.

Arrival at Stations: Allow time to navigate the large stations like Penn Station and Grand Central Terminal. Both are major transportation hubs with various services and amenities.

Baggage Policies: Check the baggage policies of the train service you're using. Amtrak, for example, allows two carry-on bags and one personal item for free, with additional fees for extra baggage.

Onboard Services: Some trains offer amenities like Wi-Fi, power outlets, and dining services. Check the services available on your specific train to enhance your journey.

Conclusion

By Car: Road Travel Tips and Routes

1. Major Highways and Routes to New York City

New York City is accessible from various regions via major highways and interstates. Depending on where you're coming from, you can take different routes into the city:

From the North (New England, Upstate New York):

I-87 (New York State Thruway): A major north-south interstate, I-87 runs from upstate New York, connecting Albany to NYC. It also connects to the George Washington Bridge (GWB) for easy access to Manhattan.

I-95: If you're coming from Connecticut or Massachusetts, I-95 (also known as the New England Thruway) will take you directly to NYC. It's a direct route into the Bronx and connects to other boroughs.

From the South (New Jersey, Pennsylvania, Washington D.C.):

I-95 (New Jersey Turnpike): I-95 runs along the East Coast, and if you're coming from New Jersey, Philadelphia, or further south, this is the most direct route to New York City. The highway leads to the Lincoln Tunnel (into Midtown Manhattan) or the George Washington Bridge (into Upper Manhattan).

I-78: This highway connects Central New Jersey with New York City and terminates at the Holland Tunnel, which brings you into Lower Manhattan.

I-80: Another option from the west, I-80 runs from Pennsylvania to the GWB, providing access to Upper Manhattan.

From the West (New Jersey, Pennsylvania):

I-280: This interstate provides a connection from Central New Jersey to the Holland Tunnel, bringing you directly into Lower Manhattan.

I-495 (Lincoln Tunnel): I-495 is a major artery from New Jersey to Manhattan, feeding into the Lincoln Tunnel, which drops you into Midtown Manhattan.

From Long Island:

I-495 (Long Island Expressway): If you're coming from Long Island, I-495 leads straight into Queens and Manhattan via the Queens-Midtown Tunnel.

Belt Parkway: For those driving from southern Long Island, the Belt Parkway provides access to Brooklyn and lower Manhattan via the Verrazano-Narrows Bridge and the Brooklyn Bridge.

2. Road Travel Tips for Driving into NYC

Timing is Key:

Avoid Rush Hour: Rush hour in NYC can be brutal. The heaviest traffic is typically between 7:00 AM - 10:00 AM and 4:00 PM - 7:00 PM, especially on weekdays. Plan to arrive or leave outside of these times to avoid gridlock.

Weekends and Holidays: Traffic can also be heavy on weekends, especially during holidays, as tourists flock to the city. If possible, travel during off-peak hours.

Tolls:

Expect Toll Roads: Many of the major highways leading into New York City, including the George Washington Bridge, Lincoln Tunnel, Holland Tunnel, and Verrazano-Narrows Bridge, have tolls. The costs can range from $10 to $16, depending on the route and payment method.

EZPass: If you frequently travel in and around NYC or the Northeast, consider getting an EZPass. It reduces toll costs and speeds up the process at toll booths. Most NYC bridges and tunnels use cashless tolling, meaning you'll need EZPass or be billed via license plate.

GPS and Navigation:

Use a Reliable GPS App: Apps like Google Maps or Waze can help you navigate traffic, find alternative routes, and alert you to accidents or delays. Real-time updates are crucial when driving in a busy city like NYC.

Keep Your Map Updated: NYC frequently undergoes road repairs, and routes may change. Make sure your GPS app is updated to avoid detours and unnecessary delays.

Speed Limits and Traffic Laws:

Speed Limits: The speed limit in New York City is 25 mph unless otherwise posted. Major highways and bridges often have limits between 40-50 mph.

No Right on Red: Unlike other cities, turning right at a red light is generally not allowed in NYC unless a sign specifically permits it.

Driving in NYC:

Prepare for Heavy Traffic: NYC is known for its congested streets. Be patient, especially in Manhattan, where pedestrian and vehicle traffic can be intense. Taxi cabs, buses, and delivery trucks may also make quick stops.

Watch for Pedestrians and Cyclists: NYC has many pedestrian crossings, and the city has embraced bike lanes. Keep an eye out for people and cyclists, especially when making turns.

Bridges and Tunnels: Be mindful of height and weight restrictions if you're driving a large vehicle, especially when navigating bridges and tunnels.

3. Parking in New York City

Street Parking:

Limited Availability: Street parking in Manhattan is scarce and often restricted to specific hours or permits. Many streets have "alternate side parking" regulations, which means cars must be moved to the opposite side of the street at certain times for street cleaning.

Pay Attention to Signs: Always read parking signs carefully. Parking violations can result in hefty fines or even towing.

Metered Parking: Many streets offer metered parking, especially in commercial areas. Meters generally operate during business hours, and you can pay using coins, credit cards, or parking apps like ParkNYC.

Parking Garages:

Costly but Convenient: Parking garages are a more reliable option but can be expensive, especially in Manhattan, where daily rates range from $30 to $60 or more.

Reserve Ahead: Apps like SpotHero and ParkWhiz allow you to reserve parking spots ahead of time, often at discounted rates. This can be a huge time-saver and can help you avoid last-minute searches for parking.

Park-and-Ride Options:

Avoid Driving into Manhattan: If you prefer not to deal with the hassle of driving in Manhattan, park at a commuter-friendly location in New Jersey, Long Island, or upstate New York, and take public transportation into the city. Many train stations and transit hubs offer park-and-ride services.

4. Scenic Drives into New York City

Palisades Parkway: This scenic highway runs along the west side of the Hudson River in New Jersey and offers beautiful views of the river and the George Washington Bridge as you approach the city.

Taconic State Parkway: If you're driving from upstate New York, the Taconic offers a more rural and picturesque drive compared to the interstates. It connects to the city via the Saw Mill River Parkway.

Route 9W: Running parallel to the Hudson River, this route offers a scenic alternative to I-87 and provides access to the George Washington Bridge with sweeping views of the Manhattan skyline.

By Ferry: Arrival from Neighboring Countries

1. International Ferry Connections

Although there are no direct international ferries from neighboring countries like Canada to New York City, there are ways to integrate ferry travel as part of a larger trip to the city:

From Canada to the U.S. (Great Lakes Region):

Ferries Across the Great Lakes: While no ferries connect directly from Canada to New York City, ferries operate across the Great Lakes between the U.S. and Canada. These routes are useful if you're traveling through regions like Michigan or upstate New York on your way to NYC.

S.S. Badger (Lake Michigan): A car ferry that connects Ludington, Michigan, to Manitowoc, Wisconsin, offering a scenic route that can be part of a longer road trip toward New York.

Ferries from Ontario: There are ferries from Kingston, Ontario, to upstate New York (Cape Vincent), which could be an option if you're planning a road or train trip from there to NYC.

While no ferry route directly links Canada to New York City, travelers from Canada can combine train or car travel with local ferry services once they reach the New York metropolitan area.

2. Regional and Domestic Ferry Routes to NYC

Several domestic ferry routes connect nearby locations, particularly across the Hudson River, Long Island Sound, and other parts of the New York metropolitan area. These ferries are useful for travelers coming from nearby states or regions.

Staten Island Ferry:

Overview: The Staten Island Ferry is a free, iconic ferry service between Staten Island and Lower Manhattan. It's not an international route but offers a great way to approach NYC from Staten Island with stunning views of the Statue of Liberty and the Manhattan skyline.

Route: Staten Island (St. George Terminal) to Lower Manhattan (Whitehall Terminal).

Travel Time: Approximately 25 minutes, with frequent service throughout the day.

NY Waterway (Hudson River Ferries):

Overview: NY Waterway operates ferries across the Hudson River, connecting New Jersey to various points in Manhattan. This service is popular with commuters but is also an excellent option for tourists traveling from New Jersey.

Routes:

Weehawken, Hoboken, and Jersey City (New Jersey) to Manhattan (West 39th Street, Battery Park, and Pier 11).

Edgewater, New Jersey to Midtown or Downtown Manhattan.

Travel Time: Generally between 10 and 20 minutes, depending on the route.

Seastreak Ferry:

Overview: Seastreak operates high-speed ferries between New Jersey and Manhattan, as well as routes to other destinations such as Long Island and Martha's Vineyard.

Routes:

Atlantic Highlands and Highlands (New Jersey) to East 35th Street or Wall Street (Manhattan).

Seasonal services to destinations like Sandy Hook and Martha's Vineyard.

Travel Time: Typically 40 to 60 minutes, depending on the route.

New York Water Taxi:

Overview: While primarily a sightseeing service, New York Water Taxi also offers some transportation routes across the city's waterways, connecting tourists to major landmarks like Brooklyn Bridge Park, DUMBO, and Battery Park.

Route: Brooklyn (DUMBO) to Lower Manhattan and Midtown Manhattan.

Travel Time: Varies by route, generally 15 to 30 minutes.

Port Jefferson Ferry:

Overview: This ferry connects Bridgeport, Connecticut, to Port Jefferson on Long Island. From there, you can drive or take the Long Island Rail Road (LIRR) into Manhattan.

Route: Bridgeport, Connecticut to Port Jefferson, Long Island.

Travel Time: About 1 hour and 15 minutes for the ferry crossing.

Cross Sound Ferry (Long Island Sound):

Overview: This ferry service operates between New London, Connecticut, and Orient Point, Long Island, providing a convenient route for travelers from New England looking to drive or take public transport into New York City.

Route: New London, Connecticut, to Orient Point, Long Island.

Travel Time: Approximately 1 hour and 20 minutes.

3. Scenic Advantages of Arriving by Ferry

Views of NYC Skyline: One of the biggest advantages of arriving in New York City by ferry is the breathtaking view of the Manhattan skyline. Whether you're coming from New Jersey or a nearby borough, the ferry allows you to experience the city's iconic landmarks from the water.

Landmarks Along the Way: Many ferry routes pass close to the Statue of Liberty, Ellis Island, and the Brooklyn Bridge, providing a scenic introduction to the city for first-time visitors.

4. Practical Tips for Ferry Travel

Ferry Tickets: For most ferries, you can purchase tickets online in advance or at the terminal. Services like the Staten Island Ferry are free, but other routes, like NY Waterway or Seastreak, have varying ticket prices, often ranging from $5 to $30 depending on the distance and time of day.

Schedules: Ferry schedules vary by route and season, so it's important to check timetables ahead of time, especially for commuter-focused services that may run less frequently during off-peak hours or on weekends.

Weather Considerations: Ferry services may be affected by weather conditions such as fog, storms, or high winds. Be sure to check for updates, especially in winter or during inclement weather.

Luggage: While most ferries allow you to bring luggage, space may be limited, especially on commuter routes. Check specific luggage policies on the ferry service website, particularly if you're traveling with larger bags or equipment.

Grace Bennett

The Ultimate New York City Travel Guide (2025 Edition)

Chapter 3: Top Cities in New York City

Jersey City, New Jersey

1. Proximity and Accessibility to NYC

Quick Commute to Manhattan: One of the primary advantages of staying in or visiting Jersey City is its close proximity to New York City. You can easily reach Lower Manhattan in just a few minutes via the PATH train, ferry, or by car through the Holland Tunnel. The PATH train connects Jersey City to popular areas such as the World Trade Center, Greenwich Village, and Midtown, making it a highly convenient base for exploring NYC.

Ferry Access: For those preferring a scenic commute, ferries operated by NY Waterway provide regular service from Jersey City to various points in Manhattan, including Wall Street and Midtown.

Affordable Accommodation: Compared to the expensive hotel rates in Manhattan, Jersey City offers more affordable accommodation options, including mid-range hotels, luxury apartments, and boutique hotels, making it an appealing choice for budget-conscious travelers.

2. Vibrant Neighborhoods and Local Attractions

Downtown Jersey City (Paulus Hook and Exchange Place): This area is known for its stunning views of the Manhattan skyline, especially from the waterfront parks. Paulus Hook is a historic neighborhood with cobblestone streets, trendy restaurants, and cafés, while Exchange Place serves as a business hub with a direct connection to the World Trade Center via the PATH.

Liberty State Park: One of Jersey City's most iconic attractions, Liberty State Park offers expansive green space with unobstructed views of the Statue of Liberty, Ellis Island, and the Manhattan skyline. The park features walking paths, picnic areas, and the Liberty Science Center, a popular museum with interactive exhibits. Visitors can also catch the ferry to Liberty Island and Ellis Island from here, avoiding the crowds at Manhattan's Battery Park.

Journal Square: This historic and cultural neighborhood is home to a diverse range of restaurants, shops, and cultural institutions. The Loew's Jersey Theatre, a restored movie palace, offers classic film screenings and live performances.

Historic Downtown: Known for its brownstone-lined streets and artistic vibe, Jersey City's Historic Downtown offers a great blend of old-world charm and modern conveniences. The area is popular for its lively arts scene, and local galleries, cafes, and boutiques attract creative residents and visitors.

3. Cultural and Culinary Scene

Jersey City boasts a rich and diverse cultural and culinary scene, reflecting the city's melting-pot population. Its neighborhoods are filled with restaurants offering a range of international cuisines, including Indian, Filipino, Mexican, and Italian.

Culinary Diversity:

Little India (Newark Avenue): Often referred to as "Little India," Newark Avenue in Jersey City is lined with Indian restaurants, grocery stores, and shops. It's a go-to destination for authentic South Asian cuisine and cultural experiences.

The Heights: This neighborhood has become a trendy area with a mix of old and new. It features a variety of cuisines, from Latin American to European, and has become known for its vibrant street food and pop-up markets.

Farmers Markets and Food Trucks: Jersey City also hosts multiple farmers' markets and food truck events, allowing visitors to sample fresh, local, and artisanal products from the region.

Arts and Entertainment: Jersey City has a growing arts community, with numerous galleries, performance spaces, and street art installations. The **Mana Contemporary** is a renowned arts center offering galleries, studios, and performances, while **Art House Productions** organizes live theater, comedy, and arts events.

4. Family-Friendly and Outdoor Activities

Liberty Science Center: A top destination for families, this interactive science museum offers hands-on exhibits, planetarium shows, and immersive learning experiences. It's an ideal attraction for children and adults alike.

Outdoor Recreation: In addition to Liberty State Park, Jersey City offers numerous parks and waterfront spaces for outdoor activities. Visitors can rent kayaks, enjoy scenic bike rides along the waterfront, or simply relax in the many green spaces. **Van Vorst Park** and **Hamilton Park** are charming neighborhood parks perfect for picnicking or spending time with family.

Skyline Views: The waterfront area along Jersey City offers some of the best views of the New York City skyline, particularly from **Liberty State Park** and the **Colgate Clock** area near Exchange Place. These spots are ideal for photography, sunsets, and even nighttime views of Manhattan's illuminated skyline.

5. Growing Popularity and Development

Booming Real Estate: Jersey City has experienced rapid development in recent years, particularly along its waterfront areas. Modern high-rise buildings and luxury apartment complexes are springing up, catering to people who want to live close to New York City without the higher costs of living in Manhattan.

Cultural Festivals and Events: Jersey City hosts numerous cultural events and festivals throughout the year. The **Jersey City Art & Studio Tour (JCAST)** is an annual event showcasing local artists and galleries. In addition, the city celebrates its diversity with events like **Indian Independence Day** parades, **Puerto Rican Day Festival**, and **LGBTQ+ Pride Month celebrations**.

6. Affordability and Relaxed Atmosphere

Lower Costs: Compared to Manhattan, Jersey City offers more affordable hotel and restaurant options without sacrificing convenience or entertainment. This affordability, combined with a relaxed, less hectic atmosphere, makes it a desirable alternative for visitors who want easy access to New York City but prefer a quieter environment for lodging.

Escape from Manhattan Crowds: While Jersey City is just a short trip from Manhattan, it offers a more laid-back vibe. After a busy day exploring the crowded streets of New York, many visitors enjoy returning to Jersey City for a more peaceful evening by the waterfront.

The Ultimate New York City Travel Guide (2025 Edition)

Hoboken, New Jersey

1. Proximity and Accessibility to NYC

Quick Access to Manhattan: Hoboken is conveniently located less than 3 miles from Manhattan, making it one of the closest towns to New York City. The town is well-connected to the city via several transportation options:

PATH Train: The PATH train provides a direct, fast connection between Hoboken and Manhattan. Trains run frequently, and you can get to popular destinations like the World Trade Center and Midtown (33rd Street) in about 10 to 15 minutes.

Ferries: For a more scenic option, NY Waterway ferries run between Hoboken's waterfront and various points in Manhattan, including Wall Street, the World Financial Center, and Midtown.

Driving and Taxis: Hoboken is also accessible by car via the Holland Tunnel, and taxis or rideshare services like Uber and Lyft are readily available for quick trips into the city.

With this range of transportation options, Hoboken is an excellent base for travelers who want to stay outside of the bustling NYC core while still enjoying easy access to all the city's major attractions.

2. Scenic Waterfront and Skyline Views

Stunning Views of Manhattan: Hoboken's location along the Hudson River provides some of the best panoramic views of the Manhattan skyline. The waterfront is lined with parks and promenades, making it a perfect spot for leisurely walks, jogging, or simply enjoying the iconic skyline. **Pier A Park** and **Pier C Park** are especially popular for their wide-open spaces, ideal for picnics, sunsets, and skyline photography.

Hoboken Waterfront Walkway: This pedestrian pathway stretches along the river, offering beautiful views of the skyline and the Hudson River. It's a peaceful place to stroll or bike, with plenty of benches and spots to relax while admiring the New York skyline.

3. Rich History and Cultural Significance

Birthplace of Frank Sinatra: Hoboken is famously known as the birthplace of music legend Frank Sinatra. Fans of "Ol' Blue Eyes" can visit landmarks like **Frank Sinatra Park** and **Sinatra Drive**, named in his honor. Sinatra's legacy is celebrated throughout the town, and his influence is a point of pride for locals.

Stevens Institute of Technology: Located on a hill overlooking the river, this historic university contributes to Hoboken's vibrant atmosphere. The campus features beautiful green spaces, and visitors can enjoy the panoramic views from **Castle Point**, the highest point in Hoboken.

First Baseball Game: Hoboken also claims to be the site of the first officially recorded baseball game, played at **Elysian Fields** in 1846. While the fields are no longer there, a plaque commemorates the event, making it a must-see for baseball enthusiasts.

4. Small-Town Charm with Urban Vibes

Boutique Shopping and Local Markets: Hoboken's main street, **Washington Street**, is known for its array of boutique shops, cafés, and specialty stores. Here, visitors can enjoy a more relaxed shopping experience compared to the hustle of New York City, with plenty of unique, locally-owned businesses offering everything from artisanal goods to vintage clothing.

Hoboken Farmers Market: During the warmer months, the town hosts a vibrant farmers market where visitors can sample fresh, local produce, baked goods, and artisanal products. It's a great way to experience the community vibe of Hoboken.

Charming Brownstones and Architecture: Much like parts of Brooklyn, Hoboken is filled with tree-lined streets and historic brownstone buildings. The charming architecture adds to the town's appeal, giving it a quintessential small-town feel despite its proximity to New York City.

5. Food and Nightlife Scene

Culinary Diversity: Despite its small size, Hoboken boasts a diverse and exciting food scene. From casual eateries to fine dining, the town is home to a wide range of restaurants that reflect the multicultural character of the area.

Italian Cuisine: Hoboken is known for its Italian-American heritage, and some of the best Italian restaurants and bakeries in the region are found here. **Carlo's Bakery**, made famous by the TV show *Cake Boss*, is a popular spot for desserts, especially cannoli.

Waterfront Dining: Hoboken's riverside restaurants offer both delicious food and fantastic views of the New York City skyline. Places like **The Ainsworth** and **Blue Eyes** offer outdoor seating with unbeatable vistas.

Vibrant Nightlife: Hoboken's nightlife is lively and varied, making it a great place for a night out. **Washington Street** is lined with bars, pubs, and lounges, ranging from casual spots to more upscale venues. The town is known for its vibrant bar scene, and many spots offer rooftop views of the skyline. Popular venues like **The Brass Rail** and **Moran's** attract both locals and visitors for drinks, socializing, and live music.

6. Family-Friendly Atmosphere and Outdoor Activities

Parks and Recreation: Hoboken is home to numerous parks that offer space for relaxation, recreation, and family-friendly activities. In addition to **Pier A Park** and **Pier C Park**, the town features **Maxwell Place Park**, a waterfront space with playgrounds, walking paths, and picnic areas. These parks are great for families, offering outdoor activities with a view.

Biking and Jogging: Hoboken is also a bike-friendly town, with many locals and visitors taking advantage of the relatively flat terrain and scenic routes along the Hudson River. The **Hoboken Cove Boathouse** even offers free kayaking sessions during the summer months, allowing visitors to enjoy the river up close.

7. Community Events and Festivals

Hoboken Arts & Music Festival: This popular annual event showcases local artists, musicians, and vendors along Washington Street. It's a great way for visitors to experience the local culture and enjoy live music, crafts, and food in a lively street fair setting.

Saint Ann's Italian Festival: Celebrating Hoboken's Italian heritage, this summer festival features traditional Italian food, live music, and games. It culminates with a procession honoring Saint Ann, making it a lively and cultural experience for visitors.

8. More Affordable Accommodation Option

Compared to Manhattan and even parts of Brooklyn, Hoboken offers more affordable accommodation options, making it a popular choice for visitors who want to stay close to NYC without paying Manhattan prices. Hotels,

Airbnbs, and rental apartments are available throughout the town, often offering views of the skyline or proximity to the waterfront.

Yonkers, New York

1. Proximity and Accessibility to NYC

Easy Access to Manhattan: Yonkers is just 15 miles north of Manhattan, making it a convenient base for visitors who want to explore both New York City and the greater Hudson Valley. There are several transportation options for getting to and from the city:

Metro-North Railroad: The **Hudson Line** of the Metro-North Railroad provides fast and easy access to Grand Central Terminal in Midtown Manhattan. Trains run frequently, and the journey takes about 30 minutes, making it ideal for day trips or commuting.

Driving: For those who prefer driving, Yonkers is accessible via major highways such as the Saw Mill River Parkway, the Bronx River Parkway, and I-87 (New York State Thruway), allowing for easy road travel to and from New York City and other areas in Westchester County.

Bus Services: Multiple bus lines also connect Yonkers to neighboring areas and the Bronx, from where visitors can transfer to New York City's subway system.

2. Rich History and Landmarks

Philipse Manor Hall: One of the most historically significant sites in Yonkers, **Philipse Manor Hall** is a colonial-era mansion that dates back to the late 1600s. It served as the estate of the powerful Philipse family and is now a museum that offers insights into Yonkers' early history. The building itself is a striking example of Georgian architecture and is listed on the National Register of Historic Places.

Sherwood House: This historic farmhouse, built in 1740, is one of the oldest buildings in Yonkers and offers a glimpse into colonial life. Visitors can tour the house and learn about the city's role during the Revolutionary War.

St. John's Episcopal Church: Located in the heart of Yonkers, this church was built in 1752 and is one of the city's oldest landmarks. Its historic graveyard includes tombs of notable Yonkers residents and adds to the city's rich historical fabric.

3. Scenic Waterfront and Outdoor Spaces

Hudson River Waterfront: Yonkers is situated along the Hudson River, providing stunning views and waterfront attractions. The revitalized **Yonkers Waterfront** area has transformed into a lively hub with restaurants, parks, and a beautiful esplanade where visitors can enjoy scenic walks along the river.

Yonkers Pier: The historic pier is a great spot to relax, take in views of the Hudson River, and watch the sunset. The waterfront area also hosts seasonal events, concerts, and festivals.

Untermyer Gardens Conservancy: One of Yonkers' hidden gems, **Untermyer Gardens** is a beautifully landscaped public garden featuring a blend of formal and naturalistic design. Originally part of a grand private estate, the gardens are now open to the public and include striking features like a walled Persian garden, a Grecian amphitheater, and terraced lawns with sweeping views of the Hudson River. It's a peaceful retreat that feels worlds away from the bustle of the city.

Sprain Ridge Park: Located just outside the city center, Sprain Ridge Park offers outdoor enthusiasts a range of activities, including hiking, biking, and swimming. The park's network of trails is perfect for a day of exploring nature without venturing far from the city.

4. Diverse Food and Dining Scene

Ethnically Diverse Restaurants: Yonkers' population reflects a broad range of cultural backgrounds, and its culinary scene is equally diverse. The city is known for its mix of Italian, Irish, Caribbean, and Latin American restaurants, with eateries offering everything from casual comfort food to upscale dining experiences.

Arthur Avenue-style Italian Dining: Yonkers has a strong Italian-American community, and visitors can enjoy classic Italian dining experiences, similar to the ones found on nearby Arthur Avenue in the Bronx, with many local pizzerias and restaurants serving up authentic Italian dishes.

Yonkers Brewing Company: Located in the heart of the Yonkers waterfront district, this local brewery has become a popular spot for both residents and visitors. It offers a rotating selection of craft beers and is a great place to relax after a day of sightseeing.

Farmers Market: During the warmer months, Yonkers hosts a **farmers market** along the waterfront, where visitors can sample fresh local produce, baked goods, and artisanal products from regional vendors.

5. Arts, Culture, and Entertainment

Hudson River Museum: The **Hudson River Museum** is a key cultural attraction in Yonkers, offering a mix of art, history, and science. The museum features a permanent collection of 19th and 20th-century American art, rotating exhibitions, and an outdoor amphitheater that hosts concerts and events. The museum's **Andrus Planetarium** is also a popular destination for families and astronomy enthusiasts.

Theater and Performing Arts: Yonkers has a growing performing arts scene, with venues like the **Yonkers Arts District** supporting local artists and hosting community events. The city is also home to the **Emelin Theatre**, which presents a variety of performances, including music, dance, and theater.

Empire City Casino: For those looking for entertainment, Yonkers is home to the **Empire City Casino** at **Yonkers Raceway**. The casino offers slot machines, electronic games, and horse racing, making it a popular spot for both locals and tourists. Yonkers Raceway also hosts live harness racing events throughout the year.

6. Family-Friendly Attractions

Legoland Discovery Center: Located in nearby **Ridge Hill Mall**, **Legoland Discovery Center** is a popular attraction for families with children. It features interactive exhibits, rides, and even a replica of the New York City skyline made entirely out of Lego bricks. Ridge Hill Mall also offers a wide range of shopping and dining options, making it a convenient destination for families.

Science Barge: The **Science Barge**, docked on the Hudson River, is a floating environmental education center and greenhouse. Families can tour the barge to learn about sustainable farming practices and renewable energy while enjoying views of the river.

7. Shopping and Retail

Ridge Hill Mall: One of the largest shopping centers in Westchester County, Ridge Hill offers a wide variety of retail stores, dining options, and entertainment facilities. It's home to major retailers, as well as boutique shops, making it a one-stop destination for shopping and entertainment.

Cross County Shopping Center: Another major retail hub in Yonkers, the **Cross County Shopping Center** is an open-air mall featuring over 100 stores, including popular brands, department stores, and restaurants.

8. Affordable Accommodations

Yonkers offers more affordable accommodation options compared to staying in Manhattan or other parts of New York City. Visitors can find a range of hotels, from budget-friendly chains to more upscale options, making it a convenient and cost-effective base for exploring both New York City and the surrounding Hudson Valley.

Tarrytown, New York

1. Proximity and Accessibility to NYC

Close to New York City: Located just 40 minutes by car or train from Manhattan, Tarrytown is a convenient and peaceful escape from the hustle and bustle of the city.

Metro-North Railroad: The **Hudson Line** of the Metro-North Railroad offers frequent service between Tarrytown and Grand Central Terminal, with a scenic ride along the Hudson River. The train journey takes about 35 to 40 minutes, making it ideal for day trips.

Driving: Tarrytown is easily accessible by car via major highways such as the Tappan Zee Bridge (Governor Mario M. Cuomo Bridge) and I-87, providing a quick route from New York City and other parts of Westchester County.

2. Historical Significance and Landmarks

Lyndhurst Mansion: One of the most famous attractions in Tarrytown, **Lyndhurst Mansion** is a stunning Gothic Revival estate that once belonged to railroad tycoon Jay Gould. The mansion is set on beautifully landscaped grounds with sweeping views of the Hudson River. Visitors can tour the opulent interiors and explore the estate's gardens and walking paths. Throughout the year, Lyndhurst hosts various events, including art shows, holiday tours, and outdoor concerts.

The Tarrytown Music Hall: Opened in 1885, the **Tarrytown Music Hall** is one of the oldest theaters in Westchester County and is listed on the National Register of Historic Places. This historic venue offers a diverse array of performances, including concerts, plays, films, and comedy shows. Its intimate setting and impressive lineup of talent make it a must-visit for anyone interested in the arts.

Washington Irving's Sunnyside: Just a short distance from Tarrytown is **Sunnyside**, the former home of Washington Irving, one of America's most famous authors. Irving, best known for his short stories *The Legend of Sleepy Hollow* and *Rip Van Winkle*, lived here in the 19th century. The beautifully preserved home and gardens are open for tours, giving visitors a glimpse into the life of this literary icon.

The Old Dutch Church of Sleepy Hollow: A short drive from Tarrytown, this historic church is one of the oldest in New York State, dating back to the late 1600s. The adjoining **Sleepy Hollow Cemetery** is the final resting place of Washington Irving, as well as other notable figures like Andrew Carnegie and William Rockefeller.

3. Scenic Hudson River Views and Outdoor Activities

Scenic Riverfront: Tarrytown is located along the Hudson River, offering stunning views of the water and the surrounding landscape. The town's riverfront parks, such as **Pierson Park**, provide beautiful places to relax, picnic, or take a stroll along the water. The views of the **Tappan Zee Bridge** and the river's expanse are especially striking at sunset.

Rockefeller State Park Preserve: For nature lovers, the **Rockefeller State Park Preserve** is just minutes from Tarrytown and offers over 1,400 acres of beautiful woodlands, fields, and lakes. The park's extensive trail system is ideal for hiking, horseback riding, bird watching, and cross-country skiing in the winter. The trails wind through scenic landscapes, including the famous **Swan Lake** and the surrounding forest, offering a peaceful retreat from city life.

Tappan Zee Bridge Path: The **Governor Mario M. Cuomo Bridge** (formerly the Tappan Zee Bridge) features a pedestrian and bicycle path, allowing visitors to enjoy breathtaking views of the Hudson River and surrounding areas while walking or biking across the bridge. The path includes rest stops with scenic overlooks, art installations, and interpretive signs about the history and engineering of the bridge.

4. Quaint Town Vibe with Local Shops and Dining

Historic Main Street: Tarrytown's Main Street is lined with charming shops, cafés, and restaurants, giving visitors a quintessential small-town experience. Many of the buildings date back to the 19th century, adding to the town's historic ambiance. Whether you're browsing antique stores, enjoying a cup of coffee at a local café, or shopping for unique gifts, Tarrytown's Main Street offers a welcoming and leisurely atmosphere.

Dining in Tarrytown: The town has an impressive selection of dining options, ranging from casual eateries to upscale restaurants. Many restaurants in Tarrytown emphasize farm-to-table dining, using fresh, local ingredients from the Hudson Valley.

The RiverMarket Bar & Kitchen: This popular restaurant on the Hudson River waterfront offers a farm-to-table menu with a focus on local, sustainable ingredients. Its seasonal dishes and craft cocktails make it a favorite for both locals and visitors.

Horsefeathers: A cozy and casual spot near Lyndhurst Mansion, **Horsefeathers** is a favorite for its comfort food, craft beers, and inviting atmosphere. It's a great place to grab a bite after a day of exploring the town's historic sites.

5. Festivals and Community Events

Tarrytown Halloween Festivities: Tarrytown and neighboring Sleepy Hollow are famous for their Halloween celebrations, drawing visitors from all over. Events such as the **Great Jack O'Lantern Blaze** feature thousands of hand-carved pumpkins lit up in intricate designs, creating a magical and spooky atmosphere. The town's Halloween parade, haunted hayrides, and tours of Sleepy Hollow Cemetery make this area a must-visit for those who love the holiday.

Tarrytown Arts & Crafts Fair: Held annually, this fair brings together local artisans and vendors offering handmade crafts, jewelry, artwork, and more. It's a great way to experience the local culture and pick up unique souvenirs from the region.

Farmers Market: The **Tarrytown and Sleepy Hollow Farmers Market** is a popular event during the warmer months. Held on Saturdays, the market offers fresh produce, baked goods, artisanal foods, and handmade crafts from local vendors. It's a great place to experience the bounty of the Hudson Valley and support local businesses.

6. Family-Friendly Attractions

Stone Barns Center for Food & Agriculture: Located just a short drive from Tarrytown, the **Stone Barns Center** is a working farm and educational center dedicated to promoting sustainable agriculture. Families can tour the farm, visit the animals, and learn about organic farming practices. The center also offers hands-on workshops and seasonal events, making it a fun and educational destination for both kids and adults.

Kykuit, the Rockefeller Estate: Just outside of Tarrytown in Pocantico Hills is **Kykuit**, the former estate of the Rockefeller family. This grand mansion is open for tours, which include the estate's impressive art collection, beautifully manicured gardens, and panoramic views of the Hudson River. The estate also has a museum showcasing modern art, including works by Picasso, Warhol, and Calder.

7. Affordable Lodging and Stay Options

Tarrytown offers a range of accommodation options to suit different budgets, making it an appealing choice for both short stays and longer getaways. Visitors can find charming inns, bed-and-breakfasts, and more modern hotels, many of which offer views of the Hudson River or are set in historic buildings.

Tarrytown House Estate: This historic estate offers luxury accommodations in a beautiful setting overlooking the Hudson River. With well-appointed rooms, manicured gardens, and an on-site restaurant, it's a perfect choice for visitors looking for a more upscale stay.

Comfortable B&Bs: There are also several charming bed-and-breakfasts in the area, providing a cozy and personal lodging experience for travelers who prefer a more intimate stay.

Sleepy Hollow, New York

1. The Legend of Sleepy Hollow and Washington Irving

Washington Irving's Influence: Sleepy Hollow owes much of its fame to Washington Irving, who set his famous tale *The Legend of Sleepy Hollow* in the area. Published in 1820, this haunting story introduced readers to Ichabod Crane and the Headless Horseman, and it forever linked the village to tales of ghosts and eerie happenings.

Sunnyside, Irving's Home: Located nearby in Tarrytown, **Sunnyside** was the home of Washington Irving, and today it serves as a museum dedicated to his life and works. Visitors can tour the house and gardens, gaining insight into the author's life and the area that inspired his most famous stories.

2. Halloween Festivities and Haunted Attractions

The Great Jack O'Lantern Blaze: Perhaps one of Sleepy Hollow's most famous events is the **Great Jack O'Lantern Blaze**, held each fall. This dazzling display features thousands of intricately carved pumpkins illuminated in stunning designs across the grounds of the historic Van Cortlandt Manor. It's a family-friendly event that attracts visitors from all over, with the pumpkins carved into everything from mythical creatures to life-size dinosaurs.

Horseman's Hollow: For those who love a good scare, **Horseman's Hollow** is a haunted experience that brings Washington Irving's tale to life. Set in the heart of Sleepy Hollow, this immersive attraction turns Philipsburg Manor into a dark, eerie landscape inhabited by creatures and ghouls inspired by *The Legend of Sleepy Hollow*. It's one of the most popular Halloween events in the region and offers a thrilling experience for those who dare.

Sleepy Hollow Cemetery Tours: Sleepy Hollow is home to one of the most famous cemeteries in the United States, the **Sleepy Hollow Cemetery**. Here, visitors can take guided tours of the historic grounds, where they'll learn about some of the notable figures buried there, including Washington Irving himself. The cemetery is also the resting place of famous individuals like Andrew Carnegie, William Rockefeller, and Elizabeth Arden. The tours are especially popular around Halloween, when the spooky atmosphere adds to the allure.

3. Historical Landmarks and Attractions

Philipsburg Manor: A key historical site in Sleepy Hollow, **Philipsburg Manor** is a restored 18th-century estate that offers a glimpse into colonial life in the Hudson Valley. Visitors can tour the manor house, working farm, and gristmill, learning about the lives of the Dutch settlers and enslaved Africans who once lived and worked there. The site is beautifully preserved, and reenactments bring history to life, making it a great educational stop for history enthusiasts.

Old Dutch Church: The **Old Dutch Church of Sleepy Hollow** is one of the oldest churches in New York, dating back to the late 1600s. The church and its adjoining cemetery play a key role in Irving's *The Legend of Sleepy Hollow*, with Ichabod Crane famously chased by the Headless Horseman to the church's bridge. The church and its graveyard, filled with tombstones from the 17th and 18th centuries, are a major attraction for fans of the legend. Visitors can explore the grounds or attend special services and events held throughout the year.

Kykuit, the Rockefeller Estate: Just outside Sleepy Hollow is **Kykuit**, the former estate of the Rockefeller family. This grand estate, with its breathtaking gardens and stunning views of the Hudson River, is open for tours and showcases the family's art collection, including works by Picasso and Calder. The meticulously landscaped grounds and impressive architecture make Kykuit one of the most iconic homes in the region.

4. Scenic Riverfront and Outdoor Activities

Hudson River Views: Sleepy Hollow's location along the Hudson River offers beautiful scenic views, particularly at sunset. Visitors can enjoy a peaceful stroll along the riverfront or relax in one of the many parks that dot the area.

Rockefeller State Park Preserve: Just minutes away from Sleepy Hollow is the **Rockefeller State Park Preserve**, offering more than 1,400 acres of pristine woodlands, fields, and wetlands. The preserve is a haven for outdoor enthusiasts, with miles of hiking and walking trails that meander through some of the most scenic landscapes in the Hudson Valley. Whether you're looking for a quiet place to enjoy nature or seeking adventure through horseback riding or birdwatching, the preserve is a fantastic option.

Kingsland Point Park: Another beautiful outdoor space in Sleepy Hollow is **Kingsland Point Park**, which offers spectacular views of the Hudson River and the iconic Tarrytown Lighthouse. The park is perfect for picnicking, fishing, and waterfront walks, and its proximity to the river makes it a peaceful retreat from the town's more bustling areas.

5. Small-Town Charm and Dining

Quaint Village Atmosphere: Despite its proximity to New York City, Sleepy Hollow maintains a quaint, small-town charm. The village's picturesque streets are lined with historic buildings, cozy cafés, and local shops. It's a perfect destination for those who want to escape the fast pace of city life while still enjoying a rich cultural and historical experience.

Dining in Sleepy Hollow: The village offers a variety of dining options, ranging from casual spots to upscale restaurants. Many of the eateries here emphasize farm-to-table dining, using fresh ingredients from the Hudson Valley. Whether you're grabbing a bite at a cozy café or enjoying a gourmet meal at one of the town's fine dining establishments, Sleepy Hollow's food scene won't disappoint.

6. Family-Friendly Activities

Sleepy Hollow Farmers Market: Held on weekends, the **Sleepy Hollow Farmers Market** offers fresh produce, baked goods, and artisan products from local vendors. It's a great spot to pick up some Hudson Valley specialties and enjoy a leisurely morning with the family.

Sleepy Hollow Lighthouse: The **Tarrytown Lighthouse** (often called the Sleepy Hollow Lighthouse) is an iconic structure that dates back to the 19th century. Visitors can walk along the riverfront to the lighthouse and take in the beautiful views of the Hudson River and the Tappan Zee Bridge. The lighthouse also serves as a great spot for photography, especially at sunset.

7. Easy Access to New York City

Close to Manhattan: Sleepy Hollow is located just 30 miles north of Manhattan, making it easily accessible for day trips. The **Metro-North Railroad** offers regular train service from Sleepy Hollow to Grand Central Terminal, with the trip taking just under an hour. For those driving, it's an easy drive up the scenic **Hudson River Parkway** or via the **Tappan Zee Bridge**.

Grace Bennett

Beacon, New York

1. Dia

– A Contemporary Art Mecca

Dia

is one of the town's main draws, a world-renowned contemporary art museum that houses large-scale installations and works from prominent artists of the 1960s to today. Housed in a former Nabisco box-printing factory, the museum's massive, light-filled spaces make it a unique setting for modern and contemporary art exhibitions.

Artists such as Richard Serra, Dan Flavin, and Donald Judd are prominently featured, and the museum's location right on the banks of the Hudson River adds to its serene yet industrial atmosphere. For art lovers, Dia

alone makes the trip to Beacon worth it, offering a premier art experience just a short train ride from New York City.

2. Main Street – A Bustling Hub of Creativity

Main Street in Beacon is known for its array of independent boutiques, galleries, and restaurants. Strolling down this vibrant street, visitors will find everything from handmade crafts and vintage shops to contemporary art galleries and chic cafés. It's a place where old meets new, with historic buildings repurposed into trendy venues that reflect the town's artistic spirit.

Art Galleries and Studios: Many local artists have set up studios and galleries along Main Street, making it a great spot to discover emerging talent. Monthly events such as Second Saturday allow visitors to explore the galleries during evening art walks.

Boutique Shopping: For shoppers, Main Street offers a unique blend of antique stores, curated fashion boutiques, and specialty shops selling artisanal products, making it perfect for those seeking one-of-a-kind finds.

3. Scenic Outdoor Beauty and Hiking Trails

Mount Beacon: For outdoor enthusiasts, Mount Beacon offers one of the best hiking experiences in the Hudson Valley. The Mount Beacon Incline Railway Trail takes visitors on a moderately challenging hike up the mountain, where the summit rewards them with sweeping views of the Hudson River and surrounding valleys. At the top, hikers can also explore the ruins of the former incline railway, which was once the steepest funicular railway in North America.

Hudson Riverfront Park: Down by the river, Beacon Riverfront Park is a peaceful spot for walking, picnicking, or just enjoying the views of the Hudson River. The park is also home to Long Dock Park, where visitors can rent kayaks, take paddleboarding lessons, or relax by the water.

4. Rich Historical Significance

Beacon's Industrial Past: Beacon's history as an industrial center is still visible in the town's architecture and layout. In the 19th and early 20th centuries, Beacon was known for its textile mills, hat factories, and brick-making. Many of these factories have now been converted into creative spaces, like Dia and artist studios, but the town's history is still honored in local museums and historic sites.

Madam Brett Homestead: For a deeper dive into Beacon's history, a visit to the Madam Brett Homestead, the oldest building in the town, offers a glimpse into colonial life in the Hudson Valley. Built in 1709, this Dutch-style home has been preserved as a museum, showcasing early American life and Beacon's development through the centuries.

5. Culinary Scene and Craft Beverages

Farm-to-Table Dining: Beacon's food scene reflects the Hudson Valley's emphasis on fresh, locally sourced ingredients. Many of the town's restaurants offer farm-to-table dining, with menus featuring seasonal produce, artisanal cheeses, and locally raised meats. Popular spots like The Roundhouse and Kitchen Sink Food & Drink have become go-to destinations for foodies visiting the area.

Craft Breweries and Distilleries: Beacon is also known for its craft beer and spirits. Hudson Valley Brewery is a local favorite, offering unique brews in an industrial setting that perfectly matches the town's creative vibe. Visitors can also explore nearby distilleries, such as Denning's Point Distillery, which produces small-batch spirits using local ingredients.

6. A Hub for Art Festivals and Events

Beacon Open Studios: This annual event showcases the work of local artists, giving visitors the chance to tour studios, meet the artists, and view art in progress. It's a great way to experience the creative energy that defines the town.

Beacon Independent Film Festival: Held annually in the fall, the Beacon Independent Film Festival draws filmmakers and cinema enthusiasts from across the region. The festival screens independent films, documentaries, and short films, offering a platform for emerging filmmakers and a unique cultural event for attendees.

7. Easy Access from New York City

Metro-North Railroad: Beacon's location on the Metro-North Hudson Line makes it easily accessible for visitors from New York City. The train ride from Grand Central Terminal takes about 90 minutes, offering stunning views of the Hudson River along the way. For city dwellers looking for a quick getaway, Beacon is an ideal destination that combines nature, art, and culture.

Driving: For those traveling by car, Beacon is a scenic drive up the Taconic State Parkway or Route 9, with many visitors opting to make the trip as part of a larger exploration of the Hudson Valley.

8. Music and Nightlife

Live Music and Entertainment: While Beacon is known for its relaxed, artsy atmosphere, it also has a lively music scene. Local venues like The Towne Crier Café host live performances, featuring everything from folk and jazz to indie rock. With its intimate setting and eclectic lineup of performers, the Towne Crier is a beloved venue for both locals and visitors alike.

The Beacon Theatre: Not to be confused with its famous Manhattan counterpart, Beacon's Beacon Theatre is a restored historic venue that hosts concerts, plays, and film screenings, further enhancing the town's vibrant cultural offerings.

Grace Bennett

Cold Spring, New York

1. Historic Village Charm

Preserved Architecture: Cold Spring's Main Street is lined with beautifully preserved 19th-century buildings, many of which house quaint shops, restaurants, and art galleries. Walking along this charming street feels like stepping back in time, as the village has retained much of its original character. The Victorian and Federal-style homes, along with old-fashioned storefronts, add to Cold Spring's timeless appeal.

Antique Shops and Boutiques: Cold Spring is a haven for antique lovers. The village's many antique shops offer a wide range of unique finds, from vintage furniture and collectibles to rare books and jewelry. Whether you're a serious collector or just looking for a memorable keepsake, Cold Spring's Main Street is the perfect place to browse for treasures.

2. Outdoor Adventures and Hiking Trails

Breakneck Ridge: One of the most popular hiking spots in the Hudson Valley, **Breakneck Ridge** offers breathtaking views of the Hudson River and surrounding mountains. This challenging trail is known for its steep climbs and rocky scrambles, but hikers are rewarded with panoramic vistas at the summit. It's a must-do for outdoor enthusiasts visiting Cold Spring.

Hudson Highlands State Park: Cold Spring is surrounded by the scenic beauty of **Hudson Highlands State Park**, which offers a variety of hiking trails ranging from easy to strenuous. In addition to Breakneck Ridge, the park features trails like the **Cornish Estate Trail**, which leads to the ruins of a historic mansion, and the **Bull Hill (Mt. Taurus) Trail**, offering more stunning views of the Hudson River and the town below.

Kayaking on the Hudson River: For those who prefer water activities, Cold Spring is a great starting point for kayaking trips on the Hudson River. Several local outfitters offer kayak rentals and guided tours, allowing visitors to explore the river's calm waters while taking in the majestic mountain and river views.

3. Cold Spring's Riverside Beauty

Cold Spring Waterfront: The village's location along the Hudson River makes it a peaceful spot to relax by the water. The **Cold Spring Dock** offers beautiful views of the river and the mountains on the opposite bank. It's a great place to enjoy a picnic, watch the sunset, or simply take in the natural beauty of the Hudson Valley.

Scenic Hudson River Views: From nearly anywhere in Cold Spring, visitors are treated to sweeping views of the Hudson River and the surrounding Hudson Highlands. The riverfront park is an ideal spot for a quiet afternoon, with benches and walking paths where you can enjoy the serene environment.

4. Historical Sites and Attractions

West Point Foundry Preserve: Cold Spring played an important role during the Industrial Revolution, and the **West Point Foundry Preserve** is a fascinating historic site that tells the story of the town's industrial past. Once one of the country's leading ironworks, the foundry produced everything from steam engines to Civil War cannons. Today, the area has been turned into a scenic park where visitors can explore the ruins of the foundry, view interpretive exhibits, and walk along nature trails.

Stonecrop Gardens: Just a short drive from Cold Spring is **Stonecrop Gardens**, a 12-acre public garden that features a stunning variety of plants, including alpine plants, woodland flora, and an exquisite collection of flowers. The garden is a hidden gem and provides a tranquil escape for visitors who appreciate horticulture and natural beauty.

Boscobel House and Gardens: Located just outside of Cold Spring, **Boscobel House** is a historic Federal-style mansion overlooking the Hudson River. The house, built in the early 19th century, has been beautifully restored and is now a museum that offers tours of the elegant interiors. The surrounding gardens and grounds are equally impressive, offering stunning views of the Hudson River and Constitution Marsh.

5. Culinary Delights and Farm-to-Table Dining

Farm-to-Table Restaurants: Cold Spring's dining scene emphasizes local ingredients and farm-to-table cuisine, making it a popular destination for food lovers. Restaurants like **Hudson House River Inn** and **Cold Spring Depot** offer delicious meals with locally sourced ingredients, often paired with scenic views of the river. Whether you're in the mood for a casual meal or a fine dining experience, Cold Spring's restaurants deliver fresh, flavorful dishes.

Cafés and Bakeries: The village is also home to several cozy cafés and bakeries where you can enjoy a cup of coffee or a sweet treat. Popular spots like **Riverview Restaurant** and **Moo Moo's Creamery** provide everything from hearty breakfasts to homemade ice cream.

6. Easy Access to New York City

Metro-North Railroad: Cold Spring's proximity to New York City makes it an easy day trip or weekend getaway for city dwellers. The **Metro-North Railroad's Hudson Line** provides direct service from Grand Central Terminal to Cold Spring, with the trip taking about 70 minutes. The Cold Spring train station is just a short walk from the village center, making it convenient for visitors to explore without needing a car.

Driving: For those who prefer to drive, Cold Spring is accessible via the **Taconic State Parkway** or **Route 9**, offering a scenic and leisurely route through the Hudson Valley.

7. Festivals and Events

Cold Spring Farmers' Market: Held year-round, the **Cold Spring Farmers' Market** is a great place to pick up fresh, locally grown produce and artisanal goods. The market showcases the bounty of the Hudson Valley, with vendors offering everything from organic vegetables to handmade cheeses and baked goods.

Cold Spring by Candlelight: During the holiday season, Cold Spring comes alive with festive lights and decorations for the annual **Cold Spring by Candlelight** event. The village's historic homes are illuminated, and visitors can enjoy guided tours, holiday shopping, and seasonal treats, all while soaking in the village's festive charm.

Grace Bennett

Chapter 4: Where to Stay in New York City

Luxury Hotels

For those seeking the pinnacle of comfort and sophistication, New York City's luxury hotels offer an unparalleled experience. From opulent rooms with stunning city views to world-class amenities and impeccable service, these high-end accommodations cater to travelers looking for an extraordinary stay. Whether you prefer a historic landmark with classic elegance or a modern marvel with cutting-edge design, New York's luxury hotels promise an unforgettable vacation, blending convenience with lavish indulgence.

Top 5 Luxury Hotels

1. **The Ritz-Carlton New York, Central Park**

The Ritz-Carlton New York, Central Park is a premier luxury hotel known for its opulent accommodations and exceptional service. Situated in one of the most prestigious locations in New York City, this hotel epitomizes luxury with its elegant design, refined amenities, and breathtaking views of Central Park. It's an ideal choice for tourists looking to indulge in a lavish vacation experience.

Location (Address & Proximity)

Address: 50 Central Park South, New York, NY 10019, USA

Proximity:

Central Park: The hotel is located directly across the street from Central Park, offering unobstructed views and easy access to one of New York City's most iconic landmarks.

Times Square: Approximately 1 mile (1.6 km) away, easily accessible by a short walk or a quick cab ride.

Broadway Theaters: Around 1 mile (1.6 km), providing convenient access to some of the city's best shows.

Fifth Avenue Shopping: Just a short walk away, ideal for those looking to indulge in high-end retail therapy.

Subway Stations: The closest subway stations are located within walking distance, offering connections to various parts of the city.

Highlights

Views of Central Park: Many rooms offer stunning views of Central Park, providing a serene backdrop amidst the bustling city.

Luxurious Accommodations: The hotel boasts elegantly designed rooms and suites with sophisticated decor, high-end furnishings, and top-notch amenities.

Exclusive Service: Renowned for its impeccable service, including personalized concierge assistance and 24-hour room service.

Spa and Wellness

The Ritz-Carlton Spa: The hotel features a full-service spa offering a range of treatments, from massages to facials, designed to provide ultimate relaxation and rejuvenation.

Fitness Center: A state-of-the-art fitness center is available for guests to maintain their workout routines while traveling.

Bars

Audrey's: This chic bar offers a sophisticated atmosphere with a menu featuring classic cocktails and a curated selection of fine wines. It's a perfect spot for a pre-dinner drink or an evening nightcap.

Events and Conferences

Event Spaces: The Ritz-Carlton New York, Central Park offers elegant event spaces ideal for weddings, corporate meetings, and social gatherings. The hotel's venues include a grand ballroom and smaller, intimate rooms equipped with the latest technology.

Event Planning Services: Dedicated event planning professionals are available to assist with every detail, ensuring a seamless and memorable experience.

Basic Facilities and Amenities

Dining: The hotel features fine dining options, including a restaurant serving contemporary American cuisine.

Concierge Service: The concierge team can assist with dining reservations, tickets to local attractions, and other personalized requests.

Business Services: Includes high-speed internet, meeting rooms, and business center services.

Pet-Friendly: The hotel accommodates pets, ensuring a comfortable stay for both guests and their furry friends.

Opening and Closing Hours

Hotel Reception: Open 24 hours a day.

Restaurants and Bars: Vary by venue, but generally follow standard dining hours, with breakfast typically starting around 6:30 AM and dinner service extending into the evening.

Spa: Usually open from early morning until late evening, but exact hours may vary.

Price

Rates at The Ritz-Carlton New York, Central Park vary significantly depending on the time of year, room type, and booking conditions. On average, rates start around $1,000 per night for standard rooms and can go upwards of $3,000 per night for suites. It's advisable to check current rates and availability directly through the hotel's website or booking platforms.

Pros

Prime Location: Directly opposite Central Park and close to major attractions.

Luxurious Experience: High-quality accommodations and exceptional service.

Stunning Views: Many rooms offer impressive views of Central Park.

High-End Amenities: Includes a top-notch spa, fitness center, and exclusive dining options.

Cons

High Price Point: Luxury comes at a premium, making it one of the more expensive options in the city.

Crowds: The area around Central Park and Times Square can be busy, which may impact the overall experience.

Local Tips

Book Early: Due to its popularity, rooms can fill up quickly, especially during peak tourist seasons and major events.

Use the Concierge: The hotel's concierge can provide valuable local tips, such as the best times to visit nearby attractions and recommendations for dining and entertainment.

Explore Central Park: Take advantage of the hotel's location by exploring Central Park. Consider renting a bike or taking a leisurely stroll to enjoy its vast green spaces and scenic spots.

2. **The Peninsula New York**

The Peninsula New York is a distinguished luxury hotel that combines classic elegance with modern sophistication. Known for its exceptional service and refined accommodations, it offers an unparalleled experience in the heart of Manhattan. With a rich history and a commitment to luxury, The Peninsula stands out as a premier destination for both leisure and business travelers.

Location (Address & Proximity)

Address: 700 Fifth Avenue, New York, NY 10019, USA

Proximity:

Central Park: Approximately 0.5 miles (0.8 km) away, a short walk to the park's southern edge.

Times Square: About 0.7 miles (1.1 km), easily accessible by a brief walk or taxi ride.

Broadway Theaters: Roughly 0.7 miles (1.1 km), convenient for theatergoers.

Fifth Avenue Shopping: Directly on Fifth Avenue, placing you steps away from high-end retail stores and flagship boutiques.

Subway Stations: Several subway lines are nearby, including the 5th Avenue/59th Street station, offering easy access to other parts of the city.

Highlights

Luxurious Accommodations: The hotel offers elegantly designed rooms and suites with high-end furnishings, modern technology, and exceptional attention to detail.

Prime Location: Situated on Fifth Avenue, it provides immediate access to world-class shopping, dining, and entertainment.

Impeccable Service: Renowned for its personalized and attentive service, ensuring a memorable stay.

Spa and Wellness

The Peninsula Spa: The hotel features a world-class spa offering a range of treatments, including massages, facials, and body therapies. It's a sanctuary for relaxation and rejuvenation.

Fitness Center: A well-equipped fitness center is available for guests, featuring state-of-the-art exercise equipment and personal training services.

Bars

Salon de Ning: Located on the rooftop, this chic bar offers panoramic views of the city, along with a stylish ambiance and a menu of creative cocktails and light bites.

The Peninsula Lounge: An elegant spot for afternoon tea or cocktails, providing a sophisticated setting with comfortable seating and a refined atmosphere.

Events and Conferences

Event Spaces: The Peninsula New York features versatile event spaces, including a grand ballroom and several smaller meeting rooms. These venues are ideal for weddings, corporate events, and private gatherings.

Event Planning Services: The hotel provides comprehensive event planning services, including catering, audiovisual equipment, and dedicated event staff to ensure every detail is meticulously handled.

Basic Facilities and Amenities

Dining: In addition to its bars and lounges, the hotel offers fine dining at Clement, its signature restaurant serving contemporary American cuisine.

Concierge Service: The concierge team offers a range of services, from arranging tickets to local attractions to organizing bespoke experiences tailored to guest preferences.

Business Services: Includes high-speed internet, meeting rooms, and a fully equipped business center.

Pet-Friendly: The Peninsula accommodates pets, providing amenities and services to ensure a comfortable stay for both guests and their pets.

Opening and Closing Hours

Hotel Reception: Open 24 hours a day.

Restaurants and Bars: Hours vary by venue, but typically include breakfast service starting around 6:30 AM, lunch, and dinner with extended hours for bars and lounges.

Spa: Usually open from early morning until late evening; specific hours may vary.

Price

Rates at The Peninsula New York vary depending on the time of year, room type, and booking conditions. On average, prices start around $800 per night for standard rooms and can exceed $2,500 per night for suites.

Booking in advance and checking current rates directly through the hotel's website or booking platforms is recommended.

Pros

Prime Location: Situated on Fifth Avenue, close to major attractions, shopping, and dining.

Luxurious Accommodations: High-quality rooms and suites with sophisticated design and modern amenities.

Exceptional Service: Known for attentive and personalized service.

Rooftop Bar: Offers stunning city views and a unique atmosphere.

Cons

High Cost: Luxury accommodations come with a premium price, making it one of the more expensive options in the city.

Busy Area: Being on Fifth Avenue, the area can be bustling, which might affect the overall experience for some guests.

Local Tips

Explore Fifth Avenue: Take advantage of the hotel's location to explore the nearby shopping and iconic landmarks.

Visit Central Park: Enjoy a leisurely stroll or bike ride in Central Park, which is just a short walk away.

Reservations: Make dining and spa reservations well in advance to secure your preferred times, especially during peak seasons.

Theater Tickets: If you're interested in Broadway shows, consider booking tickets ahead of time to ensure availability.

3. **Four Seasons Hotel New York Downtown**

The Four Seasons Hotel New York Downtown is a luxury hotel known for its modern elegance and exceptional service. Located in the heart of the Financial District, it offers a sophisticated retreat with a focus on contemporary design and personalized guest experiences. This hotel is ideal for both business and leisure travelers looking for high-end accommodations in a vibrant part of Manhattan.

Location (Address & Proximity)

Address: 27 Barclay Street, New York, NY 10007, USA

Proximity:

World Trade Center: Directly across the street from the World Trade Center complex, including the One World Observatory and the 9/11 Memorial & Museum.

Battery Park: Approximately 1 mile (1.6 km), a short walk or quick cab ride away, offering views of the Statue of Liberty and a scenic park space.

SoHo: Around 1 mile (1.6 km), providing easy access to trendy shops, galleries, and dining options.

Chinatown: About 1 mile (1.6 km), known for its vibrant cultural scene and diverse culinary offerings.

Subway Stations: The hotel is close to several subway lines, including the 1, 2, 3, A, C, and E trains, providing convenient access to other parts of the city.

Highlights

Modern Design: The hotel features sleek, contemporary interiors with a minimalist aesthetic and luxurious finishes.

Exceptional Service: Renowned for its attentive and personalized service, ensuring a high level of comfort and convenience for guests.

Prime Location: Positioned in the Financial District, offering easy access to major business hubs, historic landmarks, and cultural attractions.

Spa and Wellness

The Spa at Four Seasons: Offers a range of indulgent treatments including massages, facials, and body therapies. The spa is designed to provide a relaxing and rejuvenating experience.

Fitness Center: A state-of-the-art fitness center is available for guests, equipped with the latest exercise equipment and amenities.

Bars

CUT Lounge: Located within the hotel, CUT Lounge offers a stylish setting for cocktails and light bites. It's an ideal spot for a pre-dinner drink or an evening relaxation.

Events and Conferences

Event Spaces: The Four Seasons Hotel New York Downtown features elegant event spaces suitable for weddings, corporate meetings, and other special occasions. The venues include a grand ballroom and smaller meeting rooms, all equipped with modern technology.

Event Planning Services: Dedicated event planners are available to assist with every detail, from catering to audiovisual needs, ensuring a seamless event experience.

Basic Facilities and Amenities

Dining: The hotel's dining options include CUT, a renowned steakhouse offering a sophisticated menu of premium cuts and contemporary dishes.

Concierge Service: The concierge team can assist with a range of services, including booking tickets, arranging transportation, and providing local recommendations.

Business Services: Includes high-speed internet, meeting rooms, and a business center to cater to professional needs.

Pet-Friendly: The hotel welcomes pets, offering amenities to ensure a comfortable stay for guests traveling with their furry companions.

Opening and Closing Hours

Hotel Reception: Open 24 hours a day.

Restaurants and Bars: Hours vary, but typically include breakfast service starting around 6:30 AM, lunch, and dinner, with bar hours extending into the evening.

Spa: Generally open from early morning until late evening; specific hours may vary.

Price

Rates at the Four Seasons Hotel New York Downtown vary depending on the season, room type, and booking conditions. On average, rates start around $750 per night for standard rooms and can exceed $2,000 per night for suites. Checking current rates and availability directly through the hotel's website or booking platforms is recommended.

Pros

Modern Luxury: Features contemporary design and high-end amenities.

Prime Location: Close to major attractions and business centers in the Financial District.

Excellent Service: Known for its high level of personalized service and attention to detail.

On-Site Dining: Includes CUT, a celebrated steakhouse, and CUT Lounge for drinks.

Cons

High Cost: The luxury experience comes with a premium price, making it one of the more expensive hotel options in New York City.

Business District: Being in the Financial District, the area may be quieter on weekends and evenings compared to more tourist-centric neighborhoods.

Local Tips

Explore the Financial District: Take advantage of the hotel's location to visit nearby landmarks like the 9/11 Memorial & Museum and the World Trade Center.

Visit SoHo and Chinatown: Enjoy shopping, dining, and cultural experiences in the neighboring SoHo and Chinatown areas.

Advance Reservations: Make dining and spa reservations in advance, especially during peak travel seasons.

Public Transit: Utilize the nearby subway stations for convenient travel throughout the city.

4. **The St. Regis New York**

The St. Regis New York is a historic luxury hotel renowned for its classic elegance, unparalleled service, and prime location in Midtown Manhattan. With a legacy of opulence and refined hospitality, the St. Regis combines timeless charm with modern amenities, making it a top choice for discerning travelers seeking a sophisticated stay in New York City.

Location (Address & Proximity)

Address: 2 East 55th Street at Fifth Avenue, New York, NY 10022, USA

Grace Bennett

Proximity:

Central Park: Approximately 0.5 miles (0.8 km) away, easily accessible by a short walk, offering a serene escape from the city's hustle and bustle.

Times Square: About 0.8 miles (1.3 km), a brief walk or a quick cab ride from the hotel.

Broadway Theaters: Roughly 0.8 miles (1.3 km), ideal for theatergoers looking to catch a show.

Fifth Avenue Shopping: Directly on Fifth Avenue, placing you steps away from high-end boutiques and flagship stores.

Subway Stations: The closest subway stations are within walking distance, including the 5th Avenue/53rd Street and 59th Street/Columbus Circle stations.

Highlights

Historic Elegance: The hotel is housed in a historic building, featuring classic décor, luxurious furnishings, and a sophisticated ambiance.

Astor Court: The hotel's main dining venue, renowned for its refined cuisine and elegant setting.

Personalized Service: Known for its exceptional and personalized service, including the signature St. Regis Butler Service.

Spa and Wellness

Spa: While The St. Regis New York does not have a dedicated spa on-site, guests have access to nearby wellness facilities and can arrange for in-room treatments through the concierge.

Fitness Center: The hotel features a well-equipped fitness center, allowing guests to maintain their workout routines while traveling.

Bars

King Cole Bar: Famous for being the birthplace of the Bloody Mary, this elegant bar offers a sophisticated atmosphere with a menu of classic cocktails, light bites, and a selection of fine wines and spirits.

Events and Conferences

Event Spaces: The St. Regis New York offers a range of elegant event spaces, including ballrooms and smaller meeting rooms, suitable for weddings, corporate events, and social gatherings.

Event Planning Services: The hotel provides comprehensive event planning services, including catering, audiovisual equipment, and dedicated event staff to ensure a seamless experience.

Basic Facilities and Amenities

Dining: In addition to King Cole Bar, the hotel offers Astor Court, which serves a menu of refined American cuisine in a luxurious setting.

Concierge Service: The concierge team is available to assist with dining reservations, event tickets, transportation arrangements, and other personalized requests.

Business Services: Includes high-speed internet, meeting rooms, and a business center to cater to professional needs.

Pet-Friendly: The St. Regis welcomes pets, providing amenities and services to ensure a comfortable stay for both guests and their furry friends.

Opening and Closing Hours

Hotel Reception: Open 24 hours a day.

Restaurants and Bars: King Cole Bar typically opens in the afternoon and operates into the evening, while Astor Court usually serves breakfast, lunch, and dinner, with specific hours varying.

Fitness Center: Generally open 24 hours for guests, though hours may vary.

Price

Rates at The St. Regis New York can vary based on the season, room type, and booking conditions. On average, rates start around $800 per night for standard rooms and can exceed $2,500 per night for suites. For the best rates, it's advisable to book in advance and check availability directly through the hotel's website or booking platforms.

Pros

Historic Charm: Combines classic elegance with modern amenities in a historic setting.

Prime Location: Situated on Fifth Avenue, close to major attractions, shopping, and dining.

Exceptional Service: Known for personalized and attentive service, including the signature Butler Service.

Elegant Dining: Offers refined dining experiences at Astor Court and classic cocktails at King Cole Bar.

Cons

High Cost: Luxury accommodations come with a premium price, making it one of the more expensive options in the city.

Limited Spa Facilities: No dedicated spa on-site, although guests can arrange for treatments through the concierge.

Local Tips

Explore Fifth Avenue: Enjoy world-class shopping and iconic landmarks right outside the hotel's door.

Visit Central Park: Take advantage of the hotel's proximity to Central Park for a leisurely stroll or bike ride.

Theater and Shows: If attending Broadway shows, book tickets in advance to secure the best seats.

Dining Reservations: Make dining reservations early, especially for popular spots like Astor Court.

5. The Langham, New York, Fifth Avenue

The Langham, New York, Fifth Avenue is a luxury hotel renowned for its refined elegance, exceptional service, and prime location. Situated in the heart of Midtown Manhattan, it offers a blend of classic sophistication and modern comfort, making it a top choice for both business and leisure travelers seeking an upscale experience.

Location (Address & Proximity)

Address: 400 Fifth Avenue, New York, NY 10018, USA

Proximity:

Empire State Building: Approximately 0.2 miles (0.3 km), a short walk from the hotel, offering stunning city views from its observation decks.

Times Square: About 0.5 miles (0.8 km), easily accessible by a brief walk or quick cab ride.

Bryant Park: Roughly 0.3 miles (0.5 km), providing a scenic park space and a host of seasonal activities.

Broadway Theaters: Around 0.5 miles (0.8 km), conveniently located for theatergoers.

Central Park: About 1 mile (1.6 km), a short walk or quick cab ride away.

Highlights

Elegant Design: The Langham, New York, Fifth Avenue features a blend of classic and contemporary design elements, creating a sophisticated and inviting atmosphere.

Luxury Accommodations: The hotel offers spacious and well-appointed rooms and suites with high-end furnishings and modern amenities.

Personalized Service: Known for its attentive and personalized service, including a dedicated concierge team to assist with various guest needs.

Spa and Wellness

The Langham Club: Offers exclusive access to a private lounge with enhanced amenities, including a range of wellness options such as yoga mats and wellness literature.

Fitness Center: The hotel features a state-of-the-art fitness center equipped with the latest exercise equipment, allowing guests to maintain their workout routines.

Bars

Aria: This stylish lounge provides a relaxing setting for cocktails, light bites, and afternoon tea. It's an excellent spot for a pre-dinner drink or a leisurely afternoon.

Events and Conferences

Event Spaces: The Langham, New York, Fifth Avenue features elegant event spaces suitable for weddings, corporate meetings, and social gatherings. The hotel's venues include sophisticated ballrooms and intimate meeting rooms.

Event Planning Services: The hotel offers comprehensive event planning services, including catering, audiovisual equipment, and dedicated event staff to ensure a seamless experience.

Basic Facilities and Amenities

Dining: In addition to Aria, the hotel offers a range of in-room dining options with a menu of refined dishes and beverages.

Concierge Service: The concierge team is available to assist with dining reservations, tickets to local attractions, transportation arrangements, and other personalized requests.

Business Services: Includes high-speed internet, meeting rooms, and a business center to cater to professional needs.

Pet-Friendly: The Langham accommodates pets, providing amenities and services to ensure a comfortable stay for both guests and their furry companions.

Opening and Closing Hours

Hotel Reception: Open 24 hours a day.

Restaurants and Bars: Aria typically operates in the late morning through evening, with specific hours for breakfast, lunch, and dinner. The hotel's in-room dining service is available around the clock.

Fitness Center: Generally open 24 hours for guests, though exact hours may vary.

Price

Rates at The Langham, New York, Fifth Avenue can vary depending on the season, room type, and booking conditions. On average, rates start around $750 per night for standard rooms and can exceed $2,500 per night for suites. For the best rates, it's advisable to book in advance and check availability directly through the hotel's website or booking platforms.

Pros

Prime Location: Situated on Fifth Avenue, close to major attractions, shopping, and dining.

Elegant Accommodations: Features spacious and stylish rooms with high-end furnishings and modern amenities.

Exceptional Service: Known for personalized and attentive service.

On-Site Dining and Lounge: Offers a stylish lounge for cocktails and afternoon tea.

Cons

High Cost: The luxury experience comes with a premium price, making it one of the more expensive hotel options in the city.

Limited Dining Options: Dining is primarily focused on the lounge and in-room options, with fewer on-site restaurant choices compared to some other luxury hotels.

Local Tips

Explore Nearby Attractions: Take advantage of the hotel's location to visit iconic landmarks such as the Empire State Building and Bryant Park.

Broadway Shows: If you're interested in Broadway, book tickets in advance to ensure availability and the best seats.

Central Park Visits: Make time for a visit to Central Park, which is within walking distance and offers a peaceful retreat from the city's hustle.

Public Transit: Utilize nearby subway stations for convenient travel throughout New York City.

Mid-Range Hotels

Mid-range hotels in New York City provide a perfect balance of comfort and affordability. Offering quality amenities, convenient locations, and stylish accommodations, these hotels cater to travelers who want a comfortable stay without breaking the bank. With options ranging from boutique hotels to established chains, mid-range hotels deliver excellent value, making them an ideal choice for a pleasant and budget-friendly New York experience.

Top 5 Mid-Range Hotels

1. **Hotel Giraffe by Library Hotel Collection**

Hotel Giraffe, part of the Library Hotel Collection, is a stylish and contemporary mid-range hotel located in the NoMad (North of Madison Square Park) neighborhood of Manhattan. Known for its welcoming atmosphere, modern amenities, and personalized service, Hotel Giraffe offers a comfortable and upscale experience without the premium price tag of luxury hotels. Its design incorporates a chic, playful theme with a focus on guest comfort and convenience.

Location (Address & Proximity)

Address: 365 Park Avenue South, New York, NY 10016, USA

Proximity:

Madison Square Park: Approximately 0.2 miles (0.3 km), a short walk from the hotel, providing green space and local eateries.

Empire State Building: About 0.8 miles (1.3 km), easily accessible by a brief walk or a short subway ride.

Times Square: Roughly 1 mile (1.6 km), accessible via a short subway ride or a longer walk.

Fifth Avenue Shopping: About 0.6 miles (1 km), offering access to high-end retail stores and boutiques.

Subway Stations: The hotel is close to the 28th Street subway station (6 train) and the 33rd Street subway station (6 train), providing easy access to various parts of the city.

Highlights

Chic Design: Hotel Giraffe features a modern, stylish design with playful accents, creating a vibrant and comfortable atmosphere.

Complimentary Amenities: The hotel offers a range of complimentary amenities, including a daily breakfast, evening wine and cheese reception, and snacks throughout the day.

Personalized Service: Known for its attentive and friendly service, ensuring a pleasant and personalized guest experience.

Spa and Wellness

No On-Site Spa: While Hotel Giraffe does not have an on-site spa, guests can access nearby wellness facilities and services. The hotel can assist in arranging spa appointments and treatments through local partners.

Fitness Center: The hotel features a well-equipped fitness center for guests to maintain their workout routines while traveling.

Bars

Lobby Lounge: The hotel has a cozy and inviting lobby lounge area where guests can relax and enjoy a complimentary wine and cheese reception in the evenings. It's a great spot for casual socializing and unwinding after a day of sightseeing.

Events and Conferences

Event Spaces: Hotel Giraffe offers versatile event spaces suitable for small meetings, private gatherings, and social events. The hotel's event spaces are designed to accommodate a variety of setups and needs.

Event Planning Services: The hotel provides event planning assistance to help coordinate details such as catering, audiovisual equipment, and room setup.

Basic Facilities and Amenities

Dining: The hotel provides a complimentary continental breakfast each morning, including a selection of pastries, fruits, and beverages.

Concierge Service: The concierge team can assist with restaurant reservations, theater tickets, and other personalized requests to enhance your stay.

Business Services: Includes high-speed internet, meeting rooms, and a business center to cater to professional needs.

Pet-Friendly: The hotel welcomes pets, offering amenities and services to ensure a comfortable stay for guests traveling with their furry companions.

Opening and Closing Hours

Hotel Reception: Open 24 hours a day.

Lobby Lounge: Typically available throughout the day, with the evening wine and cheese reception usually starting around 5 PM and ending around 7 PM.

Fitness Center: Generally open 24 hours for guests, though exact hours may vary.

Price

Rates at Hotel Giraffe are generally more affordable compared to luxury hotels, with average prices starting around $300 to $400 per night for standard rooms. Rates can vary based on the season, room type, and booking conditions. For the best rates, it's advisable to book in advance and check availability directly through the hotel's website or booking platforms.

Pros

Stylish and Comfortable: Features modern, chic design and a comfortable atmosphere.

Complimentary Amenities: Includes daily breakfast, evening wine and cheese reception, and snacks.

Great Location: Located in a vibrant neighborhood with easy access to major attractions.

Personalized Service: Known for friendly and attentive service.

Cons

No On-Site Spa: Lacks a dedicated spa, though spa services can be arranged through local partners.

Room Size: Rooms are generally comfortable but may be smaller compared to some other mid-range hotels.

Local Tips

Explore NoMad: Take advantage of the hotel's location to explore the NoMad neighborhood, which offers a variety of dining and shopping options.

Visit Nearby Parks: Enjoy nearby green spaces like Madison Square Park for a leisurely break.

Public Transit: Utilize the nearby subway stations for convenient travel throughout the city.

Reservations: For popular attractions and dining spots, consider making reservations in advance to secure your spot.

2. The Standard, High Line

The Standard, High Line is a trendy and vibrant hotel situated in the Meatpacking District of Manhattan. Known for its modern design, lively atmosphere, and stunning views, this hotel is a popular choice for both leisure and business travelers seeking a dynamic and stylish stay in New York City. It offers a unique blend of contemporary comfort and cutting-edge style, complemented by a range of on-site dining and entertainment options.

Location (Address & Proximity)

Address: 848 Washington Street, New York, NY 10014, USA

Proximity:

High Line Park: Directly adjacent to the hotel, offering easy access to this elevated park with scenic views, walking paths, and art installations.

Chelsea Market: Approximately 0.3 miles (0.5 km), a short walk from the hotel, featuring a variety of food vendors, shops, and unique experiences.

Greenwich Village: About 0.8 miles (1.3 km), easily accessible by a brief walk or quick cab ride.

Times Square: Roughly 1.5 miles (2.4 km), a short subway ride or longer walk away.

Subway Stations: The hotel is close to the 14th Street subway station (A, C, E trains) and the 8th Avenue subway station (L train), providing convenient access to other parts of the city.

Highlights

Modern Design: The hotel features sleek, contemporary design with floor-to-ceiling windows, modern furnishings, and an emphasis on style.

Unique Atmosphere: Known for its lively and social atmosphere, with a range of dining and entertainment options that attract both locals and visitors.

Stunning Views: Many rooms offer panoramic views of the city, the Hudson River, and the High Line park.

Spa and Wellness

No On-Site Spa: The Standard, High Line does not have a dedicated spa on-site, but guests can access nearby wellness facilities and services. The hotel's concierge can assist with booking spa treatments through local partners.

Fitness Center: The hotel features a well-equipped fitness center, allowing guests to maintain their workout routines while traveling.

Bars

Le Bain: A chic rooftop bar and nightclub with stunning views of the Hudson River and the city skyline. It's known for its vibrant atmosphere, eclectic cocktails, and lively DJ sets.

The Standard Grill: Located on the ground floor, this popular spot offers a range of classic American dishes in a stylish setting, with a lively bar scene and outdoor seating.

Events and Conferences

Event Spaces: The Standard, High Line offers a variety of event spaces, including stylish meeting rooms and flexible event venues with modern amenities. The hotel's event spaces are designed to accommodate a range of functions, from corporate meetings to social gatherings.

Event Planning Services: The hotel provides comprehensive event planning services, including catering, audiovisual equipment, and dedicated event staff to ensure a seamless experience.

Basic Facilities and Amenities

Dining: In addition to Le Bain and The Standard Grill, the hotel offers a range of dining options, including a rooftop bar and a stylish restaurant serving American cuisine.

Concierge Service: The concierge team is available to assist with reservations, tickets, transportation, and other personalized requests to enhance your stay.

Business Services: Includes high-speed internet, meeting rooms, and a business center to cater to professional needs.

Pet-Friendly: The Standard, High Line is pet-friendly, offering amenities and services to ensure a comfortable stay for guests traveling with their pets.

Opening and Closing Hours

Hotel Reception: Open 24 hours a day.

Le Bain: Typically operates in the evening and late into the night, with specific hours varying based on events and season.

The Standard Grill: Usually open for breakfast, lunch, and dinner, with specific hours varying.

Fitness Center: Generally open 24 hours for guests, though exact hours may vary.

Price

Rates at The Standard, High Line can vary depending on the season, room type, and booking conditions. On average, prices start around $350 to $500 per night for standard rooms and can exceed $1,000 per night for suites. For the best rates, it's advisable to book in advance and check availability directly through the hotel's website or booking platforms.

Pros

Prime Location: Adjacent to the High Line and close to Chelsea Market and other attractions.

Modern Design: Features contemporary style and luxurious amenities.

Lively Atmosphere: Offers vibrant dining and nightlife options, including the popular Le Bain.

Stunning Views: Many rooms provide panoramic views of the city and the Hudson River.

Cons

High Cost: Luxury accommodations come with a premium price, making it one of the more expensive options in the city.

No On-Site Spa: Lacks a dedicated spa, though spa services can be arranged through local partners.

Lively Atmosphere: The vibrant nightlife and social scene may not be ideal for guests seeking a quieter experience.

Local Tips

Explore the High Line: Take advantage of the hotel's proximity to the High Line Park for a scenic walk and unique urban experience.

Visit Chelsea Market: Check out the diverse food options and unique shops at Chelsea Market, just a short walk away.

Rooftop Views: Enjoy the panoramic views and lively atmosphere at Le Bain, the hotel's rooftop bar.

Public Transit: Utilize nearby subway stations for convenient travel throughout the city.

3. CitizenM New York Times Square

CitizenM New York Times Square is a modern and trendy hotel known for its innovative design and affordable luxury. As part of the CitizenM brand, the hotel offers a contemporary, tech-savvy experience with a focus on comfort, convenience, and style. It caters to both business and leisure travelers with its strategic location, smart technology, and vibrant atmosphere.

Location (Address & Proximity)

Address: 218 West 50th Street, New York, NY 10019, USA

Proximity:

Times Square: Approximately 0.2 miles (0.3 km), just a short walk from the hotel, offering a bustling entertainment hub with theaters, restaurants, and shops.

Broadway Theaters: About 0.3 miles (0.5 km), making it very convenient for catching Broadway shows.

Central Park: Roughly 1 mile (1.6 km), easily accessible by a brief walk or a short cab ride.

Rockefeller Center: About 0.5 miles (0.8 km), home to attractions like the Top of the Rock Observation Deck and the ice skating rink.

Subway Stations: The hotel is close to several subway stations, including the 49th Street (N, Q, R, W trains) and Times Square-42nd Street (1, 2, 3, 7, N, Q, R, W trains) stations.

Highlights

Innovative Design: The hotel features a contemporary and vibrant design with a focus on technology and modern comfort.

Smart Technology: Rooms are equipped with mood lighting, tablet controls for room settings, and large smart TVs, allowing guests to customize their stay.

Affordable Luxury: Offers high-quality amenities and a stylish experience at a mid-range price point.

Spa and Wellness

No On-Site Spa: CitizenM New York Times Square does not have a dedicated spa. However, guests can access nearby wellness facilities and services, with the concierge available to assist in arranging treatments.

Fitness Center: The hotel features a compact but well-equipped fitness center, allowing guests to keep up with their workout routines.

Bars

CitizenM Bar: The hotel has a stylish bar area in the lobby where guests can enjoy a selection of cocktails, wines, and snacks. The bar is a lively spot, perfect for socializing and relaxing after a day exploring the city.

Events and Conferences

Meeting Rooms: CitizenM offers several flexible meeting rooms equipped with the latest technology, suitable for business meetings and small events.

Event Planning Services: The hotel provides event planning assistance, including audiovisual support and catering options to ensure successful events.

Basic Facilities and Amenities

Dining: The hotel offers a 24-hour canteenM with a selection of fresh, high-quality food and beverages. Guests can enjoy breakfast, lunch, and dinner with a variety of international and local options.

Concierge Service: The concierge team is available to assist with reservations, recommendations, and travel arrangements to enhance your stay.

Business Services: Includes high-speed internet and meeting rooms to cater to professional needs.

Pet-Friendly: The hotel welcomes pets, providing amenities and services to ensure a comfortable stay for guests traveling with their furry friends.

Opening and Closing Hours

Hotel Reception: Open 24 hours a day.

canteenM: The hotel's 24-hour dining area offers continuous service throughout the day.

Bar: Typically open in the evenings and into the night, with specific hours varying.

Fitness Center: Generally open 24 hours for guests, though exact hours may vary.

Price

Rates at CitizenM New York Times Square are generally more affordable compared to luxury hotels, with average prices starting around $250 to $350 per night for standard rooms. Prices can vary based on the season, room type, and booking conditions. For the best rates, it's advisable to book in advance and check availability directly through the hotel's website or booking platforms.

Pros

Prime Location: Situated close to Times Square, Broadway theaters, and other major attractions.

Modern Design: Features contemporary design with smart technology and stylish amenities.

Affordable Luxury: Offers a high-quality experience at a mid-range price point.

24-Hour Dining: Provides continuous food and beverage service in the canteenM.

Cons

No On-Site Spa: Lacks a dedicated spa, though spa services can be arranged through local partners.

Compact Rooms: Rooms are stylish but may be smaller compared to other mid-range hotels.

Lively Atmosphere: The vibrant bar and common areas may be bustling, which might not appeal to guests seeking a quieter environment.

Local Tips

Explore Times Square: Take advantage of the hotel's proximity to Times Square for entertainment, shopping, and dining.

Catch a Broadway Show: With theaters nearby, it's easy to enjoy a Broadway performance; consider booking tickets in advance.

Visit Central Park: Make time to explore Central Park, which is a short walk or quick ride away.

Public Transit: Utilize the nearby subway stations for convenient travel throughout the city.

4. Arlo Soho

Arlo Soho is a chic, modern hotel located in the trendy SoHo neighborhood of Manhattan. Known for its stylish design, vibrant atmosphere, and focus on creating a unique guest experience, Arlo Soho caters to both business and leisure travelers with a blend of contemporary comfort and urban flair. The hotel emphasizes space-efficient design and a social, community-oriented atmosphere.

Location (Address & Proximity)

Address: 231 Hudson Street, New York, NY 10013, USA

Proximity:

SoHo Shopping: Directly situated in SoHo, providing immediate access to high-end boutiques, art galleries, and trendy shops.

Greenwich Village: Approximately 0.8 miles (1.3 km), easily accessible by a brief walk or a short cab ride.

Chinatown: About 1 mile (1.6 km), with vibrant street life and diverse dining options.

Tribeca: Roughly 0.6 miles (1 km), known for its upscale dining and cultural venues.

Subway Stations: The hotel is close to the Canal Street subway station (1, 2, 4, 6, N, Q, R, W trains), providing easy access to other parts of the city.

Highlights

Stylish Design: The hotel features modern, minimalist design with an emphasis on functionality and comfort.

Rooftop Bar: Offers stunning views of the Manhattan skyline and a relaxed setting for enjoying cocktails and small plates.

Community Vibe: Emphasizes a social atmosphere with communal spaces and regular events, fostering a sense of community among guests.

Spa and Wellness

No On-Site Spa: Arlo Soho does not have a dedicated spa. However, guests can access nearby wellness facilities and services, with the concierge available to assist in arranging treatments.

Fitness Center: The hotel features a compact but well-equipped fitness center, allowing guests to maintain their workout routines.

Bars

Arlo Rooftop: The hotel's rooftop bar offers a stylish setting with panoramic views of the city. It's a popular spot for enjoying drinks, light bites, and socializing in a relaxed environment.

Arlo Lobby Bar: Located in the hotel's lobby, this bar provides a casual setting for grabbing a drink or a quick bite.

Events and Conferences

Event Spaces: Arlo Soho offers flexible event spaces that can be used for meetings, small events, and social gatherings. The hotel's design allows for adaptable setups to suit various needs.

Event Planning Services: The hotel provides event planning assistance, including catering, audiovisual equipment, and dedicated staff to ensure a successful event.

Basic Facilities and Amenities

Dining: In addition to Arlo Rooftop and the lobby bar, the hotel offers a 24-hour café with a range of fresh, high-quality food and beverages.

Concierge Service: The concierge team is available to assist with reservations, recommendations, and travel arrangements to enhance your stay.

Business Services: Includes high-speed internet and meeting rooms to cater to professional needs.

Pet-Friendly: The hotel is pet-friendly, providing amenities and services to ensure a comfortable stay for guests traveling with their pets.

Opening and Closing Hours

Hotel Reception: Open 24 hours a day.

Arlo Rooftop: Typically open in the evening, with specific hours varying based on the season and events.

Lobby Bar: Usually open throughout the day, with specific hours varying.

Fitness Center: Generally open 24 hours for guests, though exact hours may vary.

Price

Rates at Arlo Soho are generally more affordable compared to luxury hotels, with average prices starting around $250 to $350 per night for standard rooms. Prices can vary based on the season, room type, and booking conditions. For the best rates, it's advisable to book in advance and check availability directly through the hotel's website or booking platforms.

Pros

Prime Location: Situated in the trendy SoHo neighborhood, close to shopping, dining, and cultural attractions.

Stylish Design: Features modern, minimalist design with a focus on comfort and functionality.

Rooftop Bar: Offers panoramic city views and a stylish environment for socializing.

Community Atmosphere: Emphasizes a social vibe with communal spaces and regular events.

Cons

No On-Site Spa: Lacks a dedicated spa, though spa services can be arranged through local partners.

Compact Rooms: Rooms are stylish but may be smaller compared to some other mid-range hotels.

Lively Atmosphere: The hotel's social and communal focus might not appeal to guests seeking a quieter environment.

Local Tips

Explore SoHo: Take advantage of the hotel's location to explore the fashionable boutiques, art galleries, and dining options in SoHo.

Visit Greenwich Village: Enjoy the vibrant culture and eclectic dining options in nearby Greenwich Village.

Rooftop Views: Make time to visit the rooftop bar for stunning views and a relaxed atmosphere.

Public Transit: Utilize nearby subway stations for convenient travel throughout the city.

5. The Beekman, A Thompson Hotel

The Beekman, A Thompson Hotel is a luxurious and historic hotel located in Lower Manhattan. Renowned for its stunning architecture, elegant design, and refined ambiance, The Beekman offers a blend of classic sophistication and modern amenities. The hotel is housed in a beautifully restored 19th-century building, combining historic charm with contemporary comforts, making it an excellent choice for travelers seeking a high-end experience in New York City.

Location (Address & Proximity)

Address: 123 Nassau Street, New York, NY 10038, USA

Proximity:

Brooklyn Bridge: Approximately 0.5 miles (0.8 km), offering a scenic walk and access to one of New York City's iconic landmarks.

One World Trade Center: About 0.7 miles (1.1 km), easily reachable by a short walk or quick cab ride.

Financial District: Roughly 0.3 miles (0.5 km), close to Wall Street and the New York Stock Exchange.

SoHo: Approximately 1 mile (1.6 km), accessible by a brief subway ride or a longer walk.

Subway Stations: The hotel is close to the Fulton Street subway station (2, 4, 5, A, C, J, Z trains) and the Park Place subway station (2, 4 trains), providing convenient access to other parts of the city.

Highlights

Historic Charm: The Beekman is known for its beautifully restored architecture, including the iconic nine-story atrium with a glass dome, which adds to its historic allure.

Elegant Design: The hotel combines classic design elements with modern luxury, featuring richly appointed rooms and stylish public spaces.

Exceptional Service: Offers high-end service with a focus on personalized guest experiences and attention to detail.

Spa and Wellness

No On-Site Spa: The Beekman does not have a dedicated spa on-site. However, guests can access nearby wellness facilities and services, with the concierge available to assist in arranging treatments.

Fitness Center: The hotel features a well-equipped fitness center for guests to maintain their workout routines during their stay.

Bars

The Bar Room: Located on the ground floor, The Bar Room offers a sophisticated setting for enjoying a variety of cocktails, fine wines, and light bites. It is known for its elegant décor and relaxing ambiance.

The Roof: An exclusive rooftop bar with stunning views of the Manhattan skyline and the Brooklyn Bridge. It provides a stylish and chic environment for enjoying drinks and socializing.

Events and Conferences

Event Spaces: The Beekman offers several elegant event spaces, including the beautifully restored ballroom and intimate meeting rooms. The hotel's venues are ideal for weddings, corporate events, and social gatherings.

Event Planning Services: The hotel provides comprehensive event planning services, including catering, audiovisual equipment, and dedicated event staff to ensure a seamless experience.

Basic Facilities and Amenities

Dining: In addition to The Bar Room and The Roof, the hotel offers a range of in-room dining options with a menu of refined dishes and beverages.

Concierge Service: The concierge team is available to assist with reservations, recommendations, and travel arrangements to enhance your stay.

Business Services: Includes high-speed internet, meeting rooms, and a business center to cater to professional needs.

Pet-Friendly: The Beekman is pet-friendly, offering amenities and services to ensure a comfortable stay for guests traveling with their pets.

Opening and Closing Hours

Hotel Reception: Open 24 hours a day.

The Bar Room: Typically open throughout the day and evening, with specific hours varying.

The Roof: Usually open in the evening, with specific hours varying based on the season and events.

Fitness Center: Generally open 24 hours for guests, though exact hours may vary.

The Ultimate New York City Travel Guide (2025 Edition)

Price

Rates at The Beekman can vary depending on the season, room type, and booking conditions. On average, prices start around $500 to $700 per night for standard rooms and can exceed $1,500 per night for suites. For the best rates, it's advisable to book in advance and check availability directly through the hotel's website or booking platforms.

Pros

Historic Architecture: Features beautifully restored 19th-century architecture and a stunning atrium.

Elegant Design: Combines classic design with modern luxury and comfort.

Prime Location: Situated close to key attractions in Lower Manhattan, including the Brooklyn Bridge and the Financial District.

Rooftop Views: Offers exclusive rooftop bar with impressive city views.

Cons

High Cost: Luxury accommodations come with a premium price, making it one of the more expensive options in the city.

No On-Site Spa: Lacks a dedicated spa, though spa services can be arranged through local partners.

Busy Area: Being in a bustling part of Manhattan, the area around the hotel can be quite busy, which might not appeal to those seeking a quieter environment.

Local Tips

Explore Lower Manhattan: Take advantage of the hotel's location to explore nearby landmarks such as the Brooklyn Bridge and the Financial District.

Visit the Rooftop Bar: Enjoy the stunning views from The Roof and consider visiting during sunset for a memorable experience.

Public Transit: Utilize the nearby subway stations for convenient travel throughout the city.

Book in Advance: For popular dining spots and attractions, consider making reservations in advance to secure your spot.

Budget Accommodation

Budget accommodations in New York City offer affordable yet comfortable options for travelers looking to make the most of their visit without overspending. These choices include hostels, budget hotels, and guesthouses that provide essential amenities and a convenient location, ensuring you can explore the city without straining your budget. Ideal for those seeking value and practicality, budget accommodations make it possible to experience New York City's vibrant culture and attractions economically.

Top 5 Budget Accommodation

1. **HI New York City Hostel**

HI New York City Hostel is a well-regarded budget accommodation option located on the Upper West Side of Manhattan. As part of the Hostelling International network, this hostel offers affordable lodging with a range of amenities geared towards budget travelers and backpackers. The hostel provides a vibrant, social atmosphere with a focus on community and comfort, making it an ideal choice for travelers looking for a cost-effective stay in New York City.

Location (Address & Proximity)

Address: 891 Amsterdam Avenue, New York, NY 10025, USA

Proximity:

Central Park: Approximately 0.7 miles (1.1 km), a short walk away, offering expansive green space, walking paths, and recreational facilities.

Columbia University: About 0.8 miles (1.3 km), making it convenient for visitors to the university or nearby cultural institutions.

American Museum of Natural History: Roughly 1 mile (1.6 km), easily reachable by a brief subway ride or a longer walk.

Times Square: Approximately 2.5 miles (4 km), accessible via a short subway ride or a longer cab ride.

Subway Stations: The hostel is close to the 103rd Street subway station (1 train) and the 110th Street subway station (B, C trains), providing convenient access to other parts of the city.

Highlights

Affordable Rates: Offers budget-friendly accommodations, making it a great option for travelers looking to save on lodging while exploring the city.

Social Atmosphere: Known for its friendly and social environment, providing opportunities to meet fellow travelers through organized events and communal spaces.

Convenient Location: Situated in a relatively quiet part of Manhattan, with easy access to major attractions and public transportation.

Facilities and Amenities

Dormitory-Style Rooms: Offers a range of dormitory options, including mixed-gender and female-only rooms, with bunk beds and shared facilities.

Private Rooms: Also provides private rooms for those seeking a bit more privacy, though still at budget-friendly rates.

Shared Bathrooms: Dormitory rooms and private rooms typically include shared bathrooms, equipped with basic toiletries and showers.

Common Areas: Features communal spaces such as a lounge, game room, and kitchen, where guests can socialize, cook meals, and relax.

Free Wi-Fi: Provides complimentary high-speed internet access throughout the hostel.

24-Hour Reception: The front desk is open around the clock, offering assistance with check-ins, check-outs, and general inquiries.

Bar and Dining

Kitchen: The hostel has a fully equipped communal kitchen where guests can prepare their own meals. This includes stoves, ovens, refrigerators, and cookware.

Dining Area: A shared dining area is available for guests to eat meals, socialize, and interact.

No On-Site Bar: The hostel does not have a bar, but there are numerous dining and drinking options in the surrounding neighborhood.

Events and Activities

Organized Events: HI New York City Hostel often organizes social events, tours, and activities to help guests explore the city and meet fellow travelers.

Community Engagement: The hostel promotes a sense of community with various programs and group activities.

Opening and Closing Hours

Reception: Open 24 hours a day.

Common Areas: Typically accessible throughout the day and night, though specific hours may vary based on hostel policies.

Price

Rates at HI New York City Hostel are generally budget-friendly, with dormitory beds starting around $50 to $80 per night, and private rooms costing more depending on size and availability. Prices can vary based on the season, room type, and booking conditions. For the best rates, it's advisable to book in advance and check availability directly through the hostel's website or booking platforms.

Pros

Affordable: Offers budget accommodations with competitive rates.

Social Environment: Provides a vibrant and communal atmosphere with opportunities to meet other travelers.

Good Location: Conveniently located near Central Park and Columbia University, with easy access to public transportation.

Free Wi-Fi: Complimentary internet access throughout the hostel.

Cons

Shared Facilities: Dormitory-style rooms and shared bathrooms may not suit guests seeking more privacy.

Basic Amenities: Facilities and furnishings are basic compared to more upscale accommodations.

Noise Levels: The social atmosphere might lead to higher noise levels, which may not appeal to all guests.

Local Tips

Explore Central Park: Take advantage of the hostel's proximity to Central Park for outdoor activities and relaxation.

Visit Nearby Attractions: Explore nearby landmarks such as the American Museum of Natural History and Columbia University.

Use Public Transit: Utilize the nearby subway stations for convenient travel throughout the city.

Socialize: Participate in the hostel's organized events and activities to meet other travelers and enhance your experience.

2. The Jane Hotel

The Jane Hotel is a boutique hotel located in the West Village neighborhood of Manhattan. Known for its unique, vintage-inspired design and historical charm, The Jane offers a blend of old-world elegance with modern amenities. The hotel caters to travelers looking for a distinctive stay in a fashionable area of New York City, providing a quirky yet comfortable lodging experience.

Location (Address & Proximity)

Address: 113 Jane Street, New York, NY 10014, USA

Proximity:

Greenwich Village: Approximately 0.4 miles (0.6 km), making it easy to explore the vibrant, historic neighborhood.

West Village: Located in the heart of the West Village, a trendy area known for its charming streets, boutiques, and dining options.

The High Line: About 1 mile (1.6 km), accessible via a short walk or quick subway ride.

SoHo: Roughly 1.2 miles (1.9 km), easily reachable by public transit or a longer walk.

Times Square: Approximately 2.5 miles (4 km), accessible via a short subway ride or cab.

Highlights

Historical Charm: The Jane Hotel, originally opened in 1908, features vintage-inspired decor and historical elements that add to its unique character.

Design: The hotel's interior design reflects a classic, maritime theme, reminiscent of a ship's cabin, providing a distinctive and memorable experience.

Location: Situated in a fashionable and historic neighborhood, offering easy access to cultural attractions, dining, and nightlife.

Rooms and Amenities

Cabin Rooms: The Jane offers small, cabin-style rooms with compact, efficient designs. These rooms are reminiscent of ship cabins, featuring a cozy and nostalgic aesthetic.

Standard Rooms: In addition to cabin rooms, the hotel offers standard rooms that are slightly larger but still maintain the vintage charm.

Shared Bathrooms: Some rooms have shared bathrooms, while others feature private bathrooms. The shared facilities are maintained to high standards of cleanliness.

Basic Amenities: Rooms come with basic amenities including free Wi-Fi, flat-screen TVs, and comfortable bedding.

Bars and Dining

The Jane Ballroom: The hotel's stylish lounge and bar area, known for its elegant decor and relaxed ambiance. It offers a range of cocktails, wines, and light bites in a chic setting.

No On-Site Restaurant: The hotel does not have a full-service restaurant, but there are numerous dining options in the surrounding West Village neighborhood.

Events and Conferences

Event Spaces: The Jane Hotel does not offer extensive meeting or event facilities. However, its stylish public spaces and lounge areas can be suitable for informal gatherings or small social events.

Event Planning Services: The hotel can assist with recommendations for nearby venues and services for more formal events or meetings.

Basic Facilities and Amenities

Free Wi-Fi: Complimentary high-speed internet access throughout the hotel.

24-Hour Reception: The front desk is open around the clock for guest assistance and inquiries.

Concierge Service: Available to help with reservations, recommendations, and travel arrangements.

No On-Site Fitness Center: The hotel does not have a dedicated fitness center, but there are nearby gyms and wellness facilities.

Opening and Closing Hours

Hotel Reception: Open 24 hours a day.

The Jane Ballroom: Typically open in the evening, with specific hours varying based on events and season.

Common Areas: Generally accessible throughout the day and night, though some spaces may have restricted hours.

Price

Rates at The Jane Hotel vary depending on the season, room type, and booking conditions. On average, prices start around $150 to $250 per night for cabin-style rooms and can go higher for standard rooms or suites. For the best rates, it's advisable to book in advance and check availability directly through the hotel's website or booking platforms.

Pros

Unique Design: Offers a distinctive and charming vintage-inspired design that stands out from more conventional hotels.

Prime Location: Situated in the fashionable West Village, close to shopping, dining, and cultural attractions.

Affordable Option: Provides a relatively affordable option for staying in a trendy neighborhood compared to other boutique hotels.

Cons

Small Rooms: Cabin rooms are compact, which may not suit all guests, especially those seeking more space.

Shared Bathrooms: Some rooms have shared bathrooms, which may not be ideal for all travelers.

Basic Amenities: Limited amenities compared to more upscale hotels, including no on-site fitness center or restaurant.

Local Tips

Explore the West Village: Take advantage of the hotel's location to explore the charming streets, boutique shops, and eclectic dining options in the West Village.

Visit The High Line: Make time to walk the High Line, a unique elevated park with green space, art installations, and city views.

Public Transit: Utilize nearby subway stations for convenient travel to other parts of the city.

3. **Pod 51 Hotel**

Pod 51 Hotel is a contemporary and budget-friendly accommodation option located in Midtown East, Manhattan. Known for its efficient use of space and modern amenities, Pod 51 caters to travelers who appreciate a stylish, functional, and affordable stay. The hotel is part of the Pod Hotel chain, which is recognized for offering compact, comfortable rooms with a focus on maximizing space and providing a pleasant experience without breaking the bank.

Location (Address & Proximity)

Address: 230 East 51st Street, New York, NY 10022, USA

Proximity:

Grand Central Terminal: Approximately 0.6 miles (1 km), a short walk away, offering easy access to transportation and iconic architecture.

Times Square: About 1 mile (1.6 km), accessible via a brief subway ride or a longer walk.

Central Park: Roughly 1 mile (1.6 km), a short distance away for outdoor activities and relaxation.

Fifth Avenue Shopping: Approximately 0.5 miles (0.8 km), home to numerous high-end shops and department stores.

Subway Stations: The hotel is close to the 51st Street subway station (6 train) and the Lexington Avenue-53rd Street subway station (E, M trains), providing convenient access to various parts of the city.

Highlights

Efficient Design: Rooms are designed to maximize space with smart, compact layouts that provide comfort and functionality.

Modern Amenities: Offers contemporary features including free Wi-Fi, flat-screen TVs, and comfortable bedding.

Affordable Rates: Provides budget-friendly accommodations in a central Manhattan location, making it accessible for travelers looking to save on lodging.

Rooms and Amenities

Pod Rooms: The hotel offers a variety of Pod rooms, including Pod 1 and Pod 2 options, featuring space-efficient designs with modern decor.

Private Bathrooms: Most rooms come with private bathrooms, though some may have shared facilities, especially in the more budget-friendly options.

Basic Amenities: Includes free Wi-Fi, air conditioning, flat-screen TVs, and comfortable beds. Some rooms may also offer mini-fridges and work desks.

Shared Spaces: Features common areas such as a lounge and rooftop garden where guests can relax and socialize.

Bars and Dining

No On-Site Restaurant: The hotel does not have a full-service restaurant. However, there are numerous dining options in the surrounding area, including cafes, restaurants, and bars.

Breakfast Options: The hotel offers a continental breakfast with options like pastries, coffee, and juice in the lobby area.

Events and Conferences

Meeting Rooms: Pod 51 does not have dedicated event or conference spaces. For business meetings or larger events, nearby venues or hotels may offer suitable facilities.

Event Planning Services: While the hotel does not provide extensive event planning services, the concierge can assist with recommendations and arrangements for local event venues.

Basic Facilities and Amenities

Free Wi-Fi: Complimentary high-speed internet access throughout the hotel.

24-Hour Reception: The front desk is open around the clock for check-ins, check-outs, and guest assistance.

Concierge Service: Available to help with reservations, recommendations, and travel arrangements.

Fitness Center: The hotel does not have an on-site fitness center, but nearby gyms and fitness facilities can be accessed.

Opening and Closing Hours

Hotel Reception: Open 24 hours a day.

Common Areas: Generally accessible throughout the day and night, though specific hours may vary based on hotel policies.

Price

Rates at Pod 51 Hotel are generally budget-friendly, with average prices starting around $150 to $250 per night, depending on room type, season, and booking conditions. Prices can vary, so it's advisable to book in advance and check availability directly through the hotel's website or booking platforms for the best rates.

Pros

Affordable: Offers budget accommodations in a central Manhattan location.

Modern Design: Features contemporary and space-efficient room designs.

Prime Location: Conveniently located near key attractions and public transportation.

Free Wi-Fi: Provides complimentary internet access throughout the hotel.

Cons

Small Rooms: Rooms are compact, which may not suit travelers seeking more space or extensive amenities.

Limited Dining Options: The hotel does not have an on-site restaurant, though there are dining options nearby.

No On-Site Fitness Center: Lacks a dedicated fitness center, though nearby facilities are available.

Local Tips

Explore Midtown: Take advantage of the hotel's location to explore nearby attractions such as Grand Central Terminal, Fifth Avenue shopping, and Central Park.

Utilize Public Transit: Use the nearby subway stations for convenient access to other parts of the city.

Visit Local Eateries: Discover the diverse dining options in the surrounding area, from casual cafes to fine dining restaurants.

Enjoy the Rooftop Garden: Make time to relax in the hotel's rooftop garden for a pleasant view of the city.

4. The Bowery House

The Bowery House is a distinctive and budget-friendly hostel located in the Bowery neighborhood of Manhattan. Known for its historic charm and unique design, the hostel offers a mix of private and shared accommodations with a focus on providing a comfortable and social environment for travelers. The Bowery House is popular among budget-conscious tourists and backpackers seeking an affordable yet characterful place to stay in New York City.

Location (Address & Proximity)

Address: 220 Bowery, New York, NY 10012, USA

Proximity:

SoHo: Approximately 0.7 miles (1.1 km), within walking distance to trendy shops, restaurants, and galleries.

Greenwich Village: About 1 mile (1.6 km), a short walk or subway ride to explore the vibrant neighborhood with its eclectic dining and nightlife.

Chinatown: Roughly 0.6 miles (1 km), easily accessible for those interested in diverse dining options and bustling street life.

Times Square: Approximately 2.5 miles (4 km), accessible via a quick subway ride or taxi.

Subway Stations: The hostel is close to the Bowery subway station (J, Z trains) and the Spring Street subway station (6 train), providing convenient access to various parts of the city.

Highlights

Historic Building: Housed in a building with a rich history, The Bowery House features a vintage design that reflects its historical roots.

Unique Design: The hostel is known for its unique aesthetic, including a retro-inspired design and use of reclaimed materials.

Affordable Rates: Offers budget-friendly accommodations with a focus on providing value for money in a central location.

Rooms and Amenities

Cabin Rooms: The Bowery House offers dormitory-style cabins with bunk beds, providing an affordable option for those willing to share space with other travelers.

Private Rooms: Also provides private rooms for guests seeking more privacy, though these are also designed with a vintage charm.

Shared Bathrooms: Most rooms have access to shared bathrooms, equipped with basic toiletries and showers.

Basic Amenities: Includes free Wi-Fi, air conditioning, and simple furnishings. Common areas are available for socializing and relaxation.

Bars and Dining

No On-Site Bar or Restaurant: The Bowery House does not have a full-service restaurant or bar on-site. However, the surrounding Bowery neighborhood offers a wide range of dining and drinking options, from casual eateries to upscale restaurants.

Shared Kitchen: The hostel provides a shared kitchen where guests can prepare their own meals.

Events and Activities

Organized Activities: While The Bowery House does not offer extensive organized events or activities, its central location and social environment make it easy for guests to explore nearby attractions and events.

Community Atmosphere: The hostel fosters a communal atmosphere with common areas where guests can interact and socialize.

Basic Facilities and Amenities

Free Wi-Fi: Provides complimentary high-speed internet access throughout the hostel.

24-Hour Reception: The front desk is open around the clock for guest assistance and inquiries.

Concierge Service: Limited concierge services are available to help with recommendations and local information.

Opening and Closing Hours

Hotel Reception: Open 24 hours a day.

Common Areas: Generally accessible throughout the day and night, though specific hours may vary based on hostel policies.

Price

Rates at The Bowery House are typically budget-friendly, with prices for dormitory beds starting around $50 to $80 per night. Private rooms are available at a higher rate, often ranging from $100 to $150 per night. Prices can fluctuate based on the season, room type, and booking conditions. For the best rates, it's advisable to book in advance and check availability through the hostel's website or booking platforms.

Pros

Affordable: Offers budget accommodations in a central Manhattan location.

Unique Design: Features a distinctive and vintage-inspired design that adds character to the stay.

Central Location: Conveniently located in the Bowery, with easy access to nearby neighborhoods and attractions.

Free Wi-Fi: Provides complimentary internet access throughout the hostel.

Cons

Small Rooms: Dormitory-style cabins and private rooms may be compact, which might not suit all travelers.

Shared Bathrooms: Shared facilities may not appeal to guests seeking more privacy.

Basic Amenities: Limited amenities compared to more upscale hotels, including no on-site dining options.

Local Tips

Explore the Bowery: Take advantage of the hostel's location to explore the eclectic and vibrant Bowery neighborhood, known for its diverse dining options and nightlife.

Visit Nearby Attractions: Explore nearby neighborhoods like SoHo and Greenwich Village for shopping, dining, and cultural experiences.

Use Public Transit: Utilize nearby subway stations for convenient travel to other parts of the city.

Try Local Eateries: Discover the diverse range of dining options in the Bowery, from casual cafes to trendy restaurants.

5. Chelsea International Hostel

Chelsea International Hostel is a budget-friendly accommodation option located in the vibrant Chelsea neighborhood of Manhattan. Known for its affordability and central location, this hostel caters to travelers seeking economical lodging with a focus on a relaxed and social environment. It offers basic amenities and a variety of room types, making it suitable for both individual travelers and groups.

Location (Address & Proximity)

Address: 251 West 20th Street, New York, NY 10011, USA

Proximity:

Chelsea Market: Approximately 0.7 miles (1.1 km), a short walk or quick subway ride to this popular food market and shopping destination.

The High Line: About 0.5 miles (0.8 km), easily accessible for a scenic stroll along the elevated park.

Madison Square Garden: Roughly 1 mile (1.6 km), a short distance away for concerts and events.

Times Square: Approximately 1.5 miles (2.4 km), accessible via a brief subway ride or cab.

Subway Stations: The hostel is close to the 23rd Street subway station (C, E trains) and the 18th Street subway station (1 train), providing convenient access to various parts of the city.

Highlights

Affordable Rates: Offers budget accommodations with competitive pricing, making it an accessible option for travelers on a tight budget.

Central Location: Situated in the Chelsea neighborhood, providing easy access to major attractions, dining, and cultural experiences.

Social Atmosphere: Known for its relaxed and friendly environment, encouraging interaction among guests.

Rooms and Amenities

Dormitory-Style Rooms: The hostel provides dormitory-style accommodations with bunk beds. Options include mixed-gender and female-only dorms.

Private Rooms: Private rooms are available for those seeking more privacy, though these are basic and may be more expensive than dorm beds.

Shared Bathrooms: Bathrooms are shared among guests, and facilities are maintained to ensure cleanliness.

Basic Amenities: Includes free Wi-Fi, air conditioning, and simple furnishings. Guests have access to a shared kitchen for meal preparation.

Bars and Dining

No On-Site Bar or Restaurant: The hostel does not have a full-service restaurant or bar. However, the surrounding Chelsea neighborhood offers a wide range of dining and drinking options, from casual eateries to upscale restaurants.

Shared Kitchen: Features a communal kitchen where guests can prepare their own meals, equipped with basic appliances and utensils.

Events and Activities

Organized Activities: While Chelsea International Hostel does not offer extensive organized events or activities, the friendly atmosphere and common areas encourage social interaction among guests.

Community Space: Provides common areas such as lounges and outdoor spaces where guests can relax and meet fellow travelers.

Basic Facilities and Amenities

Free Wi-Fi: Offers complimentary high-speed internet access throughout the hostel.

24-Hour Reception: The front desk is open around the clock for guest assistance and inquiries.

Concierge Service: Limited concierge services are available to help with recommendations and local information.

Opening and Closing Hours

Hotel Reception: Open 24 hours a day.

Common Areas: Generally accessible throughout the day and night, though specific hours may vary based on hostel policies.

Price

Rates at Chelsea International Hostel are typically budget-friendly, with dormitory beds starting around $50 to $80 per night and private rooms available at higher rates, often ranging from $100 to $150 per night. Prices can vary depending on the season, room type, and booking conditions. For the best rates, it's advisable to book in advance and check availability through the hostel's website or booking platforms.

Pros

Affordable: Provides budget accommodations in a central Manhattan location.

Social Environment: Offers a friendly and social atmosphere that encourages interaction among guests.

Central Location: Conveniently located in Chelsea, with easy access to major attractions and public transportation.

Free Wi-Fi: Complimentary internet access throughout the hostel.

Cons

Basic Facilities: Rooms and amenities are basic compared to more upscale accommodations.

Shared Bathrooms: Shared facilities may not suit all travelers, especially those seeking more privacy.

No On-Site Dining: Lacks an on-site restaurant or bar, though there are dining options nearby.

Local Tips

Explore Chelsea Market: Visit the nearby Chelsea Market for a diverse range of food options and unique shopping experiences.

Walk the High Line: Take advantage of the hostel's proximity to The High Line for a scenic walk and urban greenery.

Discover Local Dining: Explore the Chelsea neighborhood for a variety of dining options, from casual cafes to trendy restaurants.

Use Public Transit: Utilize nearby subway stations for convenient travel to other parts of the city.

Boutique Hotels

Boutique hotels in New York City offer a unique and personalized lodging experience, combining stylish design with individual charm. These hotels provide distinctive rooms, often with themed décor and bespoke amenities, creating an intimate atmosphere that stands out from larger chain hotels. Perfect for travelers seeking a more curated and memorable stay, boutique hotels offer both character and comfort in some of the city's most vibrant neighborhoods.

Top 5 Boutique Hotels

1. **The Greenwich Hotel**

The Greenwich Hotel is a luxurious boutique hotel located in the heart of the Tribeca neighborhood of Manhattan. Renowned for its blend of sophisticated design and relaxed elegance, the hotel offers an intimate and high-end experience. With its attention to detail, exceptional service, and unique character, The Greenwich Hotel caters to travelers seeking a refined and personalized stay in New York City.

Location (Address & Proximity)

Address: 377 Greenwich Street, New York, NY 10013, USA

Proximity:

Tribeca: Located in the Tribeca neighborhood, known for its upscale charm, artistic vibe, and historic architecture.

SoHo: Approximately 0.8 miles (1.3 km), a short walk or quick subway ride to the trendy shopping and dining district.

Financial District: About 1 mile (1.6 km), easily reachable for business travelers or those interested in visiting Wall Street and the World Trade Center.

Central Park: Roughly 4 miles (6.4 km), accessible via a short subway ride or taxi.

Subway Stations: The hotel is close to the Chambers Street subway station (J, Z trains) and the Franklin Street subway station (1 train), providing convenient access to other parts of the city.

Highlights

Luxury and Elegance: The Greenwich Hotel is known for its opulent yet understated decor, combining classic luxury with a warm and inviting atmosphere.

Personalized Service: Offers exceptional service with a focus on personalized guest experiences and attention to detail.

Exclusive Amenities: Features a range of high-end amenities and services, including a full-service spa, an indoor pool, and a renowned restaurant.

Rooms and Suites

Room Types: The hotel offers a variety of room types, including deluxe rooms, suites, and specialty suites, each designed with a blend of traditional and contemporary styles.

Unique Design: Rooms are individually decorated with custom furnishings, rich fabrics, and artisanal touches, creating a distinctive and cozy ambiance.

Luxury Amenities: Includes features such as luxury bedding, spacious bathrooms with high-end toiletries, and state-of-the-art technology.

Private Services: Some suites offer private terraces, fireplaces, and in-room dining options for an added level of luxury.

Spa and Wellness

Shibui Spa: The Greenwich Hotel houses Shibui Spa, a tranquil retreat offering a range of treatments and therapies designed to promote relaxation and rejuvenation. The spa features a traditional Japanese design, including a serene indoor pool.

Wellness Facilities: In addition to the spa, the hotel offers a fitness center with modern equipment to cater to guests' wellness needs.

Bars and Dining

Locanda Verde: The hotel's on-site restaurant, Locanda Verde, is a popular dining spot known for its Italian cuisine and vibrant atmosphere. It serves breakfast, lunch, and dinner with a menu featuring fresh and seasonal ingredients.

Bar: The hotel features a stylish bar area where guests can enjoy cocktails and light bites in a relaxed setting.

Events and Conferences

Event Spaces: The Greenwich Hotel offers a range of elegant event spaces for meetings, private events, and social gatherings. These spaces are designed to accommodate both intimate and larger events with a focus on high-quality service and attention to detail.

Event Planning Services: The hotel provides comprehensive event planning and catering services to ensure a seamless and memorable event experience.

Basic Facilities and Amenities

Free Wi-Fi: Complimentary high-speed internet access throughout the hotel.

24-Hour Concierge: Available to assist with reservations, recommendations, and personalized guest services.

Valet Parking: Valet parking is available for guests with vehicles.

Business Services: Offers business services including meeting rooms, printing, and copying facilities.

Opening and Closing Hours

Hotel Reception: Open 24 hours a day.

Locanda Verde: Restaurant hours typically range from breakfast through dinner, with specific hours varying based on the day of the week.

Shibui Spa: Spa hours vary, so guests should check availability and book treatments in advance.

Price

Rates at The Greenwich Hotel vary based on room type, season, and booking conditions. On average, rates start around $700 to $1,200 per night for standard rooms, with suites and specialty accommodations priced higher. Prices can fluctuate, so it's advisable to book in advance and check availability directly through the hotel's website or booking platforms.

Pros

Luxurious Design: Offers a high-end, stylish atmosphere with a focus on comfort and elegance.

Personalized Service: Provides exceptional, attentive service tailored to individual guest needs.

Prime Location: Located in the trendy Tribeca neighborhood with easy access to nearby attractions and dining.

Exclusive Amenities: Features a full-service spa, upscale dining, and modern wellness facilities.

Cons

High Cost: Luxury comes with a high price tag, making it less accessible for budget travelers.

Limited Dining Options: While Locanda Verde is a renowned restaurant, dining options are limited to the hotel's facilities.

Local Tips

Explore Tribeca: Take advantage of the hotel's location to explore the chic Tribeca neighborhood, known for its art galleries, boutiques, and upscale dining.

Visit SoHo: A short walk or quick ride to SoHo offers additional shopping and dining opportunities.

Walk the High Line: Enjoy a stroll on The High Line, an elevated park that provides unique views of the city and greenery.

Utilize Public Transit: Nearby subway stations offer convenient access to other parts of Manhattan and beyond.

2. **The Crosby Street Hotel**

The Crosby Street Hotel is a chic and sophisticated boutique hotel located in the heart of SoHo, Manhattan. Renowned for its modern design, luxurious amenities, and exceptional service, the hotel offers a refined and stylish experience for discerning travelers. With its prime location, elegant accommodations, and a focus on personalized guest experiences, The Crosby Street Hotel stands out as a top choice for those seeking a high-end stay in New New York City.

Location (Address & Proximity)

Address: 79 Crosby Street, New York, NY 10012, USA

Proximity:

SoHo: Located in SoHo, a trendy and artistic neighborhood known for its high-end shopping, galleries, and dining options.

Greenwich Village: Approximately 0.8 miles (1.3 km), within walking distance or a short subway ride to explore this vibrant neighborhood.

Chinatown: About 1 mile (1.6 km), easily accessible for diverse dining experiences and bustling street life.

Times Square: Roughly 2 miles (3.2 km), accessible via a quick subway ride or taxi.

Central Park: Approximately 3.5 miles (5.6 km), reachable via a short subway ride or cab.

Highlights

Stylish Design: The hotel is known for its contemporary design and elegant decor, featuring a blend of modern luxury and artistic flair.

Exceptional Service: Offers high levels of personalized service and attention to detail, ensuring a memorable guest experience.

Prime Location: Situated in the fashionable SoHo neighborhood, providing easy access to shopping, dining, and cultural attractions.

Rooms and Suites

Room Types: The Crosby Street Hotel offers a range of room types, including deluxe rooms, suites, and specialty suites, all designed with a modern and sophisticated aesthetic.

Design and Decor: Rooms feature floor-to-ceiling windows, contemporary furnishings, and high-quality materials. Many rooms offer stunning views of the city or the hotel's private garden.

Luxury Amenities: Includes features such as luxury bedding, spacious bathrooms with premium toiletries, and state-of-the-art technology including flat-screen TVs and high-speed Wi-Fi.

Specialty Suites: Some suites offer additional features such as private terraces, fireplaces, and separate living areas for added comfort and luxury.

Spa and Wellness

No On-Site Spa: The Crosby Street Hotel does not have an on-site spa. However, the concierge can assist with recommendations and bookings for nearby wellness facilities.

Fitness Center: The hotel has a well-equipped fitness center with modern equipment to cater to guests' fitness needs.

Bars and Dining

The Crosby Bar: The hotel features a stylish bar area known for its relaxed atmosphere and high-quality cocktails. It's an ideal spot for unwinding or socializing.

On-Site Dining: While there is no full-service restaurant, the hotel's bar provides light snacks and a selection of beverages.

Events and Conferences

Event Spaces: The Crosby Street Hotel offers elegant event spaces suitable for meetings, private events, and social gatherings. The spaces are designed to accommodate both intimate and larger events.

Event Planning Services: The hotel provides comprehensive event planning and catering services to ensure a seamless and sophisticated event experience.

Basic Facilities and Amenities

Free Wi-Fi: Offers complimentary high-speed internet access throughout the hotel.

24-Hour Reception: The front desk is open around the clock for guest assistance and inquiries.

Concierge Service: Available to help with reservations, recommendations, and personalized guest services.

Business Services: Provides business services including meeting rooms, printing, and copying facilities.

Opening and Closing Hours

Hotel Reception: Open 24 hours a day.

The Crosby Bar: Generally open throughout the day and evening, though specific hours may vary.

Price

Rates at The Crosby Street Hotel can vary widely depending on room type, season, and booking conditions. On average, prices start around $600 to $1,000 per night for standard rooms, with suites and specialty accommodations priced higher. Prices are subject to change, so it's advisable to book in advance and check availability through the hotel's website or booking platforms for the best rates.

Pros

Luxurious Design: Features a contemporary and elegant design that provides a high-end and comfortable experience.

Exceptional Service: Known for attentive and personalized service.

Prime Location: Situated in the trendy SoHo neighborhood with easy access to shopping, dining, and cultural attractions.

Modern Amenities: Offers a range of luxury amenities including high-speed Wi-Fi and well-equipped fitness center.

Cons

High Cost: The luxury experience comes with a premium price tag, making it less accessible for budget travelers.

No On-Site Spa: Lacks a full-service spa, though wellness options are available nearby.

Local Tips

Explore SoHo: Take advantage of the hotel's location to explore SoHo's high-end shopping, art galleries, and vibrant dining scene.

Visit Nearby Neighborhoods: Greenwich Village and Chinatown are within walking distance or a short subway ride, offering additional dining and cultural experiences.

Walk the High Line: A short distance away, The High Line offers a unique elevated park experience with city views and art installations.

Utilize Public Transit: Nearby subway stations provide convenient access to other parts of Manhattan and beyond.

3. **The NoMad Hotel**

The NoMad Hotel is a luxury boutique hotel located in the NoMad (North of Madison Square Park) neighborhood of Manhattan. Renowned for its elegant design, sophisticated ambiance, and exceptional service, The NoMad Hotel combines classic and modern elements to provide a unique and upscale experience. The hotel is known for its stylish interiors, high-quality dining options, and a refined yet relaxed atmosphere.

Location (Address & Proximity)

Address: 1170 Broadway, New York, NY 10001, USA

The Ultimate New York City Travel Guide (2025 Edition)

Proximity:

Madison Square Park: Approximately 0.2 miles (0.3 km), a short walk to this iconic park featuring green space and public art.

Empire State Building: About 0.6 miles (1 km), within walking distance to this famous skyscraper and observation deck.

Times Square: Roughly 1 mile (1.6 km), accessible via a brief subway ride or a walk.

SoHo: Approximately 1.5 miles (2.4 km), easily reachable by subway or a longer walk.

Subway Stations: The hotel is close to the 28th Street subway station (R, W trains) and the 23rd Street subway station (C, E trains), providing convenient access to various parts of the city.

Highlights

Elegant Design: The NoMad Hotel features a blend of classic and contemporary design elements, including luxurious fabrics, antique furnishings, and modern artwork.

Exceptional Dining: Home to acclaimed dining options, including a renowned restaurant and bar that offer high-quality food and beverages.

Prime Location: Located in the vibrant NoMad neighborhood, offering easy access to key attractions, dining, and shopping.

Rooms and Suites

Room Types: The NoMad Hotel offers a range of room types, including deluxe rooms, suites, and specialty suites. Each room is designed with a blend of classic and modern aesthetics.

Design and Decor: Rooms feature luxurious furnishings, rich fabrics, and elegant details. Many rooms offer large windows with views of the city or the hotel's courtyard.

Luxury Amenities: Includes high-quality bedding, spacious bathrooms with premium toiletries, and state-of-the-art technology such as flat-screen TVs and high-speed Wi-Fi.

Specialty Suites: Some suites offer additional features such as private terraces, separate living areas, and elegant décor for an enhanced luxury experience.

Spa and Wellness

No On-Site Spa: The NoMad Hotel does not have an on-site spa. However, the concierge can assist with recommendations and bookings for nearby wellness facilities.

Fitness Center: The hotel has a well-equipped fitness center with modern equipment to cater to guests' fitness needs.

Bars and Dining

NoMad Restaurant: The hotel features an acclaimed restaurant, known for its sophisticated menu and high-quality cuisine. The dining experience includes breakfast, lunch, and dinner options with a focus on fresh, seasonal ingredients.

NoMad Bar: The hotel's stylish bar offers a refined setting for enjoying cocktails and light bites. The bar is known for its chic atmosphere and expertly crafted drinks.

Events and Conferences

Event Spaces: The NoMad Hotel offers elegant event spaces suitable for meetings, private events, and social gatherings. These spaces are designed to accommodate both intimate and larger events.

Event Planning Services: The hotel provides comprehensive event planning and catering services to ensure a seamless and memorable event experience.

Basic Facilities and Amenities

Free Wi-Fi: Offers complimentary high-speed internet access throughout the hotel.

24-Hour Reception: The front desk is open around the clock for guest assistance and inquiries.

Concierge Service: Available to help with reservations, recommendations, and personalized guest services.

Business Services: Provides business services including meeting rooms, printing, and copying facilities.

Opening and Closing Hours

Hotel Reception: Open 24 hours a day.

NoMad Restaurant: Typically serves breakfast, lunch, and dinner with specific hours varying based on the day of the week.

NoMad Bar: Generally open throughout the day and evening, though specific hours may vary.

Price

Rates at The NoMad Hotel vary based on room type, season, and booking conditions. On average, prices start around $500 to $800 per night for standard rooms, with suites and specialty accommodations priced higher. Prices can fluctuate, so it's advisable to book in advance and check availability through the hotel's website or booking platforms for the best rates.

Pros

Elegant Design: Features a stylish and sophisticated design that combines classic and modern elements.

Exceptional Dining: Offers high-quality dining options, including a renowned restaurant and bar.

Prime Location: Located in the vibrant NoMad neighborhood with easy access to key attractions and public transportation.

Luxury Amenities: Provides a range of upscale amenities including a well-equipped fitness center and personalized guest services.

Cons

High Cost: The luxury experience comes with a premium price tag, making it less accessible for budget travelers.

No On-Site Spa: Lacks a full-service spa, though wellness options are available nearby.

Local Tips

Explore NoMad: Take advantage of the hotel's location to explore the trendy NoMad neighborhood, known for its dining, shopping, and cultural attractions.

Visit Nearby Parks: Madison Square Park is a short walk away and offers a pleasant green space for relaxation.

Check Out Nearby Attractions: The Empire State Building and Times Square are within walking distance or a short subway ride, offering iconic New York City experiences.

Utilize Public Transit: Nearby subway stations provide convenient access to other parts of Manhattan and beyond.

4. The Marlton Hotel

The Marlton Hotel is a stylish boutique hotel located in Greenwich Village, Manhattan. Known for its chic, vintage-inspired design and intimate atmosphere, The Marlton combines classic charm with modern amenities. It offers a unique blend of sophistication and comfort, appealing to travelers who appreciate a well-curated, boutique experience in one of New York City's most vibrant neighborhoods.

Location (Address & Proximity)

Address: 5 West 8th Street, New York, NY 10011, USA

Proximity:

Washington Square Park: Approximately 0.2 miles (0.3 km), just a short walk to this iconic park known for its arch, street performers, and green space.

SoHo: About 1 mile (1.6 km), easily accessible by subway or a longer walk to explore trendy shops and restaurants.

Times Square: Roughly 2 miles (3.2 km), reachable via a short subway ride or taxi.

The High Line: Approximately 1.5 miles (2.4 km), accessible for a scenic walk along the elevated park.

Subway Stations: The hotel is close to the 8th Street subway station (N, R, W trains) and the West 4th Street subway station (A, C, E trains), providing convenient access to various parts of the city.

Highlights

Vintage Charm: The Marlton Hotel features a vintage-inspired design with classic furnishings, rich textures, and a warm, inviting ambiance.

Prime Location: Situated in the heart of Greenwich Village, offering easy access to a variety of dining, shopping, and cultural attractions.

Intimate Atmosphere: Provides a cozy and personalized experience, with a focus on comfort and attention to detail.

Rooms and Suites

Room Types: The hotel offers a range of room types, including classic rooms, deluxe rooms, and suites. Each room is designed with a vintage aesthetic and modern amenities.

Design and Decor: Rooms feature elegant, retro-inspired decor, including patterned wallpapers, plush bedding, and vintage furnishings. Many rooms offer views of the city or the hotel's courtyard.

Luxury Amenities: Includes features such as high-quality linens, spacious bathrooms with premium toiletries, and modern technology including flat-screen TVs and complimentary Wi-Fi.

Spa and Wellness

No On-Site Spa: The Marlton Hotel does not have an on-site spa. However, the concierge can assist with recommendations and bookings for nearby wellness facilities.

Fitness Center: The hotel does not have a dedicated fitness center. Guests can use nearby gyms or ask the concierge for recommendations on fitness options.

Bars and Dining

The Marlton Bar: The hotel features a stylish bar area known for its relaxed atmosphere and carefully crafted cocktails. The bar is designed to reflect the vintage charm of the hotel.

Dining Options: While there is no full-service restaurant, the bar serves a selection of light bites and snacks. The surrounding Greenwich Village neighborhood offers a wide range of dining options from casual eateries to upscale restaurants.

Events and Conferences

Event Spaces: The Marlton Hotel does not offer extensive event spaces. However, the intimate and stylish setting makes it a potential option for small gatherings and private events.

Event Planning Services: The hotel provides personalized assistance for organizing small-scale events or meetings.

Basic Facilities and Amenities

Free Wi-Fi: Offers complimentary high-speed internet access throughout the hotel.

24-Hour Reception: The front desk is open around the clock for guest assistance and inquiries.

Concierge Service: Available to help with reservations, recommendations, and personalized guest services.

Opening and Closing Hours

Hotel Reception: Open 24 hours a day.

The Marlton Bar: Typically open throughout the day and evening, with specific hours varying based on the day of the week.

Price

Rates at The Marlton Hotel vary based on room type, season, and booking conditions. On average, prices start around $300 to $500 per night for standard rooms, with suites and higher-end rooms priced higher. Prices can fluctuate, so it's advisable to book in advance and check availability through the hotel's website or booking platforms for the best rates.

Pros

Vintage Charm: Features stylish, vintage-inspired decor that adds character and charm to the stay.

Prime Location: Located in Greenwich Village, with easy access to a variety of local attractions and dining options.

Intimate Atmosphere: Offers a cozy and personalized experience with attention to detail.

Free Wi-Fi: Provides complimentary high-speed internet access throughout the hotel.

Cons

Limited Facilities: Lacks extensive facilities such as an on-site spa or dedicated fitness center.

No Full-Service Restaurant: The hotel's dining options are limited to the bar, with additional dining needed in the surrounding area.

Local Tips

Explore Greenwich Village: Take advantage of the hotel's location to explore the charming and historic Greenwich Village neighborhood, known for its eclectic shops, cafes, and vibrant cultural scene.

Visit Washington Square Park: A short walk away, Washington Square Park offers a lively atmosphere with street performers, a large fountain, and green space for relaxation.

Discover Local Dining: The neighborhood is home to numerous dining options, ranging from trendy eateries to classic New York delis.

Utilize Public Transit: Nearby subway stations provide convenient access to other parts of Manhattan and beyond.

5. The Ludlow Hotel

The Ludlow Hotel is a chic boutique hotel located in the Lower East Side of Manhattan. Known for its trendy design, luxurious amenities, and vibrant atmosphere, The Ludlow Hotel offers a stylish and contemporary stay for travelers seeking a mix of modern comfort and urban edge. The hotel's eclectic decor and lively atmosphere make it a standout choice for those wanting to immerse themselves in one of New York City's most dynamic neighborhoods.

Location (Address & Proximity)

Address: 180 Ludlow Street, New York, NY 10002, USA

Proximity:

SoHo: Approximately 1 mile (1.6 km), easily accessible by subway or a short cab ride for shopping and dining.

Greenwich Village: About 1 mile (1.6 km), accessible via a short subway ride or walk, offering additional dining and cultural experiences.

Chinatown: Roughly 0.6 miles (1 km), within walking distance to explore vibrant street life and diverse dining options.

Times Square: About 2 miles (3.2 km), reachable by a quick subway ride or taxi.

Subway Stations: The hotel is close to the Delancey Street subway station (F train) and the Essex Street subway station (J, Z trains), providing convenient access to various parts of the city.

Highlights

Trendy Design: The Ludlow Hotel features a stylish and contemporary design with a mix of modern and vintage elements, creating a vibrant and welcoming atmosphere.

Rooftop Bar: The hotel boasts a popular rooftop bar offering stunning views of the city and a lively ambiance.

Prime Location: Situated in the Lower East Side, known for its trendy eateries, art galleries, and nightlife.

Rooms and Suites

Room Types: The Ludlow Hotel offers a range of room types, including standard rooms, deluxe rooms, and suites. Each room is designed with a modern and eclectic style.

Design and Decor: Rooms feature floor-to-ceiling windows, contemporary furnishings, and unique design elements. Many rooms offer views of the city or the hotel's rooftop garden.

Luxury Amenities: Includes high-quality bedding, spacious bathrooms with premium toiletries, and modern technology such as flat-screen TVs and high-speed Wi-Fi.

Specialty Suites: Some suites offer additional features such as private terraces, separate living areas, and enhanced décor for a more luxurious experience.

Spa and Wellness

No On-Site Spa: The Ludlow Hotel does not have an on-site spa. However, the concierge can assist with recommendations and bookings for nearby wellness facilities.

Fitness Center: The hotel features a well-equipped fitness center with modern equipment to cater to guests' fitness needs.

Bars and Dining

The Roof: The hotel's rooftop bar, known as The Roof, offers a stylish setting with panoramic views of the city. It's a popular spot for cocktails and socializing.

The Ludlow House: The hotel has an on-site restaurant that provides a relaxed dining experience with a menu featuring a mix of American and international dishes.

Additional Dining Options: The Lower East Side is home to a variety of dining options, from trendy cafes to upscale restaurants.

Events and Conferences

Event Spaces: The Ludlow Hotel offers stylish and flexible event spaces for meetings, private events, and social gatherings. These spaces are designed to accommodate both intimate and larger events.

Event Planning Services: The hotel provides event planning and catering services to ensure a seamless and successful event experience.

Basic Facilities and Amenities

Free Wi-Fi: Offers complimentary high-speed internet access throughout the hotel.

24-Hour Reception: The front desk is open around the clock for guest assistance and inquiries.

Concierge Service: Available to help with reservations, recommendations, and personalized guest services.

Business Services: Provides business services including meeting rooms, printing, and copying facilities.

Opening and Closing Hours

Hotel Reception: Open 24 hours a day.

The Roof: Generally open throughout the day and evening, though specific hours may vary based on the season and day of the week.

The Ludlow House: Typically open for breakfast, lunch, and dinner, with specific hours varying by day.

Price

Rates at The Ludlow Hotel vary depending on room type, season, and booking conditions. On average, prices start around $400 to $600 per night for standard rooms, with suites and higher-end accommodations priced higher. Prices can fluctuate, so it's advisable to book in advance and check availability through the hotel's website or booking platforms for the best rates.

Pros

Trendy Design: Features stylish, contemporary design with modern amenities and a vibrant atmosphere.

Rooftop Bar: Offers a popular rooftop bar with stunning city views and a lively social scene.

Prime Location: Located in the Lower East Side, with easy access to a range of dining, shopping, and nightlife options.

Modern Amenities: Provides a range of upscale amenities including a well-equipped fitness center and free Wi-Fi.

Cons

Higher Cost: The luxury experience comes with a premium price tag, which may not be ideal for budget travelers.

No On-Site Spa: Lacks a full-service spa, though wellness options are available nearby.

Local Tips

Explore the Lower East Side: Take advantage of the hotel's location to explore the vibrant Lower East Side neighborhood, known for its eclectic mix of restaurants, bars, and cultural attractions.

Visit Nearby Attractions: Explore nearby neighborhoods like SoHo and Greenwich Village for additional dining, shopping, and cultural experiences.

Enjoy the Rooftop: Don't miss the opportunity to visit The Roof for cocktails and panoramic views of the city.

Utilize Public Transit: Nearby subway stations provide convenient access to other parts of Manhattan and beyond.

Business Hotel

Business hotels in New York City are designed to cater to the needs of professionals, offering efficient amenities and services tailored for work and convenience. These hotels feature well-equipped business centers, meeting rooms, high-speed internet, and comfortable workspaces. Ideal for travelers combining business with leisure, business hotels provide a streamlined stay with easy access to the city's major corporate hubs and transportation links.

Top 5 Business Hotel

1. **The Langham, New York, Fifth Avenue**

The Langham, New York, Fifth Avenue, located in the heart of Midtown Manhattan, is a premier luxury hotel renowned for its elegance, sophisticated service, and business-friendly amenities. It caters to corporate travelers with its upscale accommodations, convenient location, and state-of-the-art facilities. The hotel combines classic luxury with modern functionality, making it a top choice for business professionals seeking a refined and efficient stay in New York City.

Location (Address & Proximity)

The Ultimate New York City Travel Guide (2025 Edition)

Address: 400 Fifth Avenue, New York, NY 10018, USA

Proximity:

Empire State Building: Approximately 0.3 miles (0.5 km), within walking distance to this iconic skyscraper and observation deck.

Times Square: About 0.5 miles (0.8 km), a short walk away for dining, entertainment, and Broadway shows.

Grand Central Terminal: Roughly 0.6 miles (1 km), accessible by a brief walk or subway ride, providing connections to transportation and additional amenities.

Central Park: Approximately 1 mile (1.6 km), a short subway ride or a longer walk to enjoy the park's expansive green spaces and recreational opportunities.

Subway Stations: The hotel is near several subway stations including 42nd Street – Bryant Park (B, D, F, M trains) and 34th Street – Herald Square (B, D, F, M, N, Q, R, W trains), offering convenient access to various parts of the city.

Highlights

Luxurious Accommodations: Features elegant rooms and suites designed with high-quality materials and attention to detail, providing a comfortable and sophisticated environment for business travelers.

Prime Location: Situated on Fifth Avenue in Midtown Manhattan, offering easy access to major business districts, landmarks, and entertainment options.

Business-Focused Amenities: Includes a range of amenities tailored for business travelers, such as meeting rooms, high-speed internet, and a business center.

Rooms and Suites

Room Types: The Langham offers various room types including deluxe rooms, executive suites, and specialty suites, all designed with modern luxury and functionality in mind.

Design and Decor: Rooms feature sophisticated decor with high-end furnishings, plush bedding, and large windows providing natural light and city views.

Luxury Amenities: Includes features such as spacious work desks, high-speed Wi-Fi, advanced technology, marble bathrooms with premium toiletries, and comfortable seating areas.

Executive Club Rooms: These rooms offer additional business-oriented amenities, including access to the Langham Club Lounge with complimentary refreshments and business services.

Spa and Wellness

Chuan Body + Soul: The Langham's on-site spa, Chuan Body + Soul, offers a range of wellness treatments and therapies designed to rejuvenate and relax guests. The spa provides a serene environment with a focus on holistic health.

Fitness Center: The hotel features a modern fitness center equipped with state-of-the-art exercise machines and free weights, catering to guests' fitness needs.

Bars and Dining

Ai Fiori: The hotel's Michelin-starred restaurant, Ai Fiori, offers an upscale dining experience with a menu inspired by the flavors of Italy and the French Riviera. It's ideal for business dinners and meetings.

The Bar: The hotel's bar provides a refined setting for cocktails and light fare, offering a comfortable and stylish environment for informal business discussions or relaxation after a busy day.

Events and Conferences

Event Spaces: The Langham, New York, Fifth Avenue offers versatile meeting and event spaces that can accommodate various types of business functions, from small meetings to larger conferences.

Business Center: Equipped with modern technology and services, including printing, copying, and high-speed internet, to support business needs.

Event Planning Services: The hotel provides comprehensive event planning and catering services to ensure a successful and seamless business event.

Basic Facilities and Amenities

Free Wi-Fi: Offers complimentary high-speed internet access throughout the hotel, including guest rooms and public areas.

24-Hour Reception: The front desk is open around the clock to assist with guest needs and inquiries.

Concierge Service: Provides personalized assistance with reservations, recommendations, and special requests.

Business Services: Includes a fully equipped business center with printing, copying, and meeting room facilities.

Opening and Closing Hours

Hotel Reception: Open 24 hours a day.

Ai Fiori: Typically open for breakfast, lunch, and dinner, with specific hours varying by day.

The Bar: Generally open throughout the day and evening, with specific hours varying based on the season and day of the week.

Price

Rates at The Langham, New York, Fifth Avenue can vary depending on the room type, season, and booking conditions. On average, prices start around $700 to $1,000 per night for standard rooms, with suites and higher-end accommodations priced higher. Prices can fluctuate, so it's advisable to book in advance and check availability through the hotel's website or booking platforms for the best rates.

Pros

Luxurious Accommodations: Offers high-end rooms and suites with elegant decor and sophisticated amenities.

Prime Location: Centrally located in Midtown Manhattan with easy access to business districts, landmarks, and entertainment.

Business Amenities: Provides a range of business-friendly amenities, including meeting rooms, high-speed internet, and a business center.

On-Site Spa and Dining: Features an on-site spa and a Michelin-starred restaurant, enhancing the overall guest experience.

Cons

High Cost: The luxury experience comes with a premium price tag, which may be less accessible for budget travelers.

Limited On-Site Dining Options: While the hotel features a high-end restaurant and bar, additional dining options are needed in the surrounding area.

Local Tips

Explore Nearby Landmarks: Take advantage of the hotel's location to visit nearby attractions such as the Empire State Building, Times Square, and Central Park.

Utilize Public Transit: Nearby subway stations provide convenient access to other parts of Manhattan and beyond, making it easy to explore the city.

Dining Recommendations: Explore the diverse dining options in Midtown Manhattan, ranging from high-end restaurants to casual eateries.

2. The Westin New York Grand Central

The Westin New York Grand Central is a well-established, upscale hotel situated in the heart of Midtown Manhattan. Known for its modern amenities, comfortable accommodations, and prime location, this hotel caters to both business and leisure travelers. Its proximity to Grand Central Terminal and major business hubs makes it a convenient choice for those visiting New York City.

Location (Address & Proximity)

Address: 212 East 42nd Street, New York, NY 10017, USA

Proximity:

Grand Central Terminal: Approximately 0.1 miles (0.2 km), just a short walk to this historic transportation hub with numerous dining and shopping options.

Empire State Building: About 0.6 miles (1 km), within walking distance or a quick subway ride to this iconic skyscraper.

Times Square: Roughly 0.8 miles (1.3 km), easily reachable by a short walk or subway ride for entertainment and Broadway shows.

Central Park: Approximately 1.2 miles (2 km), a short subway ride or longer walk to enjoy the park's expansive green spaces.

Subway Stations: The hotel is close to Grand Central Station (4, 5, 6, 7, S trains) and Bryant Park (B, D, F, M trains), providing convenient access to various parts of the city.

Highlights

Convenient Location: Situated near Grand Central Terminal, offering easy access to transportation, dining, and shopping.

Modern Amenities: Features contemporary accommodations with a focus on comfort and convenience.

Business-Focused Facilities: Includes business services and meeting spaces tailored for corporate travelers.

Rooms and Suites

Room Types: The Westin New York Grand Central offers a variety of room types, including standard rooms, deluxe rooms, and suites. Each room is designed with modern amenities and comfort in mind.

Design and Decor: Rooms feature contemporary decor with plush bedding, large windows, and ergonomic workspaces. Many rooms offer views of the city or the East River.

Luxury Amenities: Includes features such as the Westin Heavenly Bed, spacious work desks, high-speed Wi-Fi, and marble bathrooms with premium toiletries.

Suites: The hotel's suites offer additional space and upgraded amenities, including separate living areas and enhanced views.

Spa and Wellness

No On-Site Spa: The Westin New York Grand Central does not have an on-site spa. However, the concierge can assist with recommendations and bookings for nearby wellness facilities.

Fitness Center: The hotel features a well-equipped fitness center with modern exercise machines, free weights, and space for yoga and stretching.

Bars and Dining

The New York Lounge: The hotel's lounge area offers a comfortable setting for casual dining and relaxation. It serves a variety of light fare, snacks, and beverages.

Nearby Dining Options: The hotel's location provides easy access to numerous dining options in Midtown Manhattan, ranging from upscale restaurants to casual eateries.

Events and Conferences

Event Spaces: The Westin New York Grand Central offers versatile meeting and event spaces suitable for business meetings, conferences, and social gatherings.

Business Center: Equipped with modern technology and services, including printing, copying, and high-speed internet, to support business needs.

Event Planning Services: The hotel provides comprehensive event planning and catering services to ensure a successful and seamless event experience.

Basic Facilities and Amenities

Free Wi-Fi: Offers complimentary high-speed internet access throughout the hotel.

24-Hour Reception: The front desk is open around the clock to assist with guest needs and inquiries.

Concierge Service: Provides personalized assistance with reservations, recommendations, and special requests.

Business Services: Includes a fully equipped business center and meeting rooms for corporate needs.

Opening and Closing Hours

Hotel Reception: Open 24 hours a day.

The New York Lounge: Typically open throughout the day, with specific hours varying based on the day of the week.

Price

Rates at The Westin New York Grand Central vary depending on the room type, season, and booking conditions. On average, prices start around $300 to $500 per night for standard rooms, with suites and higher-end accommodations priced higher. Prices can fluctuate, so it's advisable to book in advance and check availability through the hotel's website or booking platforms for the best rates.

Pros

Prime Location: Conveniently located near Grand Central Terminal, providing easy access to transportation and key attractions.

Modern Comfort: Features contemporary accommodations with comfortable furnishings and modern amenities.

Business-Friendly: Offers a range of business-focused facilities, including meeting rooms, a business center, and high-speed Wi-Fi.

Fitness Center: Provides a well-equipped fitness center for guests looking to maintain their exercise routine.

Cons

No On-Site Spa: Lacks a full-service spa, though wellness options are available nearby.

Basic Dining Options: Limited on-site dining options with additional dining needed in the surrounding area.

Local Tips

Explore Grand Central Terminal: Take advantage of the hotel's proximity to Grand Central Terminal to explore its historic architecture, dining options, and the iconic Oyster Bar.

Visit Nearby Attractions: Use the hotel's location to explore nearby attractions such as Times Square, the Empire State Building, and Bryant Park.

Public Transit: Utilize the nearby subway stations for convenient access to other parts of Manhattan and beyond.

3. Marriott Marquis Times Square

The Marriott Marquis Times Square is a landmark hotel located in the heart of one of New York City's most iconic areas. Known for its expansive accommodations, extensive amenities, and central location, the hotel caters to both business and leisure travelers. Its proximity to Broadway theaters and major attractions makes it a popular choice for visitors looking to experience the vibrant energy of Times Square.

Location (Address & Proximity)

Address: 1535 Broadway, New York, NY 10036, USA

Proximity:

Times Square: Directly located in the heart of Times Square, offering immediate access to the area's bright lights, theaters, and entertainment.

Broadway Theaters: Just steps away from numerous Broadway theaters, ideal for catching world-class performances.

Empire State Building: Approximately 0.7 miles (1.1 km), easily reachable by a short walk or subway ride.

Central Park: About 1.5 miles (2.4 km), a short subway ride or longer walk to enjoy the park's expansive green spaces.

Subway Stations: The hotel is close to several subway stations, including Times Square – 42nd Street (1, 2, 3, 7, N, Q, R, W trains) and 49th Street (N, Q, R, W trains), providing convenient access to various parts of the city.

Highlights

Prime Location: Located in the center of Times Square, offering easy access to entertainment, dining, and shopping.

Large Hotel Space: Features a vast atrium and a range of amenities catering to both business and leisure guests.

Broadway Access: Perfectly positioned for easy access to Broadway theaters and shows.

Rooms and Suites

Room Types: The hotel offers a range of room types, including standard rooms, deluxe rooms, and suites. Each room is designed to provide comfort and convenience.

Design and Decor: Rooms feature contemporary decor with modern furnishings, large windows, and city views. Some rooms offer panoramic views of Times Square.

Luxury Amenities: Includes high-speed Wi-Fi, comfortable bedding, spacious work desks, flat-screen TVs, and marble bathrooms with premium toiletries.

Suites: The hotel's suites offer additional space and enhanced amenities, including separate living areas and upgraded views of Times Square or the city skyline.

Spa and Wellness

No On-Site Spa: The Marriott Marquis Times Square does not have an on-site spa. However, the concierge can assist with recommendations and bookings for nearby wellness facilities.

Fitness Center: The hotel features a large, modern fitness center equipped with state-of-the-art exercise machines and free weights.

Bars and Dining

The View Restaurant & Lounge: The hotel's rotating rooftop restaurant offers breathtaking views of the city skyline along with a menu of American cuisine. It provides a unique dining experience with panoramic views of Times Square.

Broadway Lounge: Located in the hotel's lobby area, this lounge offers a relaxed setting for casual dining and drinks.

Additional Dining Options: The Times Square area is home to a wide range of dining options, from casual eateries to upscale restaurants.

Events and Conferences

Event Spaces: The Marriott Marquis Times Square features extensive meeting and event facilities, including a large ballroom and multiple meeting rooms. It is well-equipped to handle various types of events, from corporate meetings to social gatherings.

Business Center: Provides comprehensive business services, including printing, copying, and high-speed internet access.

Event Planning Services: The hotel offers event planning and catering services to ensure a smooth and successful event experience.

Basic Facilities and Amenities

Free Wi-Fi: Offers complimentary high-speed internet access throughout the hotel.

24-Hour Reception: The front desk is open around the clock to assist with guest needs and inquiries.

Concierge Service: Provides personalized assistance with reservations, recommendations, and special requests.

Business Services: Includes a fully equipped business center and meeting rooms for corporate needs.

Opening and Closing Hours

Hotel Reception: Open 24 hours a day.

The View Restaurant & Lounge: Typically open for dinner, with specific hours varying based on the day of the week.

Broadway Lounge: Generally open throughout the day and evening, with hours varying by day.

Price

Rates at the Marriott Marquis Times Square can vary depending on room type, season, and booking conditions. On average, prices start around $500 to $800 per night for standard rooms, with suites and higher-end accommodations priced higher. Prices can fluctuate, so it's advisable to book in advance and check availability through the hotel's website or booking platforms for the best rates.

Pros

Prime Location: Located in the heart of Times Square, providing easy access to Broadway theaters, dining, and entertainment.

Extensive Amenities: Features a range of amenities including a rotating rooftop restaurant, large fitness center, and extensive event facilities.

Modern Comfort: Offers contemporary accommodations with high-quality furnishings and amenities.

Business Facilities: Provides comprehensive business services and meeting spaces suitable for corporate needs.

Cons

High Cost: The luxury experience comes with a premium price tag, which may not be ideal for budget travelers.

Crowded Area: Being in Times Square, the area can be very crowded, which may be a consideration for those seeking a quieter stay.

Local Tips

Explore Times Square: Take full advantage of the hotel's location to explore Times Square's vibrant atmosphere, including its theaters, shops, and landmarks.

Visit Nearby Attractions: Use the hotel's central location to explore nearby attractions such as the Empire State Building, Bryant Park, and Central Park.

Dining Options: Explore the diverse dining options in the Times Square area, ranging from international cuisines to iconic New York delis.

Public Transit: Utilize the nearby subway stations for convenient access to other parts of Manhattan and beyond.

4. **Conrad New York Downtown**

The Conrad New York Downtown is a luxury hotel located in the Financial District of Manhattan. Known for its spacious suites, upscale amenities, and modern design, the Conrad offers a sophisticated stay for both business and leisure travelers. Its location provides convenient access to major financial hubs, cultural attractions, and waterfront views, making it a popular choice for those visiting New York City.

The Ultimate New York City Travel Guide (2025 Edition)

Location (Address & Proximity)

Address: 102 North End Avenue, New York, NY 10282, USA

Proximity:

One World Trade Center: Approximately 0.3 miles (0.5 km), within walking distance to this iconic skyscraper and its observation deck.

Wall Street: About 0.4 miles (0.6 km), a short walk away from the heart of the financial district.

Battery Park: Roughly 0.6 miles (1 km), providing access to waterfront views and ferries to the Statue of Liberty.

South Street Seaport: Approximately 1 mile (1.6 km), accessible by a short walk or subway ride, offering dining and shopping options.

Subway Stations: The hotel is near several subway stations including the World Trade Center (E train) and Chambers Street (J, Z trains), providing convenient access to various parts of the city.

Highlights

Spacious Suites: Known for its large, open-plan suites that offer more space and comfort compared to typical hotel rooms.

Modern Design: Features contemporary design with sleek furnishings and high-tech amenities.

Prime Location: Situated in the Financial District, providing easy access to business centers, cultural landmarks, and waterfront attractions.

Rooms and Suites

Room Types: The Conrad New York Downtown offers a range of suite types, including standard suites, one-bedroom suites, and more luxurious options.

Design and Decor: Suites feature modern decor with floor-to-ceiling windows, spacious living areas, and sleek furnishings. Many suites offer views of the Hudson River or the city skyline.

Luxury Amenities: Includes features such as plush bedding, separate living and working areas, high-speed Wi-Fi, and large flat-screen TVs. Suites also come with fully equipped kitchenettes or kitchens in some cases.

Executive Suites: These suites provide additional space and enhanced amenities, including access to the Executive Lounge and more premium furnishings.

Spa and Wellness

No On-Site Spa: The Conrad New York Downtown does not have an on-site spa. However, the concierge can assist with recommendations and bookings for nearby wellness facilities.

Fitness Center: The hotel features a well-equipped fitness center with modern exercise machines, free weights, and space for stretching and yoga.

Bars and Dining

Atrio Wine Bar & Restaurant: The hotel's main dining venue, Atrio, offers a sophisticated setting for breakfast, lunch, and dinner. The menu features contemporary American cuisine with an emphasis on fresh, seasonal ingredients.

Lobby Lounge: Provides a relaxed setting for casual dining and drinks, ideal for informal meetings or relaxation after a busy day.

Nearby Dining Options: The Financial District offers a variety of dining options, from upscale restaurants to casual eateries and trendy food markets.

Events and Conferences

Event Spaces: The Conrad New York Downtown offers versatile meeting and event spaces, including a grand ballroom and several smaller meeting rooms. These spaces are designed to accommodate various types of events, from corporate meetings to social gatherings.

Business Center: Equipped with modern technology and services, including printing, copying, and high-speed internet access.

Event Planning Services: The hotel provides comprehensive event planning and catering services to ensure a smooth and successful event experience.

Basic Facilities and Amenities

Free Wi-Fi: Offers complimentary high-speed internet access throughout the hotel.

24-Hour Reception: The front desk is open around the clock to assist with guest needs and inquiries.

Concierge Service: Provides personalized assistance with reservations, recommendations, and special requests.

Business Services: Includes a fully equipped business center and meeting rooms for corporate needs.

Opening and Closing Hours

Hotel Reception: Open 24 hours a day.

Atrio Wine Bar & Restaurant: Typically open for breakfast, lunch, and dinner, with specific hours varying based on the day of the week.

Lobby Lounge: Generally open throughout the day and evening, with hours varying by day.

Price

Rates at the Conrad New York Downtown can vary depending on room type, season, and booking conditions. On average, prices start around $500 to $700 per night for standard suites, with more luxurious accommodations priced higher. Prices can fluctuate, so it's advisable to book in advance and check availability through the hotel's website or booking platforms for the best rates.

Pros

Spacious Accommodations: Offers large suites with modern design, providing more space and comfort.

Prime Location: Located in the Financial District with easy access to major business centers, attractions, and waterfront views.

Modern Amenities: Features contemporary decor, high-tech amenities, and a range of on-site facilities.

Business-Friendly: Provides comprehensive business services and event spaces suitable for corporate needs.

Cons

No On-Site Spa: Lacks a full-service spa, though wellness options are available nearby.

Higher Cost: The luxury experience comes with a premium price tag, which may not be ideal for budget travelers.

Local Tips

Explore the Financial District: Take advantage of the hotel's location to explore landmarks such as One World Trade Center, Wall Street, and Battery Park.

Visit Nearby Attractions: Use the hotel's location to explore nearby attractions such as the Statue of Liberty, South Street Seaport, and the vibrant neighborhoods of Tribeca and SoHo.

Dining Options: Explore the diverse dining options in the Financial District, ranging from high-end restaurants to casual eateries.

Public Transit: Utilize the nearby subway stations for convenient access to other parts of Manhattan and beyond.

5. Hyatt Centric Times Square

The Hyatt Centric Times Square is a stylish and contemporary hotel located in the heart of Times Square, New York City. Known for its modern design, prime location, and comprehensive amenities, the Hyatt Centric offers a comfortable and convenient stay for both leisure and business travelers. Its central position provides easy access to major attractions, entertainment, and dining options in one of the city's most vibrant areas.

Location (Address & Proximity)

Address: 135 West 45th Street, New York, NY 10036, USA

Proximity:

Times Square: Directly located in Times Square, offering immediate access to its famous neon lights, Broadway theaters, and entertainment.

Broadway Theaters: Just steps away from numerous theaters, making it an ideal location for catching Broadway shows.

Empire State Building: Approximately 0.7 miles (1.1 km), easily reachable by a short walk or subway ride.

Central Park: About 1.5 miles (2.4 km), a short subway ride or longer walk to enjoy the park's expansive green spaces.

Subway Stations: The hotel is near several subway stations, including Times Square – 42nd Street (1, 2, 3, 7, N, Q, R, W trains) and 49th Street (N, Q, R, W trains), providing convenient access to various parts of the city.

Highlights

Prime Location: Situated in the heart of Times Square, offering unparalleled access to entertainment, dining, and shopping.

Modern Design: Features contemporary decor with sleek furnishings and high-tech amenities.

Rooftop Bar: Offers stunning views of Times Square and the Manhattan skyline.

Rooms and Suites

Room Types: The Hyatt Centric Times Square offers a variety of room types, including standard rooms, deluxe rooms, and suites. Each room is designed for comfort and modern functionality.

Design and Decor: Rooms feature contemporary decor with large windows, offering city views and plenty of natural light. Furnishings include plush bedding, ergonomic workspaces, and comfortable seating areas.

Luxury Amenities: Includes high-speed Wi-Fi, flat-screen TVs, premium bedding, and marble bathrooms with high-end toiletries. Some rooms offer additional amenities such as mini-refrigerators and coffee makers.

Suites: The hotel's suites provide additional space and upgraded amenities, including separate living areas and enhanced views of Times Square or the city skyline.

Spa and Wellness

No On-Site Spa: The Hyatt Centric Times Square does not have an on-site spa. However, the concierge can assist with recommendations and bookings for nearby wellness facilities.

Fitness Center: The hotel features a modern fitness center equipped with state-of-the-art exercise machines, free weights, and space for stretching and yoga.

Bars and Dining

Rooftop Bar: The hotel's rooftop bar offers breathtaking views of Times Square and the Manhattan skyline, along with a menu of cocktails and light fare. It's an ideal spot for relaxing after a day of exploring the city.

Dining Options: The hotel's central location provides easy access to a wide range of dining options in Times Square, from high-end restaurants to casual eateries.

Events and Conferences

Event Spaces: The Hyatt Centric Times Square offers versatile meeting and event spaces suitable for business meetings, conferences, and social gatherings.

Business Center: Equipped with modern technology and services, including printing, copying, and high-speed internet access.

Event Planning Services: The hotel provides comprehensive event planning and catering services to ensure a smooth and successful event experience.

Basic Facilities and Amenities

Free Wi-Fi: Offers complimentary high-speed internet access throughout the hotel.

24-Hour Reception: The front desk is open around the clock to assist with guest needs and inquiries.

Concierge Service: Provides personalized assistance with reservations, recommendations, and special requests.

Business Services: Includes a fully equipped business center and meeting rooms for corporate needs.

Opening and Closing Hours

Hotel Reception: Open 24 hours a day.

Rooftop Bar: Typically open in the evening, with specific hours varying based on the day of the week and season.

Price

Rates at the Hyatt Centric Times Square can vary depending on room type, season, and booking conditions. On average, prices start around $400 to $600 per night for standard rooms, with suites and higher-end accommodations priced higher. Prices can fluctuate, so it's advisable to book in advance and check availability through the hotel's website or booking platforms for the best rates.

Pros

Prime Location: Situated in Times Square, providing easy access to entertainment, dining, and major attractions.

Modern Accommodations: Features contemporary design with comfortable furnishings and high-tech amenities.

Rooftop Bar: Offers stunning views of Times Square and the Manhattan skyline.

Business-Friendly: Provides a range of business services and meeting spaces suitable for corporate needs.

Cons

Higher Cost: The luxury experience comes with a premium price tag, which may not be ideal for budget travelers.

No On-Site Spa: Lacks a full-service spa, though wellness options are available nearby.

Local Tips

Explore Times Square: Take full advantage of the hotel's location to explore Times Square's vibrant atmosphere, including its theaters, shops, and landmarks.

Visit Nearby Attractions: Use the hotel's location to explore nearby attractions such as the Empire State Building, Bryant Park, and Central Park.

Dining Options: Explore the diverse dining options in Times Square, ranging from international cuisines to iconic New York delis.

Public Transit: Utilize the nearby subway stations for convenient access to other parts of Manhattan and beyond.

Chapter 5: Top Attractions in New York City

Statue of Liberty and Ellis Island

The Statue of Liberty and Ellis Island are iconic landmarks in New York Harbor that symbolize freedom and immigration. The Statue of Liberty, a gift from France, stands as a global emblem of liberty and democracy. Ellis Island, once the main entry point for immigrants, now houses the Ellis Island National Museum of Immigration, which tells the stories of those who passed through its doors.

Location

Statue of Liberty: Liberty Island, New York Harbor, New York City.

Ellis Island: Ellis Island, New York Harbor, New York City.

Both islands are accessible by ferry from Battery Park in Manhattan or Liberty State Park in Jersey City, New Jersey.

History

Statue of Liberty: Designed by French sculptor Frédéric Auguste Bartholdi and engineered by Gustave Eiffel, the statue was dedicated on October 28, 1886. It was a gift from France to commemorate the centennial of American independence and is a symbol of freedom and democracy.

Ellis Island: Opened in 1892, Ellis Island served as the main immigration station for the United States until 1954. During its operation, it processed over 12 million immigrants, making it a crucial entry point for those seeking new opportunities in America.

Opening and Closing Hours

Statue of Liberty: Open daily from 8:30 AM to 4:00 PM. The last ferry departs from Liberty Island around 5:00 PM. Hours may vary seasonally and for special events.

Ellis Island: Open daily from 9:00 AM to 5:00 PM. The last ferry departs from Ellis Island around 5:30 PM.

Note: Ferries operate from early morning until late afternoon, with schedules subject to change based on season and weather conditions.

Top Things to Do

Statue of Liberty:

Visit the Statue: Explore the statue's pedestal and observation deck for panoramic views of New York Harbor and the city skyline.

Explore the Museum: Discover exhibits about the statue's history, construction, and significance.

Climb to the Crown: For an additional fee and advance reservation, visitors can climb up to the statue's crown for a unique view (note: this requires a fitness level due to the narrow, steep staircase).

Ellis Island:

Museum of Immigration: Visit the museum to learn about the immigrant experience through exhibits, photographs, and interactive displays.

American Immigrant Wall of Honor: Pay tribute to the contributions of immigrants by exploring this monument featuring engraved names of those who have shaped American history.

Research Family History: Use the American Immigrant Wall of Honor's database to trace your family's immigration history.

Practical Information

Ferry Tickets: Tickets include access to both Liberty Island and Ellis Island. Purchase tickets in advance online or at Battery Park.

Accessibility: Both islands are accessible to visitors with disabilities, including wheelchair access. Some areas, like the crown of the Statue of Liberty, are not wheelchair accessible.

Security: Expect security screening before boarding the ferry. No large bags or backpacks are allowed on Liberty Island or Ellis Island.

Food and Beverage: Cafés and snack bars are available on both islands. You can also bring your own food and drinks, but there are designated picnic areas.

Tips for Visiting

Plan Ahead: Book your ferry tickets and any special tours (such as the crown visit) well in advance, especially during peak tourist season.

Arrive Early: To avoid long lines and ensure you have ample time to explore, try to arrive early in the day.

Dress Comfortably: Wear comfortable shoes for walking, and dress in layers as weather conditions can change quickly.

Check Weather: The outdoor areas are subject to weather conditions, so check the forecast before you go.

Photography: Don't forget your camera for iconic photos of the Statue of Liberty and the New York City skyline from the islands.

Central Park

Central Park is an expansive urban oasis in the heart of Manhattan, offering a sprawling green space amidst the city's towering skyscrapers. Designed by Frederick Law Olmsted and Calvert Vaux, it provides a tranquil escape for both locals and visitors, featuring scenic landscapes, recreational activities, and cultural landmarks.

Location

Central Park stretches from 59th Street to 110th Street, between Fifth Avenue and Central Park West, covering approximately 843 acres in Midtown Manhattan.

History

Central Park opened in 1858, designed as a response to the rapid urbanization of New York City. Its creation aimed to provide a natural retreat and recreational space for residents. The park's design was revolutionary for its time, emphasizing naturalistic landscapes and offering a respite from the city's congestion.

Opening and Closing Hours

Opening Hours: Central Park is open daily from 6:00 AM to 1:00 AM.

Note: Specific facilities and attractions within the park may have different hours of operation.

Top Things to Do

Stroll Through the Park: Wander through picturesque pathways, including the Mall and the Bethesda Terrace, and enjoy the park's various scenic spots.

Visit the Central Park Zoo: Explore the Central Park Zoo, home to a variety of animals and educational exhibits.

Explore the Great Lawn: Relax or participate in recreational activities on the Great Lawn, a popular spot for picnics and sports.

Rowboat Rentals: Rent a rowboat at the Loeb Boathouse and enjoy a peaceful row on the Central Park Lake.

See the Alice in Wonderland Statue: Check out the whimsical Alice in Wonderland statue, a favorite among children and families.

Take a Horse-Drawn Carriage Ride: Experience a classic carriage ride through the park, offering a nostalgic and charming way to see the sights.

Practical Information

Transportation: The park is accessible by subway (various lines) and bus. Major entrances are located at 59th Street, 72nd Street, 86th Street, and 110th Street.

Accessibility: Central Park is wheelchair accessible, with paved paths and accessible restrooms available throughout the park.

Food and Beverage: Several food vendors and cafés are located within the park, including the Central Park Boathouse, which offers dining with a view.

Tips for Visiting

Plan Your Route: Central Park is large, so plan your visit to focus on specific areas or attractions you want to see.

Bring a Map: Pick up a map or use a smartphone app to navigate the park's extensive pathways and landmarks.

Wear Comfortable Shoes: The park is best explored on foot, so wear comfortable shoes and be prepared for a lot of walking.

Check the Weather: Dress appropriately for the weather, as many of the park's activities are best enjoyed outdoors.

Stay Hydrated: Bring water, especially during warmer months, as you'll be walking and exploring a large area.

The Ultimate New York City Travel Guide (2025 Edition)

Times Square

Times Square, often referred to as "The Cross-roads of the World," is a vibrant and bustling commercial and entertainment hub located in Midtown Manhattan. Known for its bright lights, massive digital billboards, and lively atmosphere, it is one of New York City's most iconic destinations and a central gathering point for tourists and locals alike.

Location

Times Square is situated at the intersection of Broadway and Seventh Avenue, spanning from 42nd Street to 47th Street. It is easily accessible and centrally located in Manhattan.

History

Times Square was originally known as Longacre Square but was renamed in 1904 when The New York Times moved its headquarters to the area. The district rapidly became famous for its theaters, neon signs, and the bustling energy that defines it today. It has since evolved into a global symbol of New York City's vibrant entertainment scene.

Opening and Closing Hours

Times Square: The area is open 24/7, with the neon lights and billboards operating throughout the night. Shops, restaurants, and attractions have varying hours, typically from around 10:00 AM to late evening.

Top Things to Do

See the Billboards: Marvel at the dazzling electronic billboards and advertisements that adorn Times Square, especially at night when they are most vibrant.

Broadway Shows: Attend a Broadway show in one of the many theaters located in and around Times Square. The area is renowned for its world-class productions and theatrical performances.

Visit the TKTS Booth: Purchase discounted theater tickets at the TKTS booth in Times Square for same-day performances.

Explore Times Square Attractions: Visit attractions such as Madame Tussauds New York or Ripley's Believe It or Not! for interactive entertainment.

People-Watch: Take a seat in the pedestrian plazas and watch the bustling crowds, street performers, and vibrant city life.

Celebrate New Year's Eve: Experience the world-famous New Year's Eve ball drop, a major annual event that draws millions of viewers.

Practical Information

Transportation: Times Square is well-served by public transportation, including subway lines (1, 2, 3, 7, N, Q, R, and W), buses, and taxis. The area is also easily accessible on foot from nearby attractions.

Accessibility: Times Square is generally accessible, with wheelchair-friendly sidewalks and entrances to many attractions and theaters.

Safety: Times Square is a highly frequented area with a strong police presence. However, be mindful of your belongings and remain alert in crowded spaces.

Tips for Visiting

Visit During Off-Peak Hours: To avoid the largest crowds, consider visiting early in the morning or late at night.

Watch Your Belongings: As a busy tourist area, be cautious of pickpockets and keep your valuables secure.

Dress Comfortably: Wear comfortable shoes for walking and be prepared for varying weather conditions, as you may spend a lot of time outdoors.

Plan for Dining: Many restaurants and eateries are located in and around Times Square, but they can be crowded. Make reservations in advance if possible.

Check Show Times: If you plan to see a Broadway show, book tickets in advance and confirm show times and locations.

The Ultimate New York City Travel Guide (2025 Edition)

Empire State Building

The Empire State Building is one of New York City's most iconic skyscrapers and a symbol of American innovation and architectural achievement. Standing at 1,454 feet (including its antenna), this Art Deco-style building was the tallest in the world upon its completion in 1931. It remains a popular tourist attraction, offering stunning panoramic views of the city from its observation decks.

Location

Located at **350 Fifth Avenue** in Midtown Manhattan, the Empire State Building is situated between 33rd and 34th Streets, near other major attractions like Times Square and Madison Square Garden.

History

Construction of the Empire State Building began in 1930 and was completed in just 13 months, a record-breaking feat at the time. It officially opened on May 1, 1931. Designed by the architectural firm Shreve, Lamb & Harmon, it quickly became a symbol of New York's economic recovery during the Great Depression. The building has appeared in countless films and remains a cultural icon.

Opening and Closing Hours

Open Daily: From **9:00 AM to 11:00 PM** (the last elevator to the observatory typically departs at 10:15 PM).

Note: Hours may vary during holidays or special events, so it's always best to check ahead.

Top Things to Do

Visit the 86th Floor Observation Deck: The open-air deck provides incredible 360-degree views of New York City, including landmarks like Central Park, the Statue of Liberty, and the Brooklyn Bridge.

Explore the 102nd Floor Observation Deck: For an even higher vantage point, the enclosed 102nd-floor deck offers unparalleled views and a more exclusive experience.

Interactive Exhibits: Learn about the building's history, construction, and role in pop culture through exhibits on the second and 80th floors.

Visit at Night: The building is beautifully lit at night, and visiting after dark provides an entirely different perspective of the city skyline.

Practical Information

Tickets: General admission tickets can be purchased online or on-site. There are different ticket options, including access to just the 86th-floor deck or both the 86th and 102nd floors. It's recommended to buy tickets in advance to avoid long lines.

Accessibility: The Empire State Building is wheelchair accessible, and elevators are available to all observation decks.

Dining: The building has several dining options, including the State Grill and Bar, and casual cafes.

Security: Expect a security screening similar to airports before entering the building.

Tips for Visiting

Buy Tickets in Advance: Purchase skip-the-line tickets online to avoid long queues, especially during peak hours.

Visit Early or Late: For a less crowded experience, visit early in the morning or late at night. Sunset is a particularly popular time for stunning views.

Weather Considerations: Check the weather before your visit to ensure clear skies for the best views.

Photography: Bring a camera for incredible photo opportunities, especially during sunrise, sunset, or nighttime.

Dress for the Weather: The outdoor 86th-floor observation deck can be windy and cold, even in warmer months, so dress appropriately.

The Ultimate New York City Travel Guide (2025 Edition)

Broadway and the Theater District

Broadway, often considered the heart of American theater, is a world-renowned destination for live performances, featuring some of the best plays, musicals, and theatrical productions. Located in Midtown Manhattan, the Theater District is home to more than 40 professional theaters that host everything from classic shows to cutting-edge performances. Seeing a Broadway show is a quintessential New York City experience for both tourists and locals alike.

Location

The Broadway Theater District is situated in **Midtown Manhattan**, primarily between **42nd Street and 53rd Street**, and between **6th Avenue and 8th Avenue**. Times Square is often considered the center of the district.

History

Broadway's rise as a theater hub began in the late 19th century. By the early 20th century, it had solidified its status as the epicenter of American theater. The district's rich history includes some of the most iconic productions and performers in theatrical history. Landmark shows like *Phantom of the Opera*, *Les Misérables*, *Hamilton*, and *The Lion King* have made Broadway globally famous.

Opening and Closing Hours

Showtimes: Broadway theaters typically offer **matinee performances** in the afternoon (usually around 2:00 PM or 3:00 PM) and **evening shows** starting between **7:00 PM and 8:00 PM**. Performances are held throughout the week, with most shows taking place Tuesday through Sunday.

Box Office Hours: Box offices are generally open from **10:00 AM to 8:00 PM**, but this can vary by theater and day.

Top Things to Do

See a Broadway Show: Whether you love musicals, dramas, or comedies, Broadway offers something for everyone. Popular shows like *Wicked*, *Hamilton*, *The Lion King*, and *Chicago* attract large audiences.

Visit the TKTS Booth: Located in Times Square, the TKTS booth offers same-day tickets to Broadway and Off-Broadway shows at discounted prices, making it a great way to see a show for less.

Take a Theater District Walking Tour: Explore the history of Broadway by walking around the Theater District, where you can see the iconic theaters and learn about their storied past.

Meet the Stars: Many Broadway stars exit through stage doors after performances, giving fans a chance to meet them, take photos, or get autographs.

Dining and Entertainment: Enjoy a pre- or post-show meal at one of the many restaurants in the district, which range from upscale dining to casual eateries.

Practical Information

Ticket Purchase: Tickets can be purchased online, at the box office, or through discount vendors like TKTS. It's often best to buy tickets in advance for popular shows to ensure availability.

Dress Code: There is no formal dress code for Broadway shows, but smart-casual attire is typical, especially for evening performances.

Accessibility: Most Broadway theaters offer accessibility options, including wheelchair seating and hearing-assist devices. Be sure to check with the theater in advance if you have specific needs.

Theater Etiquette: Arrive at least 30 minutes before showtime, silence your phone, and avoid talking or taking photos during the performance.

Tips for Visiting

Book Early: If you want to see a popular show, such as *Hamilton* or *The Lion King*, book your tickets well in advance, as these performances can sell out months ahead.

Discount Tickets: Check the TKTS booth in Times Square or online platforms like TodayTix for discounted tickets to same-day performances.

Arrive Early: The Theater District can get busy, especially near showtime, so arrive at the theater 30–45 minutes before the show to find your seat and settle in.

Post-Show Entertainment: After the show, explore Times Square or grab a late-night bite at one of the nearby restaurants that stay open late for theatergoers.

Metropolitan Museum of Art (The Met)

The Metropolitan Museum of Art, commonly known as **The Met**, is one of the largest and most prestigious art museums in the world. Spanning over 2 million square feet and housing a collection of over 2 million works of art, The Met offers a journey through 5,000 years of art history from around the globe, with pieces ranging from ancient Egyptian artifacts to modern masterpieces.

Location

The Met's main location, often called **The Met Fifth Avenue**, is situated at **1000 Fifth Avenue** on the eastern edge of Central Park, between 82nd and 86th Streets. The museum also has two other locations:

The Met Cloisters (dedicated to medieval European art) in Fort Tryon Park, uptown Manhattan.

The Met Breuer (modern and contemporary art), now closed as of 2020, with modern pieces moved to the Fifth Avenue location.

History

Founded in 1870 by a group of American citizens, The Met was established to encourage and develop the study of fine arts. Over the years, it has grown into a cultural institution that showcases art from every corner of the globe, including renowned collections of paintings, sculptures, textiles, and decorative arts. The museum's iconic Beaux-Arts building was completed in 1902 and continues to expand its galleries and exhibitions.

Opening and Closing Hours

Open Thursday through Monday: 10:00 AM to 5:00 PM.

Closed on Tuesdays and Wednesdays.

Special hours on holidays may apply, so it's recommended to check in advance.

Top Things to Do

Explore the Egyptian Art Collection: Visit the **Temple of Dendur**, an ancient Egyptian temple that was transported from Egypt and reassembled in a glass atrium.

Admire European Paintings: See masterpieces by artists like Van Gogh, Rembrandt, Vermeer, and Monet in the **European Paintings** gallery.

Visit the Costume Institute: Discover iconic fashion from the past and present through rotating exhibitions curated by the museum's renowned Costume Institute.

Sculpture and Decorative Arts: Stroll through the museum's many galleries displaying ancient Greek and Roman sculptures, as well as European decorative arts, including rooms recreated to reflect the style of different historical periods.

Modern and Contemporary Art: Don't miss the impressive collection of 20th- and 21st-century works, featuring pieces by Picasso, Pollock, and Rothko.

Roof Garden: Visit the museum's **Rooftop Garden** for contemporary art installations and panoramic views of Central Park and the New York skyline (open seasonally).

Practical Information

Admission: Suggested admission for New York residents is "pay as you wish." For out-of-state visitors, general admission is $30 for adults, $22 for seniors, and $17 for students.

Tickets: It's recommended to purchase tickets online in advance to skip the lines.

Accessibility: The Met is fully wheelchair accessible. There are elevators and accessible restrooms throughout the museum, and wheelchairs are available for rent.

Food and Drink: Several dining options are available, including cafés and a rooftop bar (seasonal).

Tips for Visiting

Plan Your Visit: The Met is enormous, so it's best to plan your visit in advance and focus on a few key areas or galleries.

Audio Guides and Tours: Consider renting an audio guide or joining a guided tour to enhance your experience and learn more about the artworks.

Best Time to Visit: Arrive early in the morning or visit on a weekday to avoid large crowds, especially in the popular galleries.

Free with Admission: Your ticket grants you same-day admission to both The Met Fifth Avenue and The Met Cloisters, allowing you to explore both locations in a single day if desired.

Photography: Non-flash photography is allowed in most areas, but certain special exhibitions may have restrictions.

Brooklyn Bridge

The **Brooklyn Bridge** is one of New York City's most iconic landmarks and a marvel of 19th-century engineering. Spanning the East River, the bridge connects **Manhattan** and **Brooklyn**, offering stunning views of the New York skyline, the Statue of Liberty, and the waterfront. It's not only a vital transportation link but also a popular destination for tourists and locals who enjoy walking or biking across its pedestrian pathway.

Location

The Brooklyn Bridge connects **Lower Manhattan** near City Hall and the Financial District to **Brooklyn Heights** and **DUMBO** (Down Under the Manhattan Bridge Overpass). It is easily accessible from both boroughs, with entrances to the pedestrian walkway at the **Brooklyn Bridge/City Hall subway station** on the Manhattan side and near **Tillary Street** in Brooklyn.

History

Completed in **1883**, the Brooklyn Bridge was the longest suspension bridge in the world at the time and an engineering masterpiece. Designed by **John A. Roebling** and completed by his son **Washington Roebling**, it took over 14 years to build. The bridge symbolizes the growth and industrial strength of New York City, and its unique design, with Gothic-style stone towers, has made it a beloved landmark.

Opening and Closing Hours

The **Brooklyn Bridge pedestrian walkway** is **open 24/7**, allowing visitors to enjoy the views any time of day or night.

Top Things to Do

Walk Across the Bridge: A walk from Manhattan to Brooklyn (or vice versa) takes about **30–40 minutes** and offers fantastic views of the skyline, the East River, and the Statue of Liberty. It's also a great spot for photos.

Biking: Rent a bike and cycle across the bridge using the designated bike lane, an efficient way to explore the bridge and nearby areas.

Photography: The bridge is a prime spot for photography, especially at **sunrise** or **sunset**. The Manhattan skyline, in particular, provides a stunning backdrop.

Visit DUMBO: After crossing into Brooklyn, explore the trendy DUMBO neighborhood with its cobblestone streets, art galleries, and waterfront parks.

Brooklyn Bridge Park: Relax at **Brooklyn Bridge Park** on the Brooklyn side, which features picnic areas, walking paths, and excellent views of the bridge and Manhattan skyline.

Practical Information

How to Get There: The pedestrian walkway entrance on the Manhattan side is near **City Hall** (accessible from the **4/5/6/J/Z/N/R** subway lines at Brooklyn Bridge/City Hall station). In Brooklyn, the entrance is near **Tillary Street** and **Cadman Plaza**.

Cost: Walking or biking across the bridge is **free**.

Length: The total length of the bridge is **1.1 miles** (1.8 kilometers), with the pedestrian walkway located above the vehicle lanes.

Safety: The bridge is usually busy with both pedestrians and cyclists, so stay in the designated lanes for walking or biking. Keep an eye on your belongings, as the bridge can get crowded.

Tips for Visiting

Best Time to Visit: Early morning or late evening are ideal times to visit for fewer crowds and cooler weather, especially in the summer.

Wear Comfortable Shoes: The bridge is a long walk, so wear comfortable shoes, especially if you plan to explore further into Brooklyn or Manhattan after crossing.

Photography Tips: For the best views of the skyline and the bridge's towers, bring a wide-angle lens or a camera with a panoramic mode.

Avoid Rush Hour: The bridge can be extremely crowded during rush hour (especially around **5:00 PM – 7:00 PM** on weekdays), so plan your visit outside these hours if possible.

The Ultimate New York City Travel Guide (2025 Edition)

Memorial and Museum

The **9/11 Memorial & Museum** is a deeply moving tribute to the nearly 3,000 victims of the September 11, 2001, terrorist attacks and the 1993 World Trade Center bombing. Located at the site of the former Twin Towers in **Lower Manhattan**, the memorial and museum provide visitors with an emotional and educational experience, offering a space for reflection and remembrance. The memorial features two massive reflecting pools, while the museum houses a comprehensive collection of artifacts, photographs, and stories related to the tragic events.

Location

The 9/11 Memorial & Museum is located at **180 Greenwich Street, New York, NY 10007**, within the **World Trade Center** site in **Lower Manhattan**. It is easily accessible by several subway lines and is close to other notable attractions such as the **One World Observatory** and **Battery Park**.

History

Opened in **2011**, ten years after the attacks, the memorial was designed by architects **Michael Arad** and **Peter Walker**. The reflecting pools, which sit in the footprints of the original Twin Towers, are surrounded by the names of the victims engraved in bronze. The museum opened in **2014**, offering an in-depth look at the events of 9/11 through multimedia displays, first-person accounts, and personal artifacts from that day.

Opening and Closing Hours

Memorial: Open daily from **10:00 AM to 5:00 PM**. The outdoor memorial is open year-round and accessible to the public without an entrance fee.

Museum: Open **Wednesday to Monday**, from **9:00 AM to 8:00 PM**, with the last entry at 6:00 PM. It is **closed on Tuesdays**.

Top Things to Do

Visit the Reflecting Pools: The twin reflecting pools are a solemn centerpiece of the memorial, with cascading waterfalls and the names of victims etched along the edges. It's a place for quiet reflection.

Explore the 9/11 Museum: The museum contains over **10,000 artifacts**, including pieces of the original World Trade Center, personal mementos of victims, and accounts from survivors and first responders.

Exhibitions: The museum features both permanent and rotating exhibits, including artifacts such as **the "Survivor Stairs"**, a piece of the **antenna from the North Tower**, and **Flight 93 artifacts**. Visitors can also listen to recorded phone calls and watch videos of the event.

"In Memoriam" Exhibition: This emotional exhibit pays tribute to the individuals who lost their lives in the attacks, presenting personal stories, photographs, and audio recordings from their loved ones.

Survivor Tree: This resilient **Callery pear tree**, found damaged but alive in the rubble after the attacks, has since been replanted at the memorial and symbolizes hope and resilience.

Practical Information

Tickets: The outdoor memorial is **free to visit**, but the museum requires a ticket. General admission is **$33** for adults, **$20** for youth (7-12 years), and **$27** for seniors. It's recommended to purchase tickets online in advance.

Accessibility: The memorial and museum are fully wheelchair accessible. Audio guides are available for those with hearing impairments.

Bag Policy: Large bags, suitcases, and items over a certain size are not allowed in the museum, and all visitors must go through security screening.

Guided Tours: The museum offers guided tours led by staff members who provide deeper insights into the exhibits and history.

Tips for Visiting

Allow Ample Time: Plan to spend at least **2–3 hours** at the museum to fully experience the exhibits. The memorial can be visited in less time.

Visit Early or Late: For a quieter experience, try to visit early in the morning or later in the afternoon. The memorial can become crowded during peak hours.

Prepare Emotionally: The museum contains powerful and emotional exhibits, so be prepared for a potentially intense experience. Visitors often find it helpful to take breaks in between exhibits.

Free Admission: Admission to the museum is free on **Mondays** between **3:30 PM and 5:00 PM**, but tickets must be reserved in advance online, as they are limited.

Photography: Photography is allowed in most areas of the memorial and museum, but be respectful of the somber nature of the site.

The Ultimate New York City Travel Guide (2025 Edition)

9/11 Rockefeller Center and Top of the Rock Observation Deck

The **9/11 Memorial & Museum** is a deeply moving tribute to the nearly 3,000 victims of the September 11, 2001, terrorist attacks and the 1993 World Trade Center bombing. Located at the site of the former Twin Towers in **Lower Manhattan**, the memorial and museum provide visitors with an emotional and educational experience, offering a space for reflection and remembrance. The memorial features two massive reflecting pools, while the museum houses a comprehensive collection of artifacts, photographs, and stories related to the tragic events.

Location

The 9/11 Memorial & Museum is located at **180 Greenwich Street, New York, NY 10007**, within the **World Trade Center** site in **Lower Manhattan**. It is easily accessible by several subway lines and is close to other notable attractions such as the **One World Observatory** and **Battery Park**.

History

Opened in **2011**, ten years after the attacks, the memorial was designed by architects **Michael Arad** and **Peter Walker**. The reflecting pools, which sit in the footprints of the original Twin Towers, are surrounded by the names of the victims engraved in bronze. The museum opened in **2014**, offering an in-depth look at the events of 9/11 through multimedia displays, first-person accounts, and personal artifacts from that day.

Opening and Closing Hours

Memorial: Open daily from **10:00 AM to 5:00 PM**. The outdoor memorial is open year-round and accessible to the public without an entrance fee.

Museum: Open **Wednesday to Monday**, from **9:00 AM to 8:00 PM**, with the last entry at 6:00 PM. It is **closed on Tuesdays**.

Top Things to Do

Visit the Reflecting Pools: The twin reflecting pools are a solemn centerpiece of the memorial, with cascading waterfalls and the names of victims etched along the edges. It's a place for quiet reflection.

Explore the 9/11 Museum: The museum contains over **10,000 artifacts**, including pieces of the original World Trade Center, personal mementos of victims, and accounts from survivors and first responders.

Exhibitions: The museum features both permanent and rotating exhibits, including artifacts such as **the "Survivor Stairs"**, a piece of the **antenna from the North Tower**, and **Flight 93 artifacts**. Visitors can also listen to recorded phone calls and watch videos of the event.

"In Memoriam" Exhibition: This emotional exhibit pays tribute to the individuals who lost their lives in the attacks, presenting personal stories, photographs, and audio recordings from their loved ones.

Survivor Tree: This resilient **Callery pear tree**, found damaged but alive in the rubble after the attacks, has since been replanted at the memorial and symbolizes hope and resilience.

Practical Information

Tickets: The outdoor memorial is **free to visit**, but the museum requires a ticket. General admission is **$33** for adults, **$20** for youth (7-12 years), and **$27** for seniors. It's recommended to purchase tickets online in advance.

Accessibility: The memorial and museum are fully wheelchair accessible. Audio guides are available for those with hearing impairments.

Bag Policy: Large bags, suitcases, and items over a certain size are not allowed in the museum, and all visitors must go through security screening.

Guided Tours: The museum offers guided tours led by staff members who provide deeper insights into the exhibits and history.

Tips for Visiting

Allow Ample Time: Plan to spend at least **2–3 hours** at the museum to fully experience the exhibits. The memorial can be visited in less time.

Visit Early or Late: For a quieter experience, try to visit early in the morning or later in the afternoon. The memorial can become crowded during peak hours.

Prepare Emotionally: The museum contains powerful and emotional exhibits, so be prepared for a potentially intense experience. Visitors often find it helpful to take breaks in between exhibits.

Free Admission: Admission to the museum is free on **Mondays** between **3:30 PM and 5:00 PM**, but tickets must be reserved in advance online, as they are limited.

Photography: Photography is allowed in most areas of the memorial and museum, but be respectful of the somber nature of the site.

The Ultimate New York City Travel Guide (2025 Edition)

The High Line

The **High Line** is a unique elevated park built on a historic former railway track in **Manhattan**, offering visitors an urban oasis with gardens, art installations, and stunning views of the city and the Hudson River. Stretching 1.45 miles, the park meanders above the streets of Manhattan's **Meatpacking District** and **Chelsea** neighborhoods, providing a tranquil space to escape the city's bustle while still enjoying its energy.

Location

The High Line runs from **Gansevoort Street** in the **Meatpacking District** to **34th Street** near Hudson Yards, following the path of the old New York Central Railroad. Key access points include:

Gansevoort Street (south entrance)

14th Street

23rd Street

34th Street–Hudson Yards (north entrance)

History

Opened in stages between **2009 and 2014**, the High Line was transformed from an abandoned freight railway into a green public space after a community-led effort to preserve it. The rail line, once used to transport goods along Manhattan's West Side, had been out of use since the 1980s. Today, the park attracts millions of visitors each year and is a testament to innovative urban design.

Opening and Closing Hours

Open daily: The park typically operates from **7:00 AM to 10:00 PM**. However, hours may vary depending on the season, so checking the official website for updates is recommended.

Top Things to Do

Stroll Through Gardens: The High Line is home to diverse plant species, ranging from wild grasses to vibrant seasonal flowers, carefully curated to reflect the natural growth that overtook the tracks after the rail line was abandoned.

Enjoy Public Art: Throughout the park, you'll find rotating **public art installations** from local and international artists, adding a creative touch to the natural surroundings.

City Views: The elevated walkway offers excellent views of the Manhattan skyline, the Hudson River, and landmarks like the **Empire State Building**.

Picnic Areas and Seating: Numerous benches and seating areas are scattered along the park, perfect for relaxing, people-watching, or enjoying a picnic.

Chelsea Market: Stop at nearby **Chelsea Market**, located at the park's 16th Street access point, to explore its array of shops and eateries.

Practical Information

Admission: The High Line is **free** to visit.

Accessibility: The park is fully accessible, with elevators and ramps available at multiple entry points for visitors with mobility needs.

Food and Drink: Food vendors can be found at various points along the park, particularly in warmer months. You can also bring your own snacks or visit nearby restaurants and cafés.

Facilities: Public restrooms are available at **Gansevoort Street** and **16th Street**.

Tips for Visiting

Best Time to Visit: The High Line is busiest on weekends, so visit on weekdays or early in the morning for a quieter experience. Sunset offers beautiful views of the city and the Hudson River.

Dress Comfortably: Wear comfortable shoes for walking, as the park stretches nearly 1.5 miles.

Explore the Surrounding Area: After your High Line walk, explore nearby attractions like the **Whitney Museum of American Art** or the **Hudson Yards Vessel**.

Seasonal Changes: The park's landscaping changes with the seasons, so there's something new to see whether you're visiting in spring, summer, fall, or winter.

The Ultimate New York City Travel Guide (2025 Edition)

Museum of Modern Art (MoMA)

The **Museum of Modern Art (MoMA)** is one of the most influential and renowned modern art museums in the world. Located in the heart of **Midtown Manhattan**, MoMA is home to an unparalleled collection of modern and contemporary art, featuring works from the late 19th century to the present. Its extensive collection includes paintings, sculptures, photography, film, design, and new media, with famous pieces by artists such as **Vincent van Gogh, Pablo Picasso, Andy Warhol**, and **Jackson Pollock**.

Location

MoMA is located at **11 West 53rd Street**, between Fifth and Sixth Avenues in Midtown Manhattan, making it easily accessible from other iconic New York landmarks such as **Rockefeller Center** and **Times Square**.

History

Founded in **1929** by philanthropists including **Abby Aldrich Rockefeller**, MoMA was one of the first museums dedicated exclusively to modern art. It has since grown into a world-class institution, undergoing several expansions, most recently in **2019**, which significantly increased its gallery space and allowed for a more diverse display of its collections.

Opening and Closing Hours

Open **daily**: Typically from **10:30 AM to 5:30 PM**. Extended hours on Fridays, when the museum stays open until **9:00 PM**.

Closed on **Thanksgiving** and **Christmas Day**.

Free Admission: Every **Friday evening** from **5:30 PM to 9:00 PM**, admission is free, but it can be quite crowded during this time.

Top Things to Do

Explore Iconic Artworks: Some of MoMA's most famous pieces include **Van Gogh's "Starry Night"**, **Picasso's "Les Demoiselles d'Avignon"**, and **Salvador Dalí's "The Persistence of Memory"**. These masterpieces are must-see highlights of the museum's collection.

Film and Media Exhibits: MoMA is known for its film screenings and innovative new media exhibitions. The museum's film library includes classics from international and independent cinema.

Temporary Exhibitions: MoMA hosts rotating exhibits that feature contemporary artists and thematic collections. These often push boundaries and showcase cutting-edge artistic movements.

Sculpture Garden: The **Abby Aldrich Rockefeller Sculpture Garden** is an outdoor space featuring modern sculptures in a peaceful environment, perfect for a break from exploring the galleries.

Interactive Spaces: Engage with hands-on installations and immersive exhibitions that focus on digital art and emerging technologies.

Practical Information

Tickets: General admission is **$25** for adults, **$18** for seniors (65+), and **$14** for students. Children under 16 get in **free**.

Free Audio Guides: Available in multiple languages, offering detailed commentary on many of the museum's most significant works.

Accessibility: MoMA is fully accessible, with elevators and wheelchair-friendly facilities. Free wheelchairs are available at the coat check.

Dining: The museum has several dining options, including the **Cafe 2** and the more upscale **The Modern**, a two-Michelin-star restaurant located within the museum.

Tips for Visiting

Buy Tickets in Advance: Purchase tickets online to skip the lines and enter the museum more quickly.

Plan for Crowds: MoMA can get busy, especially around the most famous artworks. Visit early in the day or during quieter weekdays for a more leisurely experience.

Explore Beyond the Classics: While the masterpieces are a draw, be sure to explore the museum's photography, architecture, and design collections for a broader understanding of modern art.

Take Breaks: With six floors of galleries, MoMA can be overwhelming. Take advantage of the seating areas and the outdoor sculpture garden to rest and recharge.

The Ultimate New York City Travel Guide (2025 Edition)

One World Observatory

The **One World Observatory** is a stunning observation deck located at the top of **One World Trade Center**, the tallest building in the Western Hemisphere. Offering panoramic, 360-degree views of New York City and beyond, the observatory provides a breathtaking experience for visitors, with interactive exhibits and multimedia presentations enhancing the journey from the ground floor to the sky-high observation platform on the **102nd floor**.

Location

The observatory is located at **117 West Street**, New York, NY, at **One World Trade Center** in **Lower Manhattan**. It's part of the rebuilt World Trade Center complex and is adjacent to the **9/11 Memorial & Museum**.

History

One World Trade Center, also known as the **Freedom Tower**, was completed in **2013** as part of the rebuilding efforts after the September 11, 2001, attacks. The observatory opened in **2015** and quickly became one of New York's top tourist attractions, offering unmatched views from 1,268 feet above the city.

Opening and Closing Hours

Open daily: Typically from **9:00 AM to 9:00 PM**, with extended hours during peak seasons.

The last admission is **45 minutes** before closing.

Hours may vary depending on holidays and events, so it's recommended to check the website before visiting.

Top Things to Do

SkyPod Elevator Ride: The journey begins with an exhilarating ride in the SkyPod elevator, which takes you to the 102nd floor in under **60 seconds**. The elevator features an animated time-lapse of New York City's skyline development over 500 years.

See Forever Theater: Upon arrival, visitors are greeted with a short, immersive video presentation showcasing the beauty of New York before revealing the breathtaking view.

Panoramic Views: Enjoy 360-degree views of New York's iconic landmarks, including the **Statue of Liberty**, **Empire State Building**, **Brooklyn Bridge**, and the **Hudson River**. On a clear day, visibility can extend up to **50 miles**.

Interactive Exhibits: The observatory offers digital guides, touchscreens, and informational panels to help you identify landmarks and learn about the city's history and culture.

Sky Portal: A thrilling glass floor at the observatory offers a virtual view of the streets below, providing a dramatic perspective for those brave enough to look down.

Dining: There's a high-end restaurant, **ONE Dine**, and a casual cafe, **ONE Mix**, both offering stunning views along with a meal or a drink.

Practical Information

Tickets: General admission starts at **$43** for adults, **$41** for seniors (65+), and **$37** for children (6-12). VIP and priority tickets are available for an enhanced experience with expedited entry.

Accessibility: The observatory is fully wheelchair accessible, with elevators, ramps, and facilities for guests with disabilities.

Audio Guides: Available in multiple languages, offering insights about the landmarks visible from the observatory.

Gift Shop: Visitors can stop by the gift shop to purchase souvenirs and memorabilia from their visit.

Tips for Visiting

Book Tickets Online: To avoid long lines, it's recommended to purchase tickets in advance online, especially during peak times.

Best Time to Visit: For the best views, consider visiting around sunset, when you can see the city in daylight and watch as the skyline lights up after dark.

Allow Plenty of Time: Plan for at least **1-2 hours** to fully enjoy the exhibits and the views.

Dress Warmly: Even though the observatory is indoors, the area can get chilly due to its altitude, so it's good to have an extra layer.

Skip the Crowds: Weekdays and mornings tend to be less crowded than weekends and afternoons.

Fifth Avenue Shopping

Fifth Avenue is one of the world's most famous shopping streets, stretching through the heart of Manhattan and offering a mix of high-end luxury brands, flagship stores, and iconic department stores. Known as a global shopping destination, Fifth Avenue attracts millions of visitors each year who come to explore its upscale boutiques and enjoy the vibrant energy of New York City's retail scene.

Location

Fifth Avenue runs through **Midtown Manhattan**, with its prime shopping area located between **49th Street and 60th Street**, near landmarks like **St. Patrick's Cathedral**, **Rockefeller Center**, and **Central Park**.

History

Fifth Avenue has been synonymous with luxury since the late **19th century**, when wealthy New Yorkers built mansions along the avenue. By the early **20th century**, it evolved into a premier shopping destination with department stores like **Saks Fifth Avenue** and exclusive boutiques establishing their presence, cementing its status as a global hub for fashion and retail.

Top Stores and Brands

Saks Fifth Avenue: An iconic department store known for its vast selection of designer clothing, accessories, and cosmetics. Its impressive window displays during the holidays are a must-see.

Tiffany & Co.: Famous for its exquisite jewelry and the legendary **Tiffany Blue Box**, this flagship store is a destination for anyone looking for luxury pieces or simply a window-shopping experience.

Louis Vuitton: A leader in high-end fashion, this flagship store offers the brand's latest collections of bags, shoes, and accessories.

Gucci: For those interested in contemporary luxury fashion, the Gucci store offers a wide range of apparel, footwear, and accessories.

Apple Store (Fifth Avenue): Known for its striking glass cube entrance, the 24/7 Apple Store is a landmark in its own right and a top destination for tech enthusiasts.

Practical Information

Hours: Most stores are open from **10:00 AM to 8:00 PM**, though flagship stores like the **Apple Store** remain open 24/7.

Accessibility: Fifth Avenue is easily accessible by subway, with several nearby stations including **5th Ave/53rd St** and **59th St/Columbus Circle**. Taxis and rideshares are also readily available.

Tips for Visiting

Plan Your Time: Fifth Avenue can be very crowded, especially during the holiday season and weekends, so visiting early in the day or during weekdays can make for a more relaxed experience.

Holiday Shopping: If you're visiting in the winter, the holiday window displays are a major attraction, and you can also enjoy ice skating at nearby **Rockefeller Center**.

Budget Options: While known for luxury shopping, Fifth Avenue also has a variety of more affordable stores like **Uniqlo** and **H&M**, catering to all budgets.

Dining Break: After a day of shopping, consider stopping at nearby cafes or restaurants for a quick bite. **The Plaza Food Hall** near Central Park offers a range of dining options.

The Ultimate New York City Travel Guide (2025 Edition)

Chinatown

Chinatown in **Lower Manhattan** is one of the largest and most vibrant Chinese communities outside of Asia. Known for its bustling streets, authentic cuisine, and rich cultural heritage, Chinatown offers a unique experience for tourists seeking a taste of New York's multicultural landscape. It's a place where you can immerse yourself in Chinese culture, sample traditional food, shop for unique items, and explore historical landmarks.

Location

Chinatown is located in **Lower Manhattan**, bordered by neighborhoods like **Little Italy**, **SoHo**, and the **Lower East Side**. The main streets include **Canal Street**, **Mott Street**, **Bayard Street**, and **Doyers Street**.

History

Chinatown began to form in the mid-**19th century** as Chinese immigrants arrived in New York, seeking new opportunities. Over time, it became a bustling enclave, growing to accommodate a diverse Chinese population and becoming a hub for Chinese culture in the U.S. Today, it's both a cultural and tourist hotspot.

Top Things to Do

Sample Authentic Cuisine: Chinatown is known for its incredible food. Whether you're in the mood for **dim sum**, **Peking duck**, or **bubble tea**, you'll find an array of authentic Chinese restaurants and street food stalls. Popular spots include **Joe's Shanghai**, **Nom Wah Tea Parlor**, and **Golden Unicorn**.

Chinatown Ice Cream Factory: Stop by for unique ice cream flavors inspired by Asian ingredients like **black sesame**, **taro**, and **lychee**.

Shopping: Chinatown is packed with stores selling everything from traditional Chinese herbs and teas to souvenirs, jewelry, and knock-off designer goods on **Canal Street**.

Cultural Landmarks: Visit **Columbus Park**, a lively gathering spot where locals practice tai chi and play mahjong, or the **Museum of Chinese in America** to learn about the Chinese-American experience and history.

Mahayana Buddhist Temple: Home to a 16-foot-tall golden Buddha, this temple is one of the largest Buddhist temples in the city, offering a serene retreat amid Chinatown's bustling streets.

Practical Information

Getting There: Chinatown is easily accessible by subway, with several nearby stations, including **Canal Street (N, Q, R, W, 6 lines)**. It's also walkable from other popular neighborhoods like **Little Italy** and **SoHo**.

Opening Hours: Many shops and restaurants open around **10:00 AM** and stay open until **10:00 PM** or later. Some dim sum restaurants are best visited earlier in the day for brunch.

Tips for Visiting

Cash is King: Many shops and restaurants in Chinatown still operate on a cash-only basis, so it's wise to have cash on hand.

Try the Dim Sum: Visit during the morning or lunchtime to experience traditional dim sum, a style of Chinese cuisine where you can sample a variety of small, flavorful dishes.

Bargain Shopping: Don't be afraid to haggle at the markets, especially when shopping for souvenirs or gifts on **Canal Street**.

Be Mindful of Crowds: Chinatown can get very crowded, especially on weekends. If you prefer a quieter experience, try visiting on a weekday.

The Ultimate New York City Travel Guide (2025 Edition)

St. Patrick's Cathedral

St. Patrick's Cathedral is a strikingly beautiful and historic Roman Catholic cathedral located in **Midtown Manhattan**. Known for its Gothic Revival architecture, its grandeur, and its significant role in New York City's religious and cultural life, St. Patrick's is a must-visit landmark. It serves as the seat of the Archdiocese of New York and is a central location for major religious events and services.

Location

St. Patrick's Cathedral is situated at **5th Avenue** between **50th** and **51st Streets**, directly across from **Rockefeller Center**. Its prominent location makes it easily accessible from other major attractions in Midtown.

History

Construction of St. Patrick's Cathedral began in **1858**, and the building was completed in **1878**. Designed by architect **James Renwick Jr.**, it was built to accommodate the growing Catholic population in New York City during the 19th century. The cathedral has since undergone several restorations and renovations to preserve its stunning architecture and historical integrity.

Opening and Closing Hours

Open daily: Typically from **6:30 AM to 8:00 PM**.

Mass Times: Regular Masses are held at various times throughout the day, with additional services on Sundays and special occasions.

Closed: Occasionally closed for special events, services, or maintenance. It's a good idea to check the cathedral's website or call ahead for the most up-to-date information.

Top Things to Do

Explore the Architecture: Admire the cathedral's Gothic Revival architecture, including its impressive spires, intricate stained glass windows, and ornate interior detailing.

Visit the Crypt: The cathedral's crypt contains the tombs of several prominent figures, including Cardinal John Cardinal O'Connor and other past archbishops.

Attend a Service: If you're interested in experiencing a traditional Catholic Mass, attending a service at St. Patrick's is a memorable way to see the cathedral in use.

See the Nativity Scene: During the Christmas season, St. Patrick's Cathedral features a beautiful Nativity scene that attracts many visitors.

Walk the Surroundings: Take a stroll around the cathedral and enjoy the surrounding area, including **Rockefeller Center** and **Central Park**.

Practical Information

Admission: Free, though donations are appreciated.

Accessibility: The cathedral is wheelchair accessible, with ramps and elevators available. Assistance for those with mobility challenges is also provided.

Dress Code: As a place of worship, visitors are asked to dress modestly. Avoid wearing hats inside the cathedral and ensure that shoulders and knees are covered.

Photography: Photography is generally allowed, but it's courteous to be respectful of worshippers and any ongoing services.

Tips for Visiting

Avoid Peak Times: Visit during off-peak hours, especially if you prefer a quieter experience. Early mornings or late afternoons can be less crowded.

Check for Events: If you're interested in attending a specific Mass or event, check the cathedral's calendar in advance to avoid any scheduling conflicts.

Respect the Space: Remember that St. Patrick's is an active place of worship. Be mindful of the needs and activities of those who come to pray and attend services.

Combine Visits: Given its central location, St. Patrick's is easily combined with visits to nearby attractions like **The Met, Rockefeller Center,** or **Times Square**.

Chapter 6: Getting Around New York City

Subway

The **New York City Subway** is one of the most extensive and efficient public transportation systems in the world, offering a fast and economical way to navigate the city. With **472 stations** spread across four boroughs—Manhattan, Brooklyn, Queens, and the Bronx—the subway connects nearly every part of New York City, making it an essential mode of transportation for both residents and tourists.

Cost

Single Ride: $2.90 for a one-way trip.

MetroCard: The standard fare card used to pay for subway rides.

Unlimited Ride MetroCard: Available for **7 days** at $34 or **30 days** at $132. Ideal for frequent travelers.

Reduced Fare: Available for seniors (65+) and people with disabilities at $1.35 per ride. Proper ID or eligibility card is required.

Payment

MetroCard: Purchase and refill MetroCards at subway stations using vending machines or at station booths. MetroCards can be used for both subway and local bus rides.

OMNY: The newer payment system allows you to pay using a contactless payment method such as a credit or debit card, smartphone, or wearable device. Simply tap your card or device at the turnstile reader.

Single Ride Ticket: If you're only using the subway once, you can buy a single-ride ticket for $3.00 from vending machines.

Tips for Using the Subway

Plan Your Route: Use apps like **Google Maps**, **Citymapper**, or the **MTA's trip planner** to plan your route and check subway schedules. These tools help navigate transfers and avoid getting lost.

Check the Schedule: Subways generally run from **5:00 AM to 1:00 AM**. Frequency varies by line and time of day, so check schedules and service changes, especially late at night or during weekends when some lines may be under maintenance.

Know the Lines: Familiarize yourself with the **local** and **express** lines. Local trains stop at every station, while express trains skip certain stops, speeding up travel but requiring careful navigation to ensure you board the correct train.

Stay Safe: Keep your belongings close and be aware of your surroundings. The subway is generally safe, but like any large city, it's best to remain vigilant.

Avoid Rush Hours: If possible, avoid traveling during peak hours (usually **8:00 AM to 9:30 AM** and **5:00 PM to 7:00 PM**), when trains are the most crowded.

Follow the Rules: Eating and drinking are not allowed on the subway. Use headphones to listen to music, and remember that loud conversations can be disruptive to other passengers.

Exit Strategy: Pay attention to the subway maps and signs posted inside the trains and stations to ensure you get off at the correct stop. Also, be aware that many exits at major stations lead to different street corners, so double-check your desired exit.

Buses

New York City's bus system complements the subway and provides access to areas not covered by the train network. With a comprehensive network of routes operating throughout the five boroughs, buses are a flexible and useful means of transportation for navigating the city's neighborhoods, especially where subways might not reach.

Cost

Single Ride: $2.90 per ride.

Unlimited Ride MetroCard: The **7-Day** or **30-Day** MetroCard can be used on buses, making it economical for frequent travelers.

Reduced Fare: Seniors (65+) and people with disabilities can use the Reduced Fare MetroCard for $1.35 per ride.

Payment

MetroCard: Swipe your MetroCard at the fare box located at the front of the bus. Both standard and Unlimited Ride MetroCards are accepted.

OMNY: Similar to the subway, you can use contactless payment methods such as a credit or debit card, smartphone, or wearable device by tapping it on the fare reader at the bus entrance.

Exact Fare: If you do not have a MetroCard or OMNY, you'll need to pay the exact fare in cash. Bus drivers do not give change, so have the exact amount ready.

Tips for Using the Bus

Check Routes and Schedules: Use apps like **Google Maps**, **Citymapper**, or the **MTA Bus Time** app to find routes and real-time schedules. Buses can be slower due to traffic, so plan your route and timing accordingly.

Identify Your Bus Stop: Bus stops are marked with signs indicating which routes stop there. Ensure you're waiting at the correct stop for your desired bus route.

Know the Bus Types: Familiarize yourself with local buses (which stop at all stations) and express buses (which travel faster by skipping some stops).

Pay Attention to Schedules: Buses have specific schedules, especially during off-peak hours and weekends. Be prepared for longer waits if traveling during less busy times.

Be Patient: Traffic can cause delays, so allow extra time if you're on a tight schedule. During peak hours, buses can be crowded.

Stay Safe: Similar to the subway, keep your belongings close and be mindful of your surroundings. Buses are generally safe but remain alert, especially late at night.

The Ultimate New York City Travel Guide (2025 Edition)

Additional Information

Accessibility: Most buses are wheelchair accessible and have designated spaces for wheelchairs and mobility devices. There are also audible and visual announcements for stops.

Transfers: If you're transferring from a subway to a bus (or vice versa), you can use the same MetroCard for a free transfer within **2 hours** of your initial swipe. Make sure to request a transfer slip when boarding the bus if using a MetroCard.

Night Buses: New York City operates select buses 24/7, known as "**night buses**," for late-night travel. These routes often have extended service hours, providing essential transportation during the night.

Taxis and Rideshares (Uber, Lyft)

Taxis and rideshare services like **Uber** and **Lyft** offer convenient and flexible transportation options for navigating New York City. While taxis are a quintessential part of the city's identity, rideshare services have become increasingly popular due to their ease of use and app-based convenience. Both options provide door-to-door service, making them ideal for travelers who prefer a more personalized and direct mode of transport.

Taxis

Hailing a Taxi: Yellow cabs can be hailed from the street in most parts of Manhattan, or you can use a taxi app to request one. Taxis are easily identifiable with their yellow color and "TAXI" sign on top.

Fare Structure: Taxis have a base fare of $3.50. The fare increases based on distance traveled and time spent in traffic, with additional charges for extra passengers, luggage, or travel during peak hours.

Payment: Taxis accept cash, credit, and debit cards. Most cabs are equipped with a card reader, but it's a good idea to confirm with the driver beforehand.

Tips: Tipping is customary, usually 15-20% of the total fare.

Rideshares (Uber and Lyft)

Booking a Ride: Use the Uber or Lyft app to request a ride. Simply enter your pickup location and destination, and the app will match you with a nearby driver. You can see the estimated fare, vehicle details, and driver information before confirming.

Fare Structure: Rideshare fares vary based on distance, time of day, and demand. Surge pricing may apply during high-demand periods, which can increase the cost of your ride.

Payment: Payment is handled through the app, with options for credit/debit cards or digital wallets. You'll receive an electronic receipt via email or the app after the ride.

Tips: While tipping is not mandatory, it's appreciated. The app allows you to add a tip directly after the ride.

Tips for Using Taxis and Rideshares

Verify Your Ride: When using rideshare services, always verify the vehicle's license plate, make, and model with the details provided in the app before getting in. This helps ensure you're getting into the correct car.

Safety First: For both taxis and rideshares, ensure the driver's credentials match what's provided. In rideshares, you can share your trip details with friends or family for added safety.

Check for Additional Fees: Be aware of potential extra charges, such as tolls or airport surcharges, which may apply to your fare.

Know the Peak Times: Traffic and surge pricing can affect rideshare costs. During rush hours or bad weather, fares may be higher, and finding a ride may take longer.

Plan for Accessibility: If you require an accessible vehicle, both Uber and Lyft offer options for rideshare services that can accommodate wheelchairs or other mobility devices. Check the app for availability.

Additional Information

Taxis vs. Rideshares: Taxis are often easier to find in busy areas and do not require a smartphone app, while rideshares offer more predictability with upfront pricing and driver details. Consider your needs and preferences when choosing between the two.

Airport Transfers: Taxis have a flat fare to and from JFK, LaGuardia, and Newark airports, while rideshare services have varying rates based on distance and traffic conditions.

Walking

Walking is one of the most enjoyable and immersive ways to explore New York City. With its vibrant streets, iconic landmarks, and diverse neighborhoods, walking allows you to experience the city at your own pace, soak in its atmosphere, and discover hidden gems that you might miss when using other forms of transportation.

Benefits of Walking

Scenic Exploration: Walking gives you the chance to take in the city's architecture, parks, and street life up close.

Flexibility: You can change your route spontaneously and explore areas that interest you.

Health and Fitness: Walking is a great way to stay active while traveling and burn off those extra calories from all the delicious food you'll be trying.

Cost-Effective: It's free and often faster than navigating traffic or waiting for public transport during busy times.

Tips for Walking in New York City

Wear Comfortable Shoes: New York is a city best explored on foot, so make sure to wear comfortable, supportive shoes to handle the amount of walking you'll be doing.

Stay Hydrated: Keep a water bottle with you, especially if you're walking for extended periods. NYC can get hot, particularly during the summer.

Dress Appropriately: Weather in New York can vary greatly, so dress in layers and check the forecast before heading out. During the winter, be prepared for cold temperatures and potential snow.

Plan Your Route: While you can discover a lot by wandering, having a general idea of your route can help you make the most of your time. Use maps or navigation apps to avoid getting lost and to estimate walking times.

Watch for Traffic: Even when crossing at marked crosswalks, always be alert. New York's traffic can be hectic, and drivers may not always yield to pedestrians.

Stay Aware of Your Surroundings: Like any large city, keep an eye on your belongings and be aware of your surroundings, especially in crowded areas.

Popular Walking Routes

Central Park: This massive urban park offers numerous scenic walking paths and attractions such as Bethesda Terrace, Bow Bridge, and the Central Park Zoo.

The High Line: A beautifully landscaped elevated park built on a former rail line, offering unique views of the city and the Hudson River.

Fifth Avenue: Walk along this iconic avenue to see landmarks like the Empire State Building, St. Patrick's Cathedral, and numerous high-end shops.

Greenwich Village: Wander through this historic neighborhood known for its bohemian vibe, charming streets, and cultural landmarks.

Brooklyn Bridge: Walking across the Brooklyn Bridge provides stunning views of the Manhattan skyline and leads you to the vibrant neighborhood of Brooklyn Heights and DUMBO.

Additional Information

Safety: NYC is generally safe for walkers, but always remain cautious in unfamiliar areas, especially after dark.

Navigation: Use pedestrian-friendly maps and apps to help navigate, especially when exploring less familiar neighborhoods.

Rest Stops: Take advantage of parks, cafes, and benches along your route to rest and recharge.

Biking (Citi Bike)

Citi Bike is New York City's popular bike-sharing program, offering an efficient and eco-friendly way to explore the city. With thousands of bikes and docking stations scattered throughout Manhattan, Brooklyn, and parts of Queens, Citi Bike provides a convenient alternative to traditional transportation methods, especially for short trips and leisurely rides.

Cost

Single Ride: $4.49 for a single ride up to 30 minutes. Additional charges apply for extra time.

Day Pass: $12 for a 24-hour pass, which includes unlimited 30-minute rides within the day. Extra charges apply for rides over 30 minutes.

Monthly Membership: $169 for unlimited rides of up to 45 minutes per ride. Charges apply for rides over 45 minutes.

Student and Reduced Fare Options: Discounts may be available for students and low-income riders. Check the Citi Bike website for details.

Payment

Citi Bike App: Use the Citi Bike app to purchase passes, locate bike stations, and unlock bikes. The app provides real-time information on bike availability and docking station locations.

Bike Stations: You can also pay for rides directly at docking stations using a credit or debit card. Membership options are available for purchase through the app or at kiosks.

Credit/Debit Card: All transactions are processed through credit or debit cards. Cash is not accepted at the docking stations.

Tips for Using Citi Bike

Choose the Right Plan: Select the plan that best fits your riding needs. For short trips, a single ride or day pass may be most economical. For longer stays, consider the monthly membership.

Check Bike Availability: Use the Citi Bike app to check for available bikes and docking stations near you. This helps avoid long waits and ensures you can find a bike when you need one.

Return Bikes Promptly: Return bikes to a docking station within the allotted time to avoid extra charges. If a station is full, you can use the app to find nearby stations with available docks.

Follow Traffic Rules: Ride safely by adhering to traffic rules and using bike lanes where available. Be cautious of pedestrians and other vehicles, especially in busy areas.

Wear a Helmet: While not required by law for adults, wearing a helmet is strongly recommended for safety. Some areas may offer helmet rentals or purchases.

Popular Biking Routes

The High Line: An elevated park that provides scenic views of the city and the Hudson River. While biking is not permitted on the park itself, it's a great route to reach nearby neighborhoods.

Central Park: Central Park features dedicated bike lanes and is a popular spot for both leisurely rides and more challenging routes.

Brooklyn Waterfront: Ride along the Brooklyn waterfront to enjoy views of the Manhattan skyline and explore neighborhoods like DUMBO and Brooklyn Heights.

Hudson River Greenway: This dedicated bike path runs along the Hudson River, offering a scenic route from Battery Park in the south to the George Washington Bridge in the north.

Additional Information

Bike Maintenance: Citi Bikes are regularly maintained, but if you encounter any issues, you can report them through the app or at a docking station.

Accessibility: Citi Bike is designed for general use but may not be suitable for individuals with certain mobility challenges. Alternative bike rental services or accessible transportation options may be available.

Weather Considerations: Check the weather before heading out, as biking in rain or extreme temperatures can be less comfortable and more challenging.

The Ultimate New York City Travel Guide (2025 Edition)

Ferries

New York City's ferry system provides a unique and scenic way to travel across the city's waterways, offering stunning views of the skyline, bridges, and iconic landmarks. Ferries connect Manhattan with various parts of Brooklyn, Queens, the Bronx, and New Jersey, making them a convenient and picturesque alternative to other forms of transportation.

Types of Ferries

NYC Ferry: Operated by the City of New York, this service offers routes connecting Manhattan with Brooklyn, Queens, and the Bronx.

Routes: Includes the East River, South Brooklyn, Rockaway, and Astoria routes.

Cost: $4.00 per ride. Transfers to the subway or bus system are not included.

Statue of Liberty & Ellis Island Ferry: Operated by Statue Cruises, these ferries provide transportation to the Statue of Liberty and Ellis Island.

Cost: $24.50 for adults, $12.00 for children (ages 4-12). Tickets include access to both Liberty Island and Ellis Island.

Booking: Tickets can be purchased online or at the ferry terminal.

NY Waterway: Offers commuter and tourist ferry services connecting Manhattan with New Jersey and Brooklyn.

Routes: Includes routes from Midtown to various locations in New Jersey and Brooklyn.

Cost: Fares vary depending on the route. Commuter passes are available for frequent travelers.

Seastreak: Provides ferry services between Manhattan and locations in New Jersey and the Hamptons.

Routes: Includes routes from Wall Street to locations like Atlantic Highlands and the Hamptons.

Cost: Fares vary depending on the route. Reservations are recommended.

Payment

NYC Ferry: Use a MetroCard, OMNY, or buy tickets through the NYC Ferry app. Credit and debit cards are accepted at the ticket vending machines at ferry terminals.

Statue of Liberty & Ellis Island Ferry: Purchase tickets online, through the Statue Cruises app, or at the ferry terminal.

NY Waterway & Seastreak: Tickets can be bought online, through their respective apps, or at the ferry terminals. Both services accept credit and debit cards.

Tips for Using Ferries

Check Schedules: Ferries operate on specific schedules, so check the timetable for your route in advance. Schedules can vary by day and season.

Arrive Early: Especially during peak times or tourist seasons, ferries can get crowded. Arriving early ensures you get a seat and helps with a smoother boarding process.

Weather Considerations: Ferries are subject to weather conditions. Check weather forecasts before traveling and be prepared for possible delays or cancellations due to severe weather.

Enjoy the View: Take advantage of the scenic ride by sitting on the open decks where available. Many ferries offer panoramic views of landmarks such as the Statue of Liberty, Brooklyn Bridge, and the Manhattan skyline.

Accessibility: Ferries are generally accessible to people with disabilities. Check with the ferry provider for specific accessibility features and accommodations.

Popular Ferry Routes

NYC Ferry's East River Route: Offers beautiful views of the East River, the Manhattan skyline, and landmarks like the Brooklyn Bridge.

Statue of Liberty & Ellis Island: Provides close-up views of the Statue of Liberty and access to the historical museums on Ellis Island.

Seastreak to the Hamptons: Ideal for a day trip to the Hamptons with scenic views of the New York Harbor and Long Island coastline.

Additional Information

Safety: Follow safety instructions provided by the crew. Life jackets are available, and emergency procedures are posted on board.

Bike and Pet Policies: Many ferries allow bikes and pets. Check with the specific ferry service for their policies and any associated fees.

Driving and Car Rentals

Driving and renting a car in New York City can be a convenient option for exploring the city and its surrounding areas, but it comes with its own set of challenges. Traffic congestion, limited parking, and high parking costs are significant considerations. However, for certain travelers, especially those planning day trips outside the city or needing flexibility, having a car can be beneficial.

Driving in New York City

Traffic: NYC is known for its heavy traffic, especially during rush hours (typically 7-10 AM and 4-7 PM). Expect delays and plan accordingly. Traffic can be particularly challenging in Manhattan.

Parking: Finding parking in NYC can be difficult and expensive. Street parking is limited and often subject to strict regulations. Public and private parking garages are available but can be costly.

Congestion Pricing: Manhattan's central business district has congestion pricing to reduce traffic. Vehicles entering this area during peak hours are subject to additional charges.

Rules and Regulations: Follow local traffic laws, including speed limits and parking regulations. Be aware of bike lanes and pedestrian zones. NYC is known for strict enforcement of traffic laws.

Car Rentals

Rental Agencies: Major rental companies like Enterprise, Hertz, Avis, Budget, and Alamo operate in NYC. Rental locations are often situated at airports, major train stations, and in various neighborhoods.

Cost: Rental rates vary based on the type of vehicle, rental duration, and the rental agency. Expect to pay higher rates in the city compared to other areas.

Booking: Reserve your rental car in advance to secure the best rates and availability. Online booking platforms and rental agency websites offer comparisons and discounts.

Insurance: Rental insurance is highly recommended. Check with your credit card company or personal auto insurance provider to see if coverage extends to rental vehicles.

Tips for Driving and Car Rentals

Plan Your Route: Use navigation apps like Google Maps or Waze to plan your route and avoid traffic jams. These apps provide real-time traffic updates and alternative routes.

Be Prepared for Tolls: Many highways and bridges into and out of NYC have tolls. Be prepared to pay these and check if your rental car has an electronic toll pass.

Check Parking Options: Before heading into the city, research parking options. Consider booking a parking spot in advance, particularly if you're staying overnight.

Consider Alternatives: For short trips within the city, consider using public transportation, rideshares, or taxis instead of driving. These options can save time and reduce stress.

Know Your Limits: NYC can be overwhelming for drivers unfamiliar with its layout and traffic patterns. If you're not comfortable driving in such a busy environment, consider alternative transportation options.

Additional Information

Traffic Cameras: Be aware of red light cameras and other traffic enforcement systems that monitor traffic violations.

Driving License: Ensure you have a valid driver's license. International drivers may need an International Driving Permit (IDP) in addition to their home country license.

Rental Car Features: Many rental cars come equipped with GPS and other features that can assist with navigation and comfort.

Trains (Commuter Rail)

Commuter rail services are an efficient way to travel between New York City and its surrounding regions, including nearby suburbs, other cities, and even other states. These trains offer a comfortable and scenic way to cover longer distances compared to driving or taking the bus. They are ideal for day trips, regional travel, or even commuting from outlying areas into NYC.

Major Commuter Rail Services

Long Island Rail Road (LIRR)

Overview: Connects Manhattan (Penn Station) with Long Island, including Nassau and Suffolk counties.

Routes: Various lines serve different parts of Long Island, with frequent service to popular destinations like Jamaica, Huntington, and Montauk.

Cost: Fares vary based on distance and time of day. Off-peak tickets are cheaper than peak tickets. Prices are available on the MTA website or app.

Payment: Tickets can be purchased at stations, through the MTA eTix app, or from ticket machines. Credit and debit cards are accepted.

Metro-North Railroad

Overview: Connects Manhattan (Grand Central Terminal) with parts of Westchester County, Putnam County, and parts of Connecticut.

Routes: Key lines include the Hudson Line (to Poughkeepsie), the Harlem Line (to Wassaic), and the New Haven Line (to New Haven, CT).

Cost: Fares depend on the distance traveled and the time of day. Peak and off-peak pricing applies. Check the MTA website for fare details.

Payment: Tickets can be purchased at stations, through the MTA eTix app, or from ticket machines. Credit and debit cards are accepted.

New Jersey Transit (NJ Transit)

Overview: Provides rail service between Manhattan (Penn Station) and various locations in New Jersey, including Newark, Hoboken, and Jersey City.

Routes: Includes multiple lines serving areas such as the North Jersey Coast Line, the Raritan Valley Line, and the Morristown Line.

Cost: Ticket prices vary based on distance and time of day. Check the NJ Transit website or app for up-to-date pricing.

Payment: Tickets can be purchased at stations, through the NJ Transit app, or from ticket vending machines. Credit and debit cards are accepted.

Amtrak

Overview: Provides intercity rail service between New York City (Penn Station) and other major cities along the Northeast Corridor, including Boston, Philadelphia, and Washington, D.C.

Routes: Includes the Acela Express (high-speed service) and Northeast Regional trains.

Cost: Fares depend on the destination and class of service. Booking in advance often results in lower prices. Check the Amtrak website for current rates.

Payment: Tickets can be purchased online, through the Amtrak app, or at Penn Station. Credit and debit cards are accepted.

Tips for Using Commuter Trains

Check Schedules: Train schedules vary by day and time. Use the respective transit authority's website or app to check schedules and plan your trip.

Buy Tickets in Advance: Purchase tickets ahead of time to avoid lines at the station. Many services offer mobile ticketing options for convenience.

Understand Peak Times: Peak hours are typically during weekday rush hours. Off-peak travel can be cheaper and less crowded.

Know Your Stop: Be aware of your destination and the stop where you need to disembark. Announcements and station signs will help, but keeping track of your route is important.

Seating and Luggage: Commuter trains usually have designated seating areas and luggage storage. Follow the guidelines for seating and storing bags to ensure a comfortable trip.

Additional Information

Accessibility: Most commuter rail services are equipped to accommodate passengers with disabilities. Check with the specific service for details on accessible features and assistance.

Transfers: Commuter trains often connect with other forms of public transportation, such as buses and subways, to complete your journey within NYC or the surrounding areas.

Trains (Commuter Rail)

Commuter rail services provide an essential link between New York City and the broader region, including suburbs, neighboring cities, and even other states. These trains are particularly useful for those traveling from outside the city, offering a comfortable and efficient way to commute or explore beyond the urban core.

Major Commuter Rail Services

Long Island Rail Road (LIRR)

Overview: Operates from Penn Station in Manhattan to various destinations on Long Island, including Nassau and Suffolk counties.

Key Routes:

Babylon Branch: Runs to Babylon and is a popular route for residents of South Shore Long Island.

Port Jefferson Branch: Connects to Port Jefferson and serves the North Shore.

Montauk Branch: Extends to Montauk at the eastern tip of Long Island.

Cost: Prices depend on distance and travel time. Off-peak tickets are less expensive than peak tickets. Refer to the MTA website for detailed fare information.

Payment: Purchase tickets at stations, via the MTA eTix app, or at ticket machines. Both credit and debit cards are accepted.

Metro-North Railroad

Overview: Serves commuters traveling from the northern suburbs of New York City to Grand Central Terminal in Manhattan. It covers areas in Westchester County, Putnam County, and parts of Connecticut.

Key Routes:

Hudson Line: Runs along the west side of the Hudson River, reaching up to Poughkeepsie.

Harlem Line: Extends north to Wassaic, passing through communities like White Plains.

New Haven Line: Connects to New Haven, Connecticut, providing service through Stamford and Bridgeport.

Cost: Fares vary by distance and time of day. Off-peak tickets are usually cheaper. Check the MTA website for specific pricing.

Payment: Tickets can be bought at stations, through the MTA eTix app, or from ticket machines. Credit and debit cards are accepted.

New Jersey Transit (NJ Transit)

Overview: Connects Manhattan (Penn Station) with various locations in New Jersey, including Newark, Hoboken, and Jersey City. It also extends to other parts of the state.

Key Routes:

North Jersey Coast Line: Runs from Hoboken to Long Branch and beyond.

Raritan Valley Line: Connects Newark with areas in central New Jersey.

Morristown Line: Serves areas from Hoboken to Morristown.

Cost: Prices depend on distance and time. Fares are available on the NJ Transit website.

Payment: Buy tickets at stations, through the NJ Transit app, or at vending machines. Credit and debit cards are accepted.

Amtrak

Overview: Provides long-distance rail service from New York City (Penn Station) to various destinations along the Northeast Corridor, including Boston, Philadelphia, and Washington, D.C.

Key Routes:

Acela Express: High-speed service with premium amenities, running between Boston and Washington, D.C.

Northeast Regional: A more economical option with frequent service along the corridor.

Cost: Fares vary based on destination, class, and how early you book. Check the Amtrak website for current rates.

Payment: Tickets can be purchased online, through the Amtrak app, or at Penn Station. Credit and debit cards are accepted.

Tips for Using Commuter Trains

Check Timetables: Train schedules can vary. Always verify departure times and routes using the transit authority's website or app.

Buy Tickets Early: Purchasing tickets in advance can help avoid long lines and ensure a smoother travel experience. Most services offer mobile ticketing options.

Know Peak Hours: Peak travel times are typically during weekday mornings and late afternoons. Off-peak fares are generally lower and less crowded.

Be Mindful of Stops: Pay attention to the stops and announcements to ensure you disembark at your intended destination.

Travel Comfort: Trains generally offer comfortable seating and some amenities. Be prepared for potential crowded conditions during rush hours.

Additional Information

Accessibility: Most commuter rail services are equipped to accommodate passengers with disabilities. For specific needs, check the service provider's accessibility features.

Luggage and Bikes: Many commuter trains allow luggage and bicycles. Confirm the specific policies and potential fees with the service provider.

Grace Bennett

Chapter 7: Shopping in New York City

Fifth Avenue and Luxury Shopping

Fifth Avenue, stretching from Washington Square Park in Greenwich Village to 142nd Street in Harlem, is one of the most iconic shopping streets in the world. Known for its high-end retailers and luxury boutiques, it represents the pinnacle of upscale shopping in New York City. Whether you're looking for designer fashion, fine jewelry, or high-end home goods, Fifth Avenue offers a premier shopping experience.

Key Attractions

Flagship Stores: Fifth Avenue is home to the flagship stores of some of the world's most prestigious brands. These include high-end names like Gucci, Prada, Louis Vuitton, and Chanel, offering exclusive collections and exceptional service.

Department Stores: Major department stores such as Saks Fifth Avenue and Bergdorf Goodman anchor this famous shopping street. Saks Fifth Avenue, with its opulent displays and extensive range of luxury goods, is particularly renowned for its elaborate holiday window displays. Bergdorf Goodman is known for its upscale fashion and unique designer pieces.

Jewelry and Watches: Fifth Avenue features an array of fine jewelry and watch stores, including Tiffany & Co., known for its iconic blue boxes, and Cartier, famed for its exquisite craftsmanship.

Cultural Landmarks: In addition to shopping, Fifth Avenue is lined with cultural landmarks, including the Metropolitan Museum of Art and the New York Public Library, making it a prime destination for those interested in both retail therapy and cultural exploration.

Cost

Luxury Brands: Prices at luxury boutiques and designer stores are on the higher end, reflecting the premium quality of the products. Expect to pay top dollar for high-end fashion, accessories, and jewelry.

Department Stores: While department stores may offer a range of products from high-end to more accessible price points, the luxury sections within them are still quite costly.

Payment

Accepted Methods: Most stores on Fifth Avenue accept major credit and debit cards. Some high-end boutiques may also accept American Express Centurion and other premium cards.

Tax Refunds: International tourists may be eligible for a tax refund on purchases. Look for stores that offer tax-free shopping or inquire about the process.

Tips for Shopping on Fifth Avenue

Plan Ahead: Fifth Avenue is a popular destination, and some stores can be quite busy. Plan your visit during less crowded times, such as weekdays or early mornings, to enjoy a more relaxed shopping experience.

Dress the Part: While there is no formal dress code, dressing stylishly can enhance your experience and help you feel more at ease in high-end retail environments.

Check for Sales: While luxury items often don't go on sale, department stores and some boutiques might offer seasonal promotions. Keep an eye out for special sales events.

Take Advantage of Services: Many high-end stores offer personal shopping services, alterations, and other amenities. Don't hesitate to ask for assistance to make your shopping experience more enjoyable.

Explore Beyond Shopping: Enjoy the architectural beauty of Fifth Avenue, visit nearby landmarks, and consider stopping by a café or restaurant to take a break from shopping.

Additional Information

Accessibility: Fifth Avenue is generally accessible for shoppers with disabilities. Most stores are equipped to accommodate special needs, but it's a good idea to call ahead if you have specific requirements.

Transport: Fifth Avenue is well-served by public transportation, including subway stations and bus routes. Taxis and rideshares are also readily available.

SoHo: Boutique Shops and High Fashion

SoHo, short for "South of Houston Street," is a trendy neighborhood in Manhattan renowned for its chic boutiques, high-fashion stores, and vibrant arts scene. Once known for its cast-iron architecture and cobblestone streets, SoHo has evolved into a premier shopping destination, offering a blend of designer brands, unique boutiques, and cutting-edge fashion. Its eclectic mix makes it a must-visit for fashion enthusiasts and trendsetters.

Key Attractions

Boutique Shops: SoHo is home to an array of independent boutiques and specialty stores that cater to diverse tastes. From avant-garde fashion and handcrafted jewelry to artisanal home goods, the boutiques here often feature unique items you won't find elsewhere.

High Fashion Stores: The area hosts high-end fashion retailers and flagship stores for both well-known and emerging designers. Renowned brands such as Chanel, Gucci, and Prada have a presence here, offering their latest collections in stylish settings.

Art Galleries: Beyond shopping, SoHo is known for its art galleries, which showcase contemporary and modern art. The neighborhood's artistic vibe complements its fashion-forward reputation.

Historic Architecture: The area is also noted for its historic cast-iron buildings, many of which have been converted into stylish boutiques and galleries. Exploring these architectural gems adds to the charm of shopping in SoHo.

Cost

Boutiques: Prices vary widely, with some boutiques offering affordable unique items and others specializing in luxury or artisanal goods.

High Fashion Stores: Expect higher prices at designer and high-fashion stores, reflecting the premium quality and exclusivity of the merchandise.

Payment

Accepted Methods: Most stores in SoHo accept major credit and debit cards. Some high-end boutiques may also accept premium credit cards, such as American Express Centurion.

Tax Refunds: International tourists may be eligible for tax refunds on purchases. Look for stores that offer tax-free shopping or ask about the process.

Tips for Shopping in SoHo

Explore on Foot: SoHo is best explored on foot. Wander through its charming streets to discover hidden gems and lesser-known boutiques.

Visit During Weekdays: To avoid the weekend crowds, consider shopping during weekdays. Early mornings or late afternoons can also be quieter times.

Check Out Local Designers: SoHo is a great place to discover emerging designers and local talent. Look for boutiques that offer unique, one-of-a-kind pieces.

Enjoy the Atmosphere: SoHo's vibrant atmosphere extends beyond shopping. Take breaks at trendy cafés or restaurants to soak in the neighborhood's creative energy.

Wear Comfortable Shoes: The area's cobblestone streets and frequent walking can be tough on your feet, so comfortable footwear is essential.

Additional Information

Accessibility: SoHo is generally accessible for shoppers with disabilities. However, some boutiques and galleries in historic buildings might have limited accessibility features, so check ahead if you have specific needs.

Transport: SoHo is well-connected by public transportation, including the subway (C, E, and R lines) and several bus routes. Taxis and rideshares are also readily available.

Grace Bennett

Williamsburg: Vintage and Indie Stores

Williamsburg, a vibrant neighborhood in Brooklyn, is renowned for its eclectic mix of vintage shops, indie boutiques, and creative flair. Once an industrial area, Williamsburg has transformed into a trendy hotspot with a unique shopping scene that attracts both locals and tourists. Its blend of retro charm and contemporary style offers a distinctive shopping experience away from Manhattan's more mainstream retail areas.

Key Attractions

Vintage Stores: Williamsburg is famous for its vintage shops, which offer a curated selection of clothing, accessories, and collectibles from past decades. Stores like **Beacon's Closet** and **L Train Vintage** are well-known for their extensive collections of retro fashion, vintage denim, and unique finds. These shops are perfect for those looking to add a touch of nostalgia to their wardrobe.

Indie Boutiques: The neighborhood also boasts a range of indie boutiques that feature the work of emerging designers and local artisans. Shops like **Artists & Fleas** provide a marketplace for handcrafted items, from artisanal jewelry to unique home décor. These boutiques offer one-of-a-kind pieces that reflect Williamsburg's creative spirit.

Record Stores: For music enthusiasts, Williamsburg has several record stores that cater to vinyl lovers. **Rough Trade NYC** is a notable spot, offering a wide selection of vinyl records, music merchandise, and live performances.

Artistic Vibe: Beyond shopping, Williamsburg is known for its artistic community. The neighborhood's street art, galleries, and performance spaces contribute to its dynamic and creative atmosphere.

Cost

Vintage Stores: Prices vary depending on the rarity and condition of the items. Vintage clothing can range from affordable to high-end, with unique pieces often commanding higher prices.

Indie Boutiques: Items in indie boutiques are generally reasonably priced, though some designer or handcrafted goods may be more expensive. Many boutiques offer affordable and unique items.

Payment

Accepted Methods: Most vintage and indie stores in Williamsburg accept major credit and debit cards. Some smaller boutiques may only accept cash, so it's a good idea to carry some with you.

Tax Refunds: While tax refunds are less common in small, independent shops, check with individual stores for any available options.

Tips for Shopping in Williamsburg

Explore the Neighborhood: Williamsburg is best explored on foot. The neighborhood's layout allows for easy wandering between shops, cafés, and street art.

Visit on Weekends: Many vintage and indie stores are open on weekends, and the neighborhood often hosts markets and pop-up events that showcase local talent.

Check for Sales: Look out for sales and discounts, especially in vintage stores where you might find unique items at reduced prices.

Be Patient: Vintage shopping requires patience and a keen eye. Take your time to sift through items to find hidden gems.

Enjoy the Local Scene: Take breaks at local cafés, bars, or eateries. Williamsburg's food scene is as eclectic as its shopping, offering everything from artisanal coffee to trendy eateries.

Additional Information

Accessibility: Williamsburg is generally accessible, though some vintage shops in older buildings may have limited accessibility. It's a good idea to check ahead if you have specific needs.

Transport: Williamsburg is accessible via the L train (to Bedford Avenue) and several bus routes. Biking and walking are also popular ways to get around, and rideshares are readily available.

Chelsea Flea Markets

Chelsea Flea Markets, located in the Chelsea neighborhood of Manhattan, offer a unique and eclectic shopping experience for those seeking vintage finds, antiques, and one-of-a-kind treasures. These markets are known for their diverse range of goods, from mid-century furniture to rare collectibles, making them a must-visit destination for treasure hunters and vintage enthusiasts.

Key Attractions

Vintage and Antique Goods: The Chelsea Flea Markets are renowned for their extensive selection of vintage items and antiques. Shoppers can find everything from mid-century modern furniture and retro clothing to rare books, old records, and antique jewelry. Each stall is a curated collection of unique finds.

Local Artisans: In addition to vintage goods, the markets feature items from local artisans and craftspeople. This includes handmade jewelry, custom artwork, and unique home décor pieces, providing a chance to purchase something distinctive and locally made.

Eclectic Mix: The markets offer a mix of high-end antiques and affordable vintage items. This variety ensures that there is something for every budget and taste, whether you're looking for a statement piece or a small, quirky item.

Location and Hours

Location: The Chelsea Flea Markets are typically held in the Chelsea neighborhood, often near the Chelsea Market or along 6th Avenue and 25th Street. The exact location can vary, so it's a good idea to check online for current addresses or locations.

Hours: Flea markets usually operate on weekends, typically from 10 AM to 5 PM. Some markets may open earlier or close later, depending on the season and vendor schedules. It's advisable to check the market's website or social media for up-to-date hours and specific dates.

Cost

Entry: Most Chelsea Flea Markets are free to enter. Some specialized or larger markets may charge a small entry fee.

Goods: Prices vary widely depending on the item's rarity, condition, and vendor. Vintage and antique items can range from affordable to high-end, so be prepared to negotiate and explore different stalls for the best deals.

Payment

Accepted Methods: Most vendors at Chelsea Flea Markets accept major credit and debit cards, though some smaller or independent sellers may prefer cash. It's advisable to carry cash in small denominations just in case.

Negotiation: Many vendors are open to negotiation, especially on higher-priced items. Don't hesitate to make an offer or ask for a discount.

Tips for Visiting Chelsea Flea Markets

Arrive Early: To get the best selection and avoid crowds, try to arrive early when the market opens. Early birds often get first pick of the most unique items.

Wear Comfortable Shoes: The markets can be spread out, with lots of walking involved. Comfortable footwear will make your shopping experience more enjoyable.

Bring Cash: While many vendors accept cards, having cash on hand is useful for smaller purchases and vendors who only accept cash.

Check for Updates: Market locations and hours can change, so check online for the most current information before you go.

Explore All Stalls: The charm of flea markets is in discovering unexpected finds. Take your time to explore every stall and uncover hidden gems.

Additional Information

Accessibility: Most flea markets are accessible, though some stalls may be set up in areas with uneven surfaces. It's a good idea to check for specific accessibility features if needed.

Transport: Chelsea is well-connected by subway (C, E, 1, 2, 3 lines) and several bus routes. Walking and biking are also convenient options in this pedestrian-friendly neighborhood.

The Ultimate New York City Travel Guide (2025 Edition)

Shopping Malls and Department Stores

New York City is a shopper's paradise, offering everything from luxury boutiques and vintage finds to expansive shopping malls and iconic department stores. The city's shopping malls and department stores provide a convenient and comprehensive retail experience, featuring a wide range of brands and products under one roof. Whether you're looking for high-end fashion, electronics, or everyday essentials, NYC's malls and department stores have you covered.

Key Shopping Malls

The Shops at Columbus Circle: Located in the Time Warner Center at Columbus Circle, this upscale shopping mall offers a mix of high-end retailers like Michael Kors and Coach, as well as a range of dining options and specialty stores. It's conveniently situated with stunning views of Central Park.

Brookfield Place: This luxury shopping destination in Battery Park City features designer stores such as Gucci and Louis Vuitton. It's also known for its gourmet food options and beautiful views of the Hudson River.

Westfield World Trade Center: Situated within the Oculus, this modern shopping center offers a variety of retail options, including Apple, H&M, and more. The architectural design of the Oculus makes it a unique and visually striking shopping experience.

The Manhattan Mall: Located in Midtown, this mall provides a more traditional shopping experience with a mix of chain stores and department stores. It's a great option for those looking for a wide range of products in one location.

Empire Outlets: Located in Staten Island, this outlet mall offers discounts on designer brands such as Nike, Kate Spade, and Michael Kors. It's a bit off the beaten path but worth the trip for bargain hunters.

Key Department Stores

Macy's Herald Square: As one of the largest department stores in the world, Macy's Herald Square offers an extensive range of products, from clothing and accessories to home goods and beauty products. The store is famous for its elaborate window displays and annual Thanksgiving Day Parade.

Bloomingdale's: Located on 59th Street and Lexington Avenue, Bloomingdale's is known for its high-end fashion and stylish merchandise. The store also features a range of luxury beauty and home products.

Saks Fifth Avenue: A flagship store on Fifth Avenue, Saks Fifth Avenue offers a premier shopping experience with designer clothing, accessories, and beauty products. The store's holiday window displays are a major attraction.

Nordstrom: With a flagship location in Midtown, Nordstrom offers a wide variety of high-quality merchandise, including designer fashion, beauty products, and home goods. The store is known for its excellent customer service.

Bergdorf Goodman: Located on Fifth Avenue, Bergdorf Goodman is a luxury department store offering exclusive designer fashion, high-end accessories, and premium beauty products. It's a top choice for those seeking upscale shopping.

Cost

Shopping Malls: Prices vary depending on the store and the type of merchandise. Malls typically offer both high-end and more affordable options, catering to a range of budgets.

Department Stores: Similarly, department stores provide a wide range of price points. High-end designer items can be expensive, but there are also mid-range and budget-friendly options available.

Payment

Accepted Methods: Most malls and department stores accept major credit and debit cards. Some stores may also accept mobile payments like Apple Pay or Google Wallet.

Tax Refunds: International tourists may be eligible for tax refunds on certain purchases. Look for stores that offer tax-free shopping or ask about the process.

Tips for Shopping

Plan Your Visit: Shopping malls and department stores can be large and busy, especially during weekends and holidays. Plan your visit to avoid peak times and make the most of your shopping experience.

Check for Sales and Promotions: Many stores offer sales, promotions, and loyalty rewards. Keep an eye out for special deals and discounts to maximize your shopping value.

Take Advantage of Services: Many department stores offer personal shopping services, alterations, and gift wrapping. Don't hesitate to ask for assistance to enhance your shopping experience.

Explore Nearby Attractions: NYC's shopping malls and department stores are often located near other attractions. Take the opportunity to explore the surrounding area and enjoy the city's sights.

Additional Information

Accessibility: Most malls and department stores in NYC are wheelchair accessible and equipped with amenities for shoppers with disabilities. Check individual store or mall websites for specific accessibility features.

Transport: NYC's shopping malls and department stores are well-connected by public transportation, including subways and buses. Many are also accessible by walking or rideshare services.

Chapter 8: New York's Food and Nightlife

Must-Try Dishes in New York

1. **New York-Style Pizza**

New York-style pizza is characterized by its large, foldable slices and a crispy, yet chewy crust. It's typically sold by the slice in countless pizzerias across the city, making it a convenient snack for on-the-go exploration. Rooted in Italian immigrant traditions, New York-style pizza has evolved into something unique and beloved by both locals and visitors alike.

Main Ingredients

At its core, New York-style pizza uses a simple set of ingredients:

Dough – Made from high-gluten bread flour to create a chewy, yet crisp base.

Tomato sauce – Lightly seasoned with herbs like oregano, basil, and garlic.

Mozzarella cheese – Usually a low-moisture variety that provides the signature stretchiness.

Toppings – While a classic slice is just cheese, popular toppings include pepperoni, mushrooms, sausage, and more.

The balance between a thin, airy crust and a generous layer of cheese and sauce makes this pizza distinct and flavorful.

Where to Try New York-Style Pizza in New York

There are countless places to enjoy New York-style pizza, but here are some legendary pizzerias that are known for serving the best slices:

Joe's Pizza (Carmine Street) – A Greenwich Village institution, Joe's has been serving up classic slices since 1975. A great spot for an authentic taste of New York.

Lombardi's (Little Italy) – Often recognized as America's first pizzeria, Lombardi's has been a staple since 1905 and offers both whole pies and slices.

Prince Street Pizza (Nolita) – Famous for its spicy pepperoni squares, this spot is loved by both locals and tourists alike.

John's of Bleecker Street (West Village) – A no-slice pizzeria that serves whole pies, but the experience and flavor are well worth it.

Di Fara Pizza (Brooklyn) – Run by a legendary pizza maker, this Brooklyn pizzeria has been around for decades and is a pilgrimage spot for pizza enthusiasts.

What Makes New York-Style Pizza Special?

Several elements contribute to the unique nature of New York-style pizza:

The Crust: The perfect balance between crispy and chewy is due to the high-gluten dough and the city's tap water, which is said to give the crust its unique texture.

Slice Size: New York pizza slices are large, often so big that they are folded in half to eat easily. The foldable nature allows you to eat it on the go—a necessity in fast-paced NYC life.

Simple, High-Quality Ingredients: The use of minimal, fresh ingredients like whole-milk mozzarella and crushed tomatoes for the sauce makes the flavor shine without overwhelming the palate.

The Oven: New York-style pizza is traditionally cooked in a gas-powered oven that reaches high temperatures, which contributes to the crispy exterior of the crust while leaving the interior chewy and soft.

Tips for Enjoying New York-Style Pizza

Fold the Slice: To eat like a local, fold your slice down the middle. This not only makes it easier to eat on the go but also helps prevent any toppings from falling off.

Order by the Slice: Most places sell pizza by the slice, so take the opportunity to sample different toppings without committing to a whole pie. Try a classic cheese slice first to appreciate the basics.

Explore Neighborhood Spots: While famous spots like Joe's and Lombardi's are fantastic, you'll also find hidden gems in many neighborhoods. Don't be afraid to try a random pizzeria—you might find an unexpected favorite.

Eat It Fresh: The best way to enjoy New York pizza is right when it comes out of the oven. The cheese should be molten and stretchy, and the crust crispy yet pliable.

Pair It with a Drink: Many locals pair their pizza with a cold drink like soda or a classic New York egg cream for a traditional experience. Beer is also a popular option.

2. Bagels with Lox and Cream Cheese

Bagels with lox and cream cheese is a traditional dish that features a freshly baked bagel topped with smooth cream cheese and thinly sliced lox (cured salmon). It's often enjoyed as a hearty breakfast or brunch item but can be satisfying at any time of day. The dish embodies a harmonious blend of soft, chewy bagel, creamy cheese, and flavorful lox, making it a must-try for anyone visiting New York.

Main Ingredients

Bagel – Typically, a New York bagel is boiled before baking, which gives it a dense, chewy texture and a slightly crisp crust. Common varieties include plain, sesame, poppy seed, and everything bagels.

Cream Cheese – This soft, spreadable cheese is often used generously on the bagel. It's rich and creamy, providing a smooth base that complements the salty and savory lox.

Lox – Thinly sliced, cured salmon, often brined or smoked, adds a salty, umami flavor to the bagel. While traditional lox is made from salmon, variations like gravlax (cured with herbs) and nova (a milder smoked salmon) are also popular.

Accompaniments – Common additions include capers, red onion slices, tomato slices, and fresh dill. These ingredients enhance the overall flavor and add a bit of crunch and freshness.

Where to Try Bagels with Lox and Cream Cheese in New York

New York City boasts several legendary spots where you can experience this classic dish:

Russ & Daughters (Lower East Side) – A historic appetizing store established in 1914, known for its high-quality bagels, lox, and cream cheese. Their bagel with lox is a beloved classic.

Ess-a-Bagel (Murray Hill) – Famous for its oversized, freshly baked bagels. Their lox and cream cheese offerings are a highlight, with a range of options for lox and toppings.

H&H Bagels (Upper West Side) – Known for its authentic New York bagels, this spot offers a great bagel with lox and cream cheese in a classic deli setting.

Bagel Hole (Park Slope, Brooklyn) – A favorite among locals for its traditional approach to bagels and lox. Their bagels are small, dense, and satisfyingly chewy.

Kossar's Bagels & Bialys (Lower East Side) – A historic shop specializing in both bagels and bialys. Their lox and cream cheese is a staple of their menu.

What Makes Bagels with Lox and Cream Cheese Special?

The Bagel: New York bagels are boiled before baking, creating a dense and chewy texture that's hard to replicate elsewhere. The bagel's crust and crumb are integral to the dish's overall experience.

Quality of Lox: The lox used in New York is often of the highest quality, providing a delicate balance of saltiness and smokiness.

Cream Cheese: The smooth, rich cream cheese pairs perfectly with the lox, creating a creamy, flavorful base that complements the bagel.

Accompaniments: The addition of capers, onions, tomatoes, and dill adds layers of flavor and texture, enhancing the taste and making each bite more complex and satisfying.

Tips for Enjoying Bagels with Lox and Cream Cheese

Customize Your Bagel: While the classic combination is lox and cream cheese, feel free to add extras like capers, onions, tomatoes, or even cucumber for added freshness and crunch.

Freshness Matters: For the best experience, choose a bagel that's freshly baked. The texture and taste are significantly better with a warm, soft bagel.

Spread Generously: Don't be shy with the cream cheese. A generous layer enhances the overall flavor and ensures each bite is creamy and satisfying.

Pair with a Drink: Many people enjoy their bagels with a cup of coffee or tea. For an authentic New York experience, try it with a classic diner-style coffee or a fresh-squeezed orange juice.

Try Different Types of Lox: Depending on your taste, you might prefer traditional lox, gravlax, or nova. Each type offers a slightly different flavor profile.

3. New York Cheesecake

New York cheesecake is characterized by its smooth, dense filling, which is made from cream cheese, eggs, sugar, and vanilla, set atop a graham cracker crust. Unlike other types of cheesecake, which can be lighter or fluffier, New York cheesecake is known for its rich, creamy, and often tangy flavor profile. It's typically served plain or with simple toppings like fruit compote or a drizzle of chocolate.

Main Ingredients

Cream Cheese – The star of the show, providing the rich, creamy base that defines the cheesecake. High-fat cream cheese is preferred for its smooth texture and flavor.

Graham Cracker Crust – Made from crushed graham crackers, sugar, and butter, this crust adds a buttery crunch that complements the creamy filling.

Eggs – Essential for setting the filling, eggs contribute to the cheesecake's dense texture and structure.

Sugar – Sweetens the filling and balances the tanginess of the cream cheese.

Vanilla Extract – Adds a hint of warmth and depth to the flavor profile.

Sour Cream or Heavy Cream (optional) – Sometimes added to enhance the creaminess and richness of the filling.

Where to Try New York Cheesecake in New York

New York City is home to some legendary spots where you can enjoy a slice of classic New York cheesecake:

Junior's Restaurant & Bakery (Brooklyn) – Famous for its cheesecake since 1950, Junior's is a must-visit for any cheesecake aficionado. Their version is rich, creamy, and consistently highly praised.

Eileen's Special Cheesecake (SoHo) – Known for its smooth and dense cheesecake, Eileen's has been serving up delicious treats since 1975. Their variety of flavors and perfect texture make it a favorite.

Keki Modern Cakes (Chinatown) – While known for a variety of cakes, Keki's New York cheesecake is a standout with its classic flavor and light, yet creamy, texture.

The Cheesecake Factory (Various locations) – While a national chain, their New York-style cheesecake is a reliable option if you're looking for a classic experience.

Two Little Red Hens (Upper East Side) – This charming bakery is known for its homemade desserts, including a delightful New York cheesecake that's creamy and flavorful.

What Makes New York Cheesecake Special?

Richness and Density: Unlike many cheesecakes that can be light and airy, New York cheesecake is dense and rich, thanks to the high cream cheese content.

Smooth Texture: The creamy filling is smooth and luscious, with a perfect balance between sweetness and tanginess, often enhanced by the addition of sour cream or heavy cream.

Graham Cracker Crust: The buttery, crumbly crust adds a contrast to the rich filling and complements the overall flavor.

Classic Flavor Profile: The simplicity of the ingredients—cream cheese, eggs, sugar, and vanilla—creates a timeless flavor that is both comforting and indulgent.

Tips for Enjoying New York Cheesecake

Serve at the Right Temperature: For the best texture and flavor, let the cheesecake come to room temperature before serving. Cold cheesecake can be too firm and may mask the flavors.

Try Classic and Novel Toppings: While a plain New York cheesecake is delicious on its own, consider adding fresh fruit, a fruit compote, or a drizzle of caramel or chocolate sauce for extra flavor.

Pair with Coffee or Tea: A rich cheesecake pairs beautifully with a cup of coffee or tea, which can help balance the dessert's richness.

Savor Slowly: Because New York cheesecake is rich and dense, it's best enjoyed slowly to fully appreciate its creamy texture and flavor.

Look for Variations: Some bakeries offer unique twists on the classic recipe, such as adding swirls of chocolate or fruit or experimenting with different crusts. Exploring these variations can be a fun way to enjoy different takes on this classic dessert.

4. Pretzels

Pretzels originated in Europe, with roots tracing back to ancient Rome and later to medieval monasteries. They were traditionally baked from simple ingredients and shaped to resemble a figure of a person crossing their arms. In the U.S., particularly in New York, pretzels are most commonly found as soft, salty snacks sold by street vendors.

Main Ingredients

Dough – Made from flour, water, yeast, and salt. The dough is shaped into the iconic twisted form before baking.

Baking Soda Solution – Soft pretzels are briefly boiled in a baking soda solution before baking. This step gives pretzels their distinctive dark brown color and chewy texture.

Coarse Salt – Sprinkled on top of the pretzel before baking, giving it a salty, savory flavor that contrasts nicely with the dough.

Optional Toppings – Pretzels can be topped with various seasonings or ingredients, such as cinnamon sugar, cheese, or garlic.

Where to Try Pretzels in New York

New York City is known for its street food culture, and pretzels are a staple of that scene. Here are some great spots to enjoy pretzels in NYC:

Pretzel Boys (Various locations) – Known for their freshly baked soft pretzels, Pretzel Boys offers classic salted pretzels as well as creative variations like pretzel dogs and pretzel bites.

The Big Pretzel Company (Midtown) – A popular spot for classic New York-style pretzels. Their pretzels are freshly baked and sold at various locations around the city.

NYC Street Vendors – Numerous street vendors across Manhattan, especially in areas like Times Square, Central Park, and around major tourist spots, offer warm, soft pretzels.

Sigmund's Pretzels (East Village) – Known for artisanal pretzels with unique flavors, such as sesame and mustard pretzels, Sigmund's offers a gourmet take on the classic snack.

Mason Jar NYC (Murray Hill) – Offers pretzels along with a variety of American comfort foods. Their pretzels are served warm with various dips and mustards.

What Makes New York Pretzels Special?

Street Food Tradition: Pretzels are an integral part of New York's street food scene. The classic soft pretzel, often enjoyed on the go, is a symbol of the city's vibrant street food culture.

Chewy Texture: The boiling process in a baking soda solution gives New York pretzels their unique chewy texture and deep brown color.

Salty Crust: The coarse salt on top adds a delicious contrast to the soft, warm dough, making each bite flavorful and satisfying.

Accessibility: Pretzels are readily available from numerous street vendors, making them an easy and convenient snack for tourists and locals alike.

Tips for Enjoying Pretzels

Eat Warm: Pretzels are best enjoyed warm. If possible, get a fresh pretzel from a vendor or bakery to savor its chewy texture and flavor at its peak.

Try Different Dips: Many vendors offer pretzels with a variety of dips, such as mustard, cheese sauce, or even sweet options like cinnamon sugar. Experimenting with these can enhance your pretzel experience.

Pair with a Beverage: Pretzels pair well with a range of beverages, from sodas and lemonade to beer. In New York, you might find pretzels served with craft beer at local bars and breweries.

Explore Variations: While the classic salted pretzel is a must-try, don't hesitate to explore variations like pretzel bites, pretzel dogs, or pretzels with unique toppings and fillings.

Enjoy the Experience: Eating a pretzel from a street vendor is as much about the experience as it is about the food. Enjoy the bustling street scene and the convenience of grabbing a snack on the go.

5. Pastrami on Rye

Pastrami on rye is characterized by its generous layers of pastrami—seasoned and smoked beef—sandwiched between slices of rye bread. It is often served with mustard and sometimes pickles, creating a savory, tangy, and satisfying bite. This sandwich reflects New York's deep Jewish deli tradition and remains a favorite for its bold flavors and satisfying textures.

Main Ingredients

Pastrami – Cured and smoked beef, typically brisket, which is seasoned with a mix of spices and then cooked. The result is a flavorful, tender, and juicy meat that forms the heart of the sandwich.

Rye Bread – A dense, slightly tangy bread that provides a sturdy and flavorful base for the pastrami. It often comes in varieties like caraway or plain rye.

Mustard – A classic condiment that adds tanginess and complements the rich flavor of the pastrami. Yellow mustard is traditional, but deli-style or spicy brown mustard are also common.

Pickles (optional) – Often served on the side, pickles add a crunchy, tart contrast to the richness of the pastrami.

Where to Try Pastrami on Rye in New York

New York City is home to several iconic delis where you can enjoy an authentic pastrami on rye:

Katz's Delicatessen (Lower East Side) – Arguably the most famous deli in New York, Katz's has been serving up legendary pastrami on rye since 1888. The pastrami is hand-sliced to order, ensuring each sandwich is freshly made.

Carnegie Deli (Midtown) – Known for its large portions and classic deli fare, Carnegie Deli offers a hearty pastrami on rye that has been a staple since 1937. Although the original location has closed, their sandwiches are still available through various means, including online orders.

2nd Ave Deli (Upper East Side) – A beloved institution, 2nd Ave Deli serves a flavorful pastrami on rye with a generous amount of tender pastrami. They're known for their classic deli experience and high-quality ingredients.

Mile End Delicatessen (Brooklyn) – Offering a modern take on traditional Jewish deli fare, Mile End's pastrami on rye is made with house-cured meat and served with an array of fresh, flavorful condiments.

Ben's Kosher Delicatessen (Various locations) – A popular spot for kosher deli classics, Ben's serves up a delicious pastrami on rye with all the traditional accompaniments.

What Makes Pastrami on Rye Special?

Quality of Pastrami: The key to a great pastrami on rye is the quality of the pastrami. Tender, flavorful, and properly seasoned pastrami makes the sandwich stand out.

Rye Bread: The rye bread adds a distinctive flavor and texture that complements the pastrami. Its slight tanginess and dense crumb make it the ideal vessel for the meat.

Simple Ingredients, Bold Flavor: Despite its simplicity, the combination of well-seasoned pastrami, rye bread, and mustard creates a complex and satisfying flavor profile.

Tradition: Pastrami on rye reflects a rich culinary tradition rooted in New York's Jewish delis, representing a piece of the city's cultural and gastronomic history.

Tips for Enjoying Pastrami on Rye

Pair with Pickles: If pickles are offered, enjoy them on the side. Their acidity and crunch provide a perfect contrast to the richness of the pastrami.

Try Different Mustards: While yellow mustard is traditional, experimenting with different types like spicy brown or deli mustard can add new layers of flavor.

Enjoy Freshly Sliced: For the best experience, opt for pastrami that's sliced to order. Freshly sliced pastrami retains its juiciness and flavor better than pre-sliced varieties.

Consider the Size: Pastrami on rye sandwiches are often quite large. If you're not up for a whole sandwich, consider sharing or asking for a half portion.

Experience the Atmosphere: Part of the enjoyment of eating a pastrami on rye comes from the traditional deli experience. Take in the bustling atmosphere and enjoy the classic deli vibe.

The Ultimate New York City Travel Guide (2025 Edition)

Street Food and Food Trucks

New York City's street food and food trucks offer a vibrant and diverse culinary experience that reflects the city's multicultural makeup. From classic hot dogs and pretzels to gourmet tacos and artisanal dishes, these mobile eateries provide delicious, affordable, and convenient options for tourists exploring the city. Street food in NYC is not just a meal—it's a part of the city's culture and daily life.

Key Street Food and Food Truck Offerings

Hot Dogs: A quintessential New York street food, hot dogs are a quick and iconic choice. Vendors offer a variety of toppings, including mustard, sauerkraut, onions, and relish. Try a hot dog from **Gray's Papaya** or a street vendor for a classic NYC experience.

Pretzels: Soft, salty pretzels are another staple. Street vendors throughout the city sell these warm, chewy snacks, often accompanied by mustard. Look for vendors in busy areas like Central Park or near tourist attractions.

Halal Food: Halal carts serve up flavorful Middle Eastern dishes such as chicken and lamb over rice, often accompanied by salad and pita bread. **The Halal Guys** is a famous option with a cult following, but many other halal carts are scattered throughout the city.

Tacos and Burritos: Food trucks offering Mexican fare have become increasingly popular. You can find everything from classic tacos to gourmet burritos. **Los Tacos No. 1** in Chelsea Market is a notable destination, though many food trucks also offer delicious options.

Gourmet and Artisanal Options: The NYC food truck scene has expanded to include gourmet and artisanal dishes. Expect to find trucks offering everything from gourmet grilled cheese sandwiches and lobster rolls to specialty ice cream and fusion cuisine.

Popular Locations

Midtown Manhattan: The area around Bryant Park, Times Square, and the food trucks on 6th Avenue are bustling with options. These spots are ideal for grabbing a quick bite while sightseeing.

Food Truck Lots: Designated food truck lots, like those at **The Plaza Food Hall** or **The High Line**, feature a variety of trucks and carts, offering everything from international cuisine to unique culinary creations.

Markets and Festivals: Food trucks often gather at markets and festivals. **Smorgasburg** in Williamsburg and **Hester Street Fair** are popular venues where you can sample a range of street food and artisanal offerings.

Cost

Street Food: Generally affordable, with prices for items like hot dogs and pretzels typically ranging from $2 to $5. More substantial meals from food trucks or carts may cost between $7 to $15, depending on the dish.

Food Trucks: Prices can vary widely based on the type of food and the truck's specialty. Gourmet and artisanal options may be pricier, with dishes ranging from $10 to $20.

Payment

Accepted Methods: Many food trucks and street vendors accept major credit and debit cards, though some may prefer cash. It's always a good idea to carry a small amount of cash for those vendors who might not have card facilities.

Tips: It's customary to tip food truck and street food vendors, especially if you've received excellent service. A tip of $1 to $2 is generally appreciated.

Tips for Visiting

Check the Menu: Menus are often displayed on the truck or cart, so take a moment to review options and prices before ordering. This will help you make an informed choice and avoid surprises.

Observe the Lines: Popular food trucks and carts may have long lines. If you're short on time, look for trucks with shorter waits or try visiting during off-peak hours.

Explore Different Cuisines: NYC's street food scene is incredibly diverse. Don't hesitate to try something new and explore a variety of cuisines to get a true taste of the city.

Stay Safe: Ensure that the food truck or cart you choose follows basic hygiene practices. Look for clean and well-maintained vendors to ensure a safe and enjoyable eating experience.

Additional Information

Accessibility: Many food trucks are positioned in areas with good pedestrian access, but be aware of potential crowds and busy streets. If you have specific accessibility needs, check in advance to ensure that the vendor can accommodate you.

Transport: Street food vendors and food trucks are generally located in high-traffic areas accessible by subway, bus, or walking. Use public transportation to navigate the city efficiently and reach your desired food destinations.

The Ultimate New York City Travel Guide (2025 Edition)

Best Restaurants in NYC

1. Eleven Madison Park

Overview: Renowned for its innovative cuisine and elegant setting, Eleven Madison Park is a top destination for fine dining in NYC. The restaurant offers a tasting menu that emphasizes plant-based ingredients and creative presentations.

Location: 11 Madison Ave, New York, NY 10010

Cuisine: Modern American

Tip: Reservations are essential, and the restaurant typically books up well in advance. Prepare for a high-end dining experience with exceptional service and presentation.

2. Le Bernardin

Overview: A seafood lover's paradise, Le Bernardin is celebrated for its sophisticated seafood dishes and impeccable service. The restaurant offers a refined dining experience with dishes that highlight fresh, high-quality ingredients.

Location: 155 W 51st St, New York, NY 10019

Cuisine: French Seafood

Tip: Consider trying the chef's tasting menu for a complete experience of the restaurant's best offerings. The wine pairings are also highly recommended.

3. Katz's Delicatessen

Overview: An iconic NYC eatery, Katz's Delicatessen is famous for its classic pastrami on rye, as well as its classic deli fare. It's a must-visit for an authentic taste of New York's deli culture.

Location: 205 E Houston St, New York, NY 10002

Cuisine: Jewish Deli

Tip: Be prepared for a lively atmosphere and long lines, especially during peak hours. Order the pastrami on rye and enjoy it with a pickle on the side.

4. Momofuku Noodle Bar

Overview: Part of David Chang's Momofuku empire, the Noodle Bar offers a modern take on Asian cuisine with inventive dishes like ramen, pork buns, and noodles. The casual setting is perfect for a relaxed meal.

Location: 171 1st Avenue, New York, NY 10003

Cuisine: Asian Fusion

Tip: The pork buns and ramen are particularly popular, so make sure to try these standout dishes.

5. Per Se

Overview: Thomas Keller's Per Se is a Michelin-starred restaurant known for its exquisite tasting menus and luxurious dining experience. The restaurant offers a refined and meticulously crafted meal with stunning views of Columbus Circle.

Location: Time Warner Center, 10 Columbus Circle, New York, NY 10019

Cuisine: French

Tip: Reservations are necessary, and the tasting menu is a highlight. Prepare for a multi-course experience with exceptional attention to detail.

6. The Spotted Pig

Overview: Known for its gastropub fare and casual vibe, The Spotted Pig offers delicious dishes like its famous burger with Roquefort cheese. The restaurant's relaxed atmosphere makes it a great spot for a laid-back meal.

Location: 314 W 11th St, New York, NY 10014

Cuisine: Gastropub

Tip: The burger and shoestring fries are highly recommended, and the casual setting is ideal for a more relaxed dining experience.

7. Sushi Noz

Overview: For an authentic sushi experience, Sushi Noz offers a traditional omakase dining experience with an emphasis on high-quality, seasonal ingredients. The intimate setting and meticulous preparation make for an exceptional meal.

Location: 181 E 78th St, New York, NY 10075

Cuisine: Japanese Sushi

Tip: Reservations are essential for this exclusive dining experience. Enjoy the chef's selection of fresh, seasonal sushi.

8. The Nomad Bar

Overview: Known for its stylish setting and upscale bar menu, The Nomad Bar serves inventive cocktails and delicious bar fare, including dishes like foie gras sliders and roasted marrow bones.

Location: 1170 Broadway, New York, NY 10001

Cuisine: American Bar

Tip: The bar offers a sophisticated ambiance with a great selection of cocktails and small plates. It's an ideal spot for a pre-dinner drink or a casual meal.

9. Carbone

Overview: This classic Italian-American restaurant offers a nostalgic dining experience with its high-quality pastas and old-school ambiance. Carbone's signature dishes, like the spicy rigatoni vodka, are a must-try.

Location: 181 Thompson St, New York, NY 10012

Cuisine: Italian-American

Tip: Make reservations well in advance, as this popular spot fills up quickly. The veal parmesan and spicy rigatoni vodka are standout dishes.

10. Blue Hill

Overview: Focused on farm-to-table dining, Blue Hill emphasizes locally sourced ingredients and seasonal dishes. The restaurant offers a unique culinary experience with dishes crafted from sustainable, organic produce.

Location: 75 Washington Pl, New York, NY 10011

Cuisine: Farm-to-Table

Tip: The tasting menu is a great way to experience the restaurant's focus on local and seasonal ingredients.

Broadway Shows and Off-Broadway Productions

Broadway Shows

Broadway is the pinnacle of theater in the United States, featuring large-scale productions with high budgets, elaborate sets, and star-studded casts. The Broadway Theater District, centered around Times Square, is home to over 40 theaters showcasing a variety of musicals, dramas, and comedies.

Top Shows:

Hamilton: A revolutionary musical by Lin-Manuel Miranda that tells the story of Alexander Hamilton through a mix of hip-hop and traditional musical styles.

The Lion King: Disney's visually stunning musical adaptation of the beloved animated film, featuring elaborate costumes and memorable songs.

Wicked: A prequel to "The Wizard of Oz," this musical explores the backstory of the Wicked Witch of the West and Glinda the Good.

Phantom of the Opera: Andrew Lloyd Webber's classic musical about a mysterious phantom haunting an opera house.

Moulin Rouge! The Musical: A vibrant adaptation of the film that combines pop hits and elaborate choreography in a Parisian setting.

Cost:

Ticket Prices: Broadway tickets can range from $50 to $200 or more, depending on the show, seat location, and time of purchase.

Discounts: Look for discounts through sources like TKTS booths, Today Tix, or Rush Tickets. Some theaters offer lottery tickets for a chance to purchase seats at a reduced price.

Tips:

Book in Advance: Popular shows often sell out quickly, so it's advisable to book tickets well in advance.

Dress Code: There is no strict dress code, but smart casual attire is recommended.

Arrive Early: Allow extra time for security checks and finding your seat.

Off-Broadway Productions

Off-Broadway theaters offer a more intimate and often experimental theater experience. These productions tend to be smaller in scale but are known for their creativity and innovation. Theaters are located throughout Manhattan, with a concentration in neighborhoods like Greenwich Village and the East Village.

Top Productions:

The Play That Goes Wrong: A comedy about a theater troupe struggling through a disastrous play.

Blue Man Group: An interactive and visually captivating performance combining music, comedy, and multimedia.

Sleep No More: An immersive theater experience inspired by Shakespeare's "Macbeth," where audiences explore a multi-story set.

Avenue Q: A puppet-filled musical that satirizes adult themes with humor and heart.

The Band's Visit: A musical about an Egyptian band stranded in an Israeli town, known for its subtle storytelling and beautiful score.

Cost:

Ticket Prices: Off-Broadway shows are generally more affordable, with tickets ranging from $40 to $100.

Discounts: Discount options are often available through theater box offices, websites like Today Tix, or discount ticket services.

Tips:

Explore Smaller Venues: Off-Broadway theaters often provide unique, unconventional experiences. Check out smaller venues and productions for something different.

Flexible Scheduling: Off-Broadway productions may have more flexible scheduling and availability compared to Broadway.

Practical Information

Booking: Tickets for both Broadway and Off-Broadway shows can be purchased online, at the theater box office, or through authorized ticket sellers.

Location: Broadway theaters are primarily located in the Theater District around Times Square. Off-Broadway theaters are spread throughout Manhattan, particularly in Greenwich Village, the East Village, and the Lower East Side.

Transportation: Most theaters are easily accessible via subway, bus, or walking. Be sure to check the theater's location and plan your travel accordingly.

The Ultimate New York City Travel Guide (2025 Edition)

Music Venues: Jazz Clubs, Concert Halls, and Nightclubs

Jazz Clubs

1. Village Vanguard

Overview: One of the most iconic jazz clubs in NYC, the Village Vanguard has been showcasing top jazz talent since 1935. The intimate setting and exceptional acoustics make it a favorite for both performers and audiences.

Location: 178 7th Ave S, New York, NY 10014

Tip: Reservations are recommended, especially for popular shows. Arrive early to secure a good seat and enjoy the club's legendary atmosphere.

2. Blue Note

Overview: Known for hosting jazz legends and emerging artists, Blue Note offers a premier jazz experience with an upscale setting. The club features nightly performances and a full-service restaurant.

Location: 131 W 3rd St, New York, NY 10012

Tip: Check the schedule in advance and book tickets early. Dinner reservations are also available for a complete experience.

3. The Jazz Standard

Overview: The Jazz Standard offers a cozy and relaxed atmosphere with high-quality jazz performances. The club also serves a menu of Southern-inspired dishes, making it a great spot for both music and dining.

Location: 116 E 27th St, New York, NY 10016

Tip: Arrive early to enjoy dinner before the show, and consider trying the club's signature cocktails.

4. Smalls Jazz Club

Overview: A beloved spot for jazz aficionados, Smalls Jazz Club is known for its intimate vibe and spontaneous performances. The club features a rotating lineup of talented musicians in a relaxed setting.

Location: 183 Waverly Pl, New York, NY 10014

Tip: The venue operates on a cover charge basis, and it's a good idea to check the schedule online before visiting.

Concert Halls

1. Carnegie Hall

Overview: One of the world's most prestigious concert venues, Carnegie Hall hosts classical, jazz, and contemporary performances. Its stunning architecture and exceptional acoustics make it a must-visit for music lovers.

Location: 881 7th Ave, New York, NY 10019

Tip: Book tickets well in advance for popular performances. Take a guided tour to explore the hall's history and architecture.

2. Lincoln Center

Overview: Lincoln Center is a cultural complex housing several renowned venues, including the Metropolitan Opera House and Avery Fisher Hall. It's the epicenter of New York's classical and opera scene.

Location: Lincoln Center Plaza, New York, NY 10023

Tip: Check the schedule for a variety of performances, from opera and ballet to classical concerts. Tours are available for a behind-the-scenes look at this iconic venue.

3. The Apollo Theater

Overview: Located in Harlem, the Apollo Theater is famous for its rich history in showcasing African American artists. The venue hosts a mix of live music, comedy, and special events.

Location: 253 W 125th St, New York, NY 10027

Tip: Attend an Amateur Night for a taste of emerging talent, or catch a performance by a legendary artist.

4. Radio City Music Hall

Overview: Known for its Art Deco design and the annual Christmas Spectacular, Radio City Music Hall hosts a variety of performances including concerts, musicals, and special events.

Location: 1260 6th Ave, New York, NY 10020

Tip: Book tickets in advance for popular shows. The venue offers guided tours showcasing its history and architecture.

Nightclubs

1. Webster Hall

Overview: A historic nightclub and concert venue, Webster Hall features a range of live music performances, DJ sets, and dance parties. The venue has multiple rooms, each with its own unique vibe.

Location: 125 E 11th St, New York, NY 10003

Tip: Check the event schedule for live music and DJ sets. Dress to impress, as the nightclub has a stylish atmosphere.

2. Cielo

Overview: Known for its top-notch sound system and electronic music, Cielo is a favorite spot for dance enthusiasts. The club features a lineup of renowned DJs and a vibrant dance floor.

Location: 18 Little W 12th St, New York, NY 10014

Tip: Arrive early to avoid long lines and enjoy the best music. The club has a casual yet upscale dress code.

3. Le Bain

Overview: Located on the top floor of The Standard, High Line, Le Bain offers stunning views of the city, a rooftop bar, and a dance floor featuring eclectic music from international DJs.

Location: 848 Washington St, New York, NY 10014

Tip: Dress stylishly and arrive early for the best views and access to the rooftop area.

4. Lavo

Overview: Combining a restaurant and nightclub, Lavo is known for its upscale ambiance and high-energy parties. The venue features a mix of house music and popular DJs.

Location: 39 E 58th St, New York, NY 10022

Tip: Make a reservation if you plan to dine at the restaurant. Dress to impress for a night out in style.

Practical Information

Booking: Tickets for concerts and club events can be purchased online through venue websites, ticketing services, or at the door (if available). Reservations for clubs are recommended, especially for popular nights.

Transportation: Most music venues are accessible via subway, bus, or walking. Check the venue's location and plan your route accordingly.

Dress Code: Dress codes vary by venue. Jazz clubs and concert halls typically have a smart casual to formal dress code, while nightclubs often require stylish attire.

Comedy Clubs: The Stand, Comedy Cellar, and More

The Stand

Overview: The Stand is a premier comedy club known for its intimate atmosphere and high-quality performances. It regularly features top comedians and offers a mix of stand-up, improv, and special events. The club's laid-back vibe and excellent food and drink options make it a favorite among comedy lovers.

Location: 116 E 16th St, New York, NY 10003

Tip: Arrive early to get a good seat, especially on weekends. The club offers a variety of shows, so check their schedule online and book tickets in advance.

Comedy Cellar

Overview: The Comedy Cellar is one of NYC's most iconic comedy venues, renowned for its intimate setting and surprise appearances by big-name comedians. The club has a storied history of launching the careers of many famous comics and continues to be a favorite spot for comedy enthusiasts.

Location: 117 MacDougal St, New York, NY 10012

Tip: The Comedy Cellar often has a waitlist, so it's wise to book tickets ahead of time. The club features a rotating lineup, so you never know which famous comic might drop by.

Stand Up NY

Overview: Stand Up NY has been a staple in the NYC comedy scene since 1986. The club features a diverse lineup of comedians, from newcomers to seasoned performers, and offers a welcoming environment for comedy fans.

Location: 236 W 78th St, New York, NY 10024

Tip: Check their website for a schedule of upcoming shows and comedians. The club often has drink and food specials, making it a great spot for a night out.

Gotham Comedy Club

Overview: Gotham Comedy Club is known for its stylish atmosphere and high-profile comedians. The club hosts a mix of comedy events, including stand-up performances and comedy classes. It's a popular venue for both locals and visitors looking to enjoy a night of laughter.

Location: 208 W 23rd St, New York, NY 10011

Tip: Make reservations in advance to secure your spot. Gotham also has a full-service bar and restaurant, so you can enjoy a meal and drinks while you laugh.

The PIT (People's Improv Theater)

Overview: The PIT is a hub for improv and sketch comedy, offering a variety of shows from both seasoned performers and new talent. The theater also hosts comedy classes, making it a vibrant spot for comedy enthusiasts looking to explore different aspects of the craft.

Location: 123 E 24th St, New York, NY 10010

Tip: The PIT often features themed shows and special events, so check their schedule for unique and entertaining performances.

New York Comedy Club

Overview: New York Comedy Club offers a dynamic lineup of comedians in a classic comedy club setting. Known for its supportive environment and diverse acts, the club provides a platform for both emerging and established comics.

Location: 241 E 24th St, New York, NY 10010

Tip: The club often has drink specials and a friendly atmosphere, making it a great place for a night out with friends.

Practical Information

Booking: Tickets for comedy shows can be purchased online through the club's website or third-party ticketing services. Some venues also offer tickets at the door, but it's best to book in advance.

Transportation: Most comedy clubs are accessible via subway, bus, or walking. Check the venue's location and plan your route accordingly.

Dress Code: There is typically no strict dress code, but smart casual attire is recommended for a more polished look.

Grace Bennett

Chapter 9: Parks and Outdoor Activities in New York City

Exploring Central Park

Central Park is a vast 843-acre park designed by Frederick Law Olmsted and Calvert Vaux, opened in 1858. It stretches from 59th Street to 110th Street and from Fifth Avenue to Central Park West. The park offers a mix of natural landscapes, recreational facilities, and cultural attractions.

Top Attractions and Activities

1. Bethesda Terrace and Fountain

Overview: This two-level platform overlooks the Central Park's waterfront and features intricate stone carvings and the iconic Angel of the Waters statue.

Activity: Enjoy the views, take photos, or relax by the fountain.

2. Bow Bridge

Overview: A picturesque bridge with stunning views of the city skyline and the park's natural beauty.

Activity: Ideal for a romantic stroll or a perfect photo opportunity.

3. The Mall and Literary Walk

Overview: A wide, tree-lined promenade leading to a statue of Shakespeare and other literary figures.

Activity: Perfect for a leisurely walk, people-watching, or catching street performers.

4. Strawberry Fields

Overview: A memorial dedicated to John Lennon, featuring a mosaic with the word "Imagine."

Activity: Pay your respects, enjoy the peaceful ambiance, and listen to live music often performed by local musicians.

5. Central Park Zoo

Overview: A small but charming zoo located in the southeastern corner of the park.

Activity: Explore the exhibits featuring a range of animals, including penguins, sea lions, and more.

6. The Great Lawn

Overview: A sprawling open space ideal for picnicking, sports, and relaxation.

Activity: Play a game of baseball, have a picnic, or simply enjoy the sun and the view.

7. Conservatory Garden

Overview: A formal garden with beautifully landscaped floral displays and tranquil pathways.

Activity: Stroll through the various themed gardens, including a French-style garden and an Italian garden.

8. Central Park Reservoir

Overview: A large water body with a jogging track offering stunning views of the skyline and the park.

Activity: Go for a run, take a leisurely walk, or enjoy the beautiful scenery.

Practical Information

Location: Central Park spans from 59th Street to 110th Street, between Fifth Avenue and Central Park West.

Hours: The park is open daily from 6:00 AM to 1:00 AM. Individual attractions, like the Central Park Zoo, may have different operating hours.

Transportation:

Subway: Several subway lines have stations near Central Park, including the A, B, C, D, and 1 trains. The 59th Street/Columbus Circle and 72nd Street stations are close to the park.

Bus: Several city buses also stop near the park.

Walking/Biking: Central Park is easily accessible on foot or by bike. You can rent bikes from various locations around the park.

Tips for Visiting:

Plan Your Route: Central Park is vast, so plan your route according to the attractions you want to visit.

Dress Comfortably: Wear comfortable shoes for walking and dress in layers as the weather can change.

Stay Hydrated: Carry water, especially during warmer months, to stay hydrated.

Follow Park Rules: Respect park regulations, including leash laws for dogs and prohibitions on barbecuing or alcohol in certain areas.

The Ultimate New York City Travel Guide (2025 Edition)

Prospect Park and Brooklyn Green Spaces

Designed by Frederick Law Olmsted and Calvert Vaux, the same team behind Central Park, Prospect Park is a 585-acre urban oasis in the heart of Brooklyn. It's known for its scenic beauty, diverse recreational activities, and cultural events.

Top Attractions and Activities:

Prospect Park Lake:

Overview: A picturesque 60-acre lake that offers opportunities for boating and fishing.

Activity: Rent a rowboat or pedal boat and enjoy a leisurely paddle on the water.

The Long Meadow:

Overview: A vast open space ideal for sports, picnics, and relaxation.

Activity: Play soccer, have a picnic, or simply unwind on the grass.

Brooklyn Botanic Garden:

Overview: Located at the park's entrance, the garden features various plant collections and themed gardens.

Activity: Explore the Cherry Esplanade, Japanese Hill-and-Pond Garden, and other beautiful areas.

Prospect Park Zoo:

Overview: A small but engaging zoo featuring a variety of animals including sea lions, monkeys, and birds.

Activity: Visit animal exhibits and enjoy educational programs and events.

The Prospect Park Bandshell:

Overview: An outdoor amphitheater that hosts concerts, performances, and cultural events throughout the year.

Activity: Attend a live music performance or cultural event in a beautiful open-air setting.

The Prospect Park Audubon Center:

Overview: An educational center focused on birdwatching and conservation.

Activity: Participate in birdwatching programs, nature walks, and educational workshops.

Practical Information:

Location: The park is situated between Flatbush Avenue and Prospect Park West, and between Empire Boulevard and 9th Street.

Hours: Open daily from 6:00 AM to 1:00 AM.

Transportation: Accessible via subway (B, Q, S trains to Prospect Park Station or the 2, 5 trains to the Church Avenue Station) and various bus routes. Cycling and walking are also popular options.

Tips for Visiting:

Plan Your Visit: Check the park's calendar for events and activities.

Bring Essentials: Carry water, sunscreen, and a picnic blanket for a comfortable visit.

Explore Different Areas: Prospect Park is large, so consider exploring different sections to fully appreciate its beauty.

Other Notable Brooklyn Green Spaces

1. Brooklyn Bridge Park

Overview: A waterfront park stretching 1.3 miles along the East River with stunning views of the Manhattan skyline.

Highlights: Jane's Carousel, Pier 1 Playground, and the Brooklyn Bridge Park Conservancy.

Activities: Enjoy walking paths, sports fields, playgrounds, and seasonal events.

2. Fort Greene Park

Overview: A historic park featuring a large open space, sports facilities, and the Prison Ship Martyrs' Monument.

Highlights: Tennis courts, basketball courts, and the weekly farmers' market.

Activities: Engage in sports, visit the monument, or shop at the farmers' market.

3. McCarren Park

Overview: A popular park straddling the border between Williamsburg and Greenpoint, known for its sports facilities and open spaces.

Highlights: McCarren Park Pool, baseball fields, and playgrounds.

Activities: Swim, play sports, or enjoy a stroll through the park.

4. Marine Park

Overview: Brooklyn's largest park, offering a mix of natural landscapes, sports fields, and recreational areas.

Highlights: Salt Marsh Nature Center, golf course, and sports fields.

Activities: Explore the nature center, play a round of golf, or participate in outdoor sports.

Riverside Park and the Hudson River

Riverside Park is a 330-acre linear park that runs along the Hudson River. Designed by Frederick Law Olmsted and Calvert Vaux, the park features a mix of open spaces, sports facilities, and walking paths. Its location provides stunning views of the Hudson River and New Jersey across the river.

Top Attractions and Activities

1. Riverside Walkway

Overview: A scenic path running alongside the Hudson River, perfect for walking, jogging, or cycling.

Activity: Enjoy a leisurely walk or bike ride while taking in the beautiful river views and watching the boats pass by.

2. Grant's Tomb

Overview: The final resting place of Ulysses S. Grant, the 18th President of the United States, located at 122nd Street.

Activity: Visit this grand monument and learn about Grant's life and legacy. The tomb is set within a picturesque park area.

3. The Soldiers' and Sailors' Monument

Overview: A historic monument dedicated to the Union soldiers and sailors who served in the Civil War, located at 89th Street.

Activity: Admire the impressive architecture and sculptures, and reflect on the park's historical significance.

4. Riverside Park South

Overview: The southern portion of Riverside Park, recently renovated with modern amenities including playgrounds, sports courts, and seating areas.

Activity: Use the sports facilities, let children play in the playground, or relax in the newly designed spaces.

5. Pier I Café

Overview: A café located at 70th Street on the Hudson River waterfront, offering casual dining with great views.

Activity: Enjoy a meal or a drink while taking in the panoramic views of the river and the New Jersey skyline.

6. Boat Basin

Overview: A marina located at 79th Street, where you can see a variety of boats and yachts docked.

Activity: Take a stroll around the basin, enjoy the maritime atmosphere, or watch the boats come and go.

Practical Information

Location: Riverside Park runs from 72nd Street to 158th Street, between the Hudson River and the city streets of Manhattan.

Hours: The park is open daily from 6:00 AM to 1:00 AM. Individual facilities, like the Boat Basin or Pier I Café, have their own operating hours.

Transportation:

Subway: Accessible via the 1, 2, or 3 trains, with several stations near the park (e.g., 72nd Street, 86th Street, 96th Street).

Bus: Several city buses serve the area, including the M11 and M57.

Walking/Biking: Riverside Park is a popular spot for walking and biking, with dedicated paths and entrances throughout the park.

Tips for Visiting:

Plan Your Route: The park is long and narrow, so plan which sections you want to explore.

Bring Essentials: Pack water, snacks, and sunscreen, especially if you plan to spend a lot of time outdoors.

Check Event Schedules: Riverside Park often hosts events and performances, so check the park's calendar for any activities during your visit.

The High Line and Elevated Urban Parks

The High Line is a 1.45-mile-long elevated park built on a historic freight rail line that runs from Gansevoort Street in the Meatpacking District to 34th Street in the Hudson Yards neighborhood. Opened in phases from 2009 to 2014, the park is renowned for its creative design and integration of natural elements into an urban setting.

Top Attractions and Features:

Gardens and Greenery:

Overview: The High Line features a mix of wildflowers, grasses, and trees, designed to mimic the park's original, semi-wild state.

Activity: Stroll through the beautifully landscaped areas and enjoy seasonal blooms and foliage.

Art Installations:

Overview: The park hosts various public art installations and sculptures by contemporary artists.

Activity: Explore rotating exhibitions and permanent artworks displayed along the walkway.

Viewing Platforms:

Overview: Several elevated platforms and overlooks provide stunning views of the Hudson River, city skyline, and surrounding neighborhoods.

Activity: Stop at these spots for panoramic photography opportunities and to take in the urban landscape.

The High Line Food Vendors:

Overview: The park features food vendors offering a range of snacks and beverages.

Activity: Grab a bite to eat or enjoy a refreshing drink while taking a break from your walk.

The Spur:

Overview: An expansion at the southern end of the High Line, featuring a circular open space with seating and views of the surrounding city.

Activity: Relax in the open area and enjoy the unique design and urban views.

Practical Information:

Location: The High Line stretches from Gansevoort Street to 34th Street, between 10th and 11th Avenues.

Hours: Open daily from 7:00 AM to 10:00 PM. Hours may vary seasonally.

Admission: Free to the public.

Transportation:

Subway: Accessible via the 14th Street/8th Avenue (L train) or 34th Street/Herald Square (B, D, F, M, N, Q, R trains) stations.

Bus: Several city buses serve the area, including the M11 and M14.

Walking/Biking: Easily accessible by foot and bike, with bike racks available nearby.

Tips for Visiting:

Visit Early or Late: To avoid crowds, consider visiting early in the morning or later in the evening.

Check for Events: The High Line often hosts events and tours. Check the park's website for schedules and activities.

Wear Comfortable Shoes: Expect to walk a lot, so comfortable footwear is recommended.

Other Elevated Urban Parks

1. The Promenade

Overview: An elevated park in Brooklyn Heights offering stunning views of the Manhattan skyline and the Brooklyn Bridge.

Features: Scenic walkways, benches, and historical plaques.

Activity: Enjoy a leisurely walk and take in the iconic city views.

2. The Rail Park (Philadelphia)

Overview: An ongoing project similar to the High Line, transforming an old rail line into an elevated green space.

Features: Planned to include gardens, pathways, and community spaces.

Activity: Explore the development and enjoy the green space once completed.

3. The Bloomingdale Trail (Chicago)

Overview: An elevated trail converted from an old rail line into a linear park known as "The 606."

Features: Walking and biking paths, parks, and community spaces.

Activity: Walk or bike along the trail and visit the various park areas and public art installations.

The Ultimate New York City Travel Guide (2025 Edition)

Biking in NYC: Best Routes and Bike Rentals

New York City is increasingly becoming a bike-friendly city with an expanding network of bike lanes, trails, and bike-sharing programs. Whether you're a local or a visitor, biking is an excellent way to explore the city's diverse neighborhoods and iconic landmarks. Here's a guide to the best biking routes and bike rental options in NYC:

Best Biking Routes in NYC

The Hudson River Greenway

Overview: This dedicated bike path runs from Battery Park in the southern tip of Manhattan to the George Washington Bridge in the northern part of the city.

Highlights: Scenic river views, parks, piers, and landmarks such as the High Line and Chelsea Piers.

Length: Approximately 11 miles.

Tip: Enjoy a leisurely ride with frequent spots to stop and take in the views or grab a bite.

Central Park Loop

Overview: A 6-mile loop around Central Park offering varied terrain, including flat paths and hilly sections.

Highlights: Iconic landmarks like Bethesda Terrace, the Great Lawn, and the Jacqueline Kennedy Onassis Reservoir.

Length: 6 miles.

Tip: The loop is closed to cars on weekends, making it safer for cyclists.

Brooklyn Bridge to Prospect Park

Overview: Start at the Brooklyn Bridge and ride through Brooklyn Heights, DUMBO, and into Prospect Park.

Highlights: Stunning views from the Brooklyn Bridge, historic neighborhoods, and the beautiful green spaces of Prospect Park.

Length: Approximately 6-7 miles.

Tip: Make sure to use the dedicated bike path on the Brooklyn Bridge for a safer and more enjoyable ride.

The East River Greenway

Overview: Runs from Battery Park to 125th Street along the eastern edge of Manhattan.

Highlights: Views of the East River, Roosevelt Island, and the Queens waterfront.

Length: Approximately 9 miles.

Tip: Enjoy a quieter ride compared to the Hudson River Greenway, especially in the northern sections.

The Bronx River Greenway

Overview: A scenic route along the Bronx River, connecting various parks and natural areas.

Highlights: Beautiful river views, nature reserves, and the Bronx Zoo.

Length: Approximately 8 miles.

Tip: Ideal for those looking to explore a less touristy part of NYC.

Bike Rentals in NYC

Citi Bike

Overview: NYC's bike-sharing program with thousands of bikes available at hundreds of stations throughout the city.

Cost: Single ride ($4.50 for a 30-minute ride), Day pass ($12 for unlimited 30-minute rides), Monthly membership options available.

How to Rent: Use the Citi Bike app or visit a bike station. Bikes can be picked up and dropped off at any station.

Website: Citi Bike

Bike Rental NYC

Overview: Offers a range of rental options including standard bikes, electric bikes, and tandem bikes.

Cost: Prices start at around $30 for a 24-hour rental.

How to Rent: Book online or visit one of their locations.

Website: Bike Rental NYC

Unlimited Biking

Overview: Provides bike rentals, guided tours, and bike accessories.

Cost: Starting at approximately $20 for a 1-hour rental.

How to Rent: Online booking or at their rental shops.

Website: Unlimited Biking

Central Park Bike Rentals

Overview: Specializes in rentals for exploring Central Park, including options for guided tours.

Cost: Rentals start at around $15 for 1 hour.

How to Rent: Book online or visit their shop near Central Park.

Website: Central Park Bike Rentals

Get Up and Ride

Overview: Offers a range of bike rentals and guided tours with a focus on personalized service.

Cost: Around $25 for a 2-hour rental.

How to Rent: Online booking or visit their location.

Website: Get Up and Ride

Tips for Biking in NYC

Obey Traffic Rules: Follow traffic signals, bike lane markings, and be aware of pedestrians and vehicles.

Wear a Helmet: Safety first—helmets are highly recommended.

Use Bike Lanes: Stick to bike lanes where available, and be cautious in areas without designated paths.

Stay Hydrated: Bring water, especially on hot days.

Check the Weather: NYC weather can be unpredictable; dress appropriately and check for any rain or severe weather warnings.

Beaches near New York City

1. Coney Island Beach

Overview: Coney Island Beach is one of the most iconic and accessible beaches near NYC. Located in Brooklyn, it offers a classic seaside experience with a lively boardwalk and amusement park.

Location: Coney Island, Brooklyn, NY.

Distance from NYC: Approximately 30 minutes by subway from Manhattan (D, F, N, or Q trains).

Highlights:

Coney Island Boardwalk: A bustling area with food vendors, games, and attractions.

Luna Park: An amusement park with rides and entertainment.

Nathan's Famous: Try the famous hot dogs at the historic stand.

Tips:

Visit early to secure a good spot on the sand.

Check for events and special activities, especially during summer weekends.

2. Rockaway Beach

Overview: Rockaway Beach, located in Queens, offers a less crowded, relaxed atmosphere compared to some of the other nearby beaches. It's popular among locals and surfers.

Location: Rockaway Peninsula, Queens, NY.

Distance from NYC: Approximately 1 hour by subway (A train) or a 45-minute drive.

Highlights:

Surfing: Known for its good surf conditions.

Boardwalk: A newly renovated boardwalk ideal for walking and biking.

Food: Enjoy local food trucks and casual dining spots.

Tips:

Bring your own equipment if you plan to surf.

Check the subway schedules, as service can be less frequent on weekends.

3. Brighton Beach

Overview: Adjacent to Coney Island, Brighton Beach is known for its vibrant Russian community and quieter, more laid-back environment compared to its neighbor.

Location: Brighton Beach, Brooklyn, NY.

Distance from NYC: Approximately 35 minutes by subway from Manhattan (B or Q trains).

Highlights:

Cultural Experience: Explore Russian markets and eateries along Brighton Beach Avenue.

Beachfront: Enjoy a more relaxed and family-friendly atmosphere.

Tips:

Sample the local Russian cuisine in the surrounding area.

Bring a light jacket for cooler evenings as the breeze from the water can be chilly.

4. Jacob Riis Park

Overview: Part of the Gateway National Recreation Area, Jacob Riis Park offers a broad, sandy beach with plenty of space for relaxation and various recreational activities.

Location: Queens, NY, within the Gateway National Recreation Area.

Distance from NYC: Approximately 1 hour by subway (A train) or a 45-minute drive.

Highlights:

Historic Bathhouse: Features a historic bathhouse and concessions.

Wide Beach: Plenty of space for sunbathing and beach games.

Fishing: Fishing is permitted on the beach.

Tips:

Parking can be challenging on busy days, so consider taking public transportation.

Check the schedule for any park events or activities.

5. Sandy Hook

Overview: Located in New Jersey, Sandy Hook is part of the Gateway National Recreation Area and offers a mix of natural beauty and beach amenities. It's a bit farther but worth the trip for its scenic views and less crowded beaches.

Location: Sandy Hook, New Jersey.

Distance from NYC: Approximately 1 to 1.5 hours by car or public transportation (New Jersey Transit train to Middletown and then a short bus ride).

Highlights:

Beaches: Several beaches to choose from with beautiful views of the New York Harbor.

Historical Sites: Visit Fort Hancock and the Sandy Hook Lighthouse.

Wildlife: Great for bird-watching and enjoying natural landscapes.

Tips:

Bring your own beach gear as amenities can be limited.

Consider visiting during weekdays to avoid weekend crowds.

Grace Bennett

The Ultimate New York City Travel Guide (2025 Edition)

Chapter 10: Day Trips and Excursions

Long Island: Beaches and Vineyards

Getting to Long Island

By Car:

Overview: The most flexible way to explore Long Island is by car, allowing you to visit multiple destinations at your own pace.

Driving Route: Take the Long Island Expressway (I-495) east from Queens. For a more scenic route, consider taking Route 27, which runs parallel to the South Shore.

Parking: Most beaches and vineyards have designated parking lots, but be prepared for a fee during peak season.

By Train:

Overview: The Long Island Rail Road (LIRR) offers convenient train service from Penn Station in Manhattan to various destinations on Long Island.

Routes: Direct trains to popular spots like Montauk, Huntington, and Riverhead. Check schedules and plan accordingly to maximize your day.

Tickets: Purchase tickets in advance or at the station. Consider a day pass for unlimited travel if planning to visit multiple locations.

By Bus:

Overview: Several bus services operate routes from NYC to Long Island.

Routes: Look for services such as the Hampton Jitney or the Long Island Bus. These buses often offer direct routes to major towns and attractions.

Tickets: Buy tickets in advance online or at the bus terminal.

Beaches on Long Island

1. Jones Beach State Park

Location: Wantagh, NY.

Distance: Approximately 40 miles east of Manhattan; about a 1-hour drive or 1.5 hours by train (LIRR to Wantagh).

Overview: A classic Long Island destination with a wide, sandy beach and a 2.5-mile boardwalk.

Activities: Swimming, sunbathing, beach volleyball, and a large picnic area. The park also features a mini-golf course and a nature center.

Tips: Arrive early to secure parking as it fills up quickly on weekends. Entrance fees apply during peak season.

2. Montauk Beach

Location: Montauk, NY, at the eastern tip of Long Island.

Distance: Approximately 115 miles from Manhattan; about a 2.5-hour drive or 3 hours by train (LIRR to Montauk).

Overview: Known for its picturesque views and less crowded atmosphere. Ideal for a more relaxed beach experience.

Activities: Surfing, fishing, and exploring the nearby Montauk Lighthouse.

Tips: Check train schedules in advance, as trips can be longer. Bring sunscreen and a hat for sun protection.

3. Robert Moses State Park

Location: Babylon, NY.

Distance: About 50 miles from Manhattan; roughly a 1-hour drive or 1.5 hours by train (LIRR to Babylon, then bus or taxi).

Overview: A large park with several miles of beach, including designated areas for swimming and fishing.

Activities: Swimming, kite-flying, and beachcombing. The park also has a golf course and picnic areas.

Tips: Parking fees apply. Consider visiting the park's observation tower for panoramic views.

Vineyards on Long Island

1. North Fork Wine Region

Location: The North Fork of Long Island, accessible via Route 25.

Distance: Approximately 80 miles from Manhattan; about a 1.5-hour drive or 2 hours by train (LIRR to Riverhead, then taxi or rideshare).

Overview: Known for its charming wineries and picturesque landscapes. The region is less commercialized compared to the Hamptons, offering a more relaxed wine tasting experience.

Popular Wineries:

Bedell Cellars: Renowned for its high-quality wines and beautiful tasting room.

Macari Vineyards: Offers a range of wines and stunning views of the vineyards.

Jamesport Vineyards: Known for its friendly staff and diverse wine selection.

Activities: Wine tastings, vineyard tours, and enjoying local gourmet food. Many wineries also offer outdoor seating and live music.

2. Hamptons Wine Region

Location: The Hamptons, particularly in Southampton and East Hampton.

Distance: Approximately 100 miles from Manhattan; about a 2-hour drive or 2.5 hours by train (LIRR to East Hampton, then taxi or rideshare).

Overview: The Hamptons offer upscale wineries with a more luxurious ambiance and often higher prices.

Popular Wineries:

Wölffer Estate Vineyard: Known for its Rosé and beautiful estate.

Channing Daughters Winery: Offers a range of unique wines and a welcoming atmosphere.

Pindar Vineyards: A large vineyard with a variety of wines and events.

Activities: Wine tastings, vineyard tours, and enjoying the upscale amenities of the Hamptons.

Tips for a Successful Day Trip

Plan Ahead: Check the opening hours and availability of the beaches and vineyards you plan to visit. Some wineries require reservations for tastings.

Dress Appropriately: Wear comfortable clothing and shoes for walking and consider bringing a hat and sunscreen for beach visits.

Bring Essentials: Pack essentials like water, snacks, and a camera. If visiting the vineyards, consider bringing a cooler for any purchases.

Stay Hydrated and Eat Well: Both the beach and wine tastings can be dehydrating, so drink plenty of water and eat a balanced meal.

Use Public Transport: If you don't plan to drive, use public transport options to reach Long Island. Arrange for taxis or rideshares in advance for convenience.

The Hamptons: Luxury Getaway

Getting to The Hamptons

By Car:

Overview: Driving to The Hamptons provides flexibility and convenience, allowing you to explore the area at your own pace.

Driving Route: Take the Long Island Expressway (I-495) east from Manhattan and then follow Route 27 south to reach the various towns and beaches.

Parking: Many upscale resorts and restaurants offer valet parking. Public parking is available at most beaches, though it can be limited and expensive during peak season.

By Train:

Overview: The Long Island Rail Road (LIRR) offers direct service from Penn Station in Manhattan to several Hamptons destinations.

Routes: Direct trains run to towns such as Southampton, East Hampton, and Montauk.

Tickets: Purchase tickets in advance, especially during the summer season. Consider a day pass for unlimited travel if planning multiple stops.

By Bus:

Overview: Several bus services provide routes from NYC to The Hamptons.

Routes: Services like the Hampton Jitney and Hampton Luxury Liner offer comfortable rides with multiple stops in The Hamptons.

Tickets: Buy tickets online or at the terminal. These buses often provide amenities like Wi-Fi and refreshments.

Top Attractions and Activities

1. Luxury Beaches

Main Beach, East Hampton:

Overview: Known for its soft sand and clean waters, Main Beach is one of the most prestigious beaches in the Hamptons.

Amenities: Lifeguards, restrooms, and seasonal beach services.

Tips: Arrive early to find a good spot and be prepared for a beach fee during peak season.

Coopers Beach, Southampton:

Overview: Offers stunning views of the Atlantic Ocean and is renowned for its serene atmosphere.

Amenities: Restrooms, showers, and lifeguards.

Tips: Bring beach chairs and an umbrella for added comfort. Parking is available but can be expensive.

2. Upscale Dining

The American Hotel, Sag Harbor:

Overview: An elegant restaurant offering classic American cuisine in a historic setting.

Specialties: Known for its seafood and fine dining experience.

Reservations: Highly recommended, especially on weekends.

Nick & Toni's, East Hampton:

Overview: A popular spot for gourmet Italian fare with a chic, relaxed ambiance.

Specialties: Fresh pasta, seafood, and a well-curated wine list.

Reservations: Essential, as the restaurant is a local favorite.

3. Luxury Shopping

Sag Harbor Village:

Overview: A quaint village with upscale boutiques and art galleries.

Highlights: High-end shops, unique art pieces, and local crafts.

Tips: Browse for unique gifts and luxury items in a charming setting.

East Hampton Village:

Overview: Features an array of designer stores and upscale shops.

Highlights: High fashion boutiques, home decor stores, and luxury goods.

Tips: Take your time exploring the various shops and enjoy a coffee at a local café.

4. Wine Tasting

Wölffer Estate Vineyard:

Overview: Famous for its Rosé and picturesque setting.

Experience: Enjoy wine tastings in a beautifully designed tasting room.

Reservations: Recommended for tastings and tours.

Channing Daughters Winery:

Overview: Offers a diverse range of wines and a welcoming atmosphere.

Experience: Tasting flights and vineyard tours available.

Reservations: Check availability in advance for a personalized experience.

5. Cultural Experiences

Guild Hall, East Hampton:

Overview: A cultural institution featuring art exhibitions, theater, and concerts.

Highlights: Art galleries, performances, and educational programs.

Tips: Check the schedule for current exhibitions and events.

The Parrish Art Museum, Water Mill:

Overview: Showcases American art with a focus on artists from the East End.

Highlights: Art exhibitions, educational programs, and beautiful architecture.

Tips: Spend a few hours exploring the galleries and enjoying the museum grounds.

Tips for a Luxurious Experience

Plan Ahead: Make reservations for dining and activities well in advance, especially during peak season.

Dress the Part: Embrace the Hamptons' stylish vibe with elegant beachwear, resort attire, and chic evening outfits.

Pack Wisely: Bring essentials like sunscreen, a hat, and comfortable shoes for exploring.

Check Traffic and Train Schedules: Traffic can be heavy during weekends, and train schedules can vary, so plan your journey accordingly.

Hudson Valley and Catskills

Getting to Hudson Valley and the Catskills

By Car:

Overview: Driving offers the flexibility to explore various spots at your own pace.

Driving Route: From NYC, take I-87 North (the New York State Thruway) to reach the Hudson Valley and Catskills.

Parking: Most towns and attractions offer public parking. Look for designated parking areas, especially in popular spots.

By Train:

Overview: Amtrak and Metro-North Railroad provide convenient train services to different areas in the Hudson Valley.

Routes:

Amtrak: Offers service to Hudson and Rhinecliff stations.

Metro-North: The Hudson Line reaches places like Cold Spring and Beacon.

Tickets: Purchase tickets in advance to ensure availability and get the best fares.

By Bus:

Overview: Several bus services operate routes from NYC to Hudson Valley and Catskills destinations.

Routes: Look for buses operated by companies like Trailways or ShortLine. They offer routes to key towns in the region.

Tickets: Buy tickets online or at the bus terminal. Check schedules as services can vary.

Exploring Hudson Valley

1. Beacon

Overview: Beacon is known for its vibrant arts scene and beautiful natural surroundings.

Activities:

Dia: A contemporary art museum housed in a former factory, featuring large-scale installations and artworks.

Mount Beacon: Hike up for panoramic views of the Hudson Valley and the Hudson River.

Dining: Enjoy farm-to-table dining at local restaurants like The Roundhouse or Kitchen Sink.

2. Cold Spring

Overview: A quaint village with historic charm and scenic views of the Hudson River.

Activities:

Hudson Highlands State Park: Offers hiking trails with stunning river views.

Cold Spring's Main Street: Explore unique shops, antique stores, and cozy cafes.

Dining: Grab a meal at local favorites such as The Iron Vine or The Cold Spring Depot.

3. Rhinebeck

Overview: Rhinebeck is known for its historic architecture and cultural attractions.

Activities:

The Dutchess County Fairgrounds: Check for events and fairs happening during your visit.

Omega Institute: Offers workshops and retreats in a beautiful setting.

Dining: Enjoy farm-to-table cuisine at places like The Beekman Arms or Gaskins.

Exploring the Catskills

1. Woodstock

Overview: Famous for its artistic vibe and historic association with the 1969 music festival.

Activities:

Woodstock's Art Scene: Visit local galleries and craft shops.

Karma Triyana Dharmachakra: A Tibetan Buddhist monastery offering peaceful grounds and cultural experiences.

Dining: Try local eateries such as Cucina or The Bear Café.

2. Hunter

Overview: Hunter is a popular destination for outdoor enthusiasts, particularly in winter for skiing and snowboarding.

Activities:

Hunter Mountain: Offers skiing, snowboarding, and scenic gondola rides.

Kaaterskill Falls: A stunning two-tiered waterfall with an easy hike to reach it.

Dining: Enjoy a meal at local spots like The Prospect or The Last Chance.

3. Phoenicia

Overview: A charming town known for its outdoor activities and natural beauty.

Activities:

The Esopus Creek: Perfect for tubing, kayaking, or fishing.

Hiking: Explore nearby trails for various difficulty levels and scenic views.

Dining: Check out local favorites like Brio's or The Phoenicia Diner.

Tips for a Successful Day Trip

Plan Ahead: Check train schedules, road conditions, and attraction hours. Some places may require advance reservations, especially for dining.

Dress Appropriately: Wear comfortable clothing and sturdy shoes for hiking and exploring. Bring layers as temperatures can vary.

Bring Essentials: Pack water, snacks, sunscreen, and a camera. If you plan on hiking, bring appropriate gear and a map.

Stay Hydrated and Eat Well: Enjoy local cuisine and stay hydrated, especially if you're engaging in outdoor activities.

Bear Mountain State Park

Bear Mountain State Park is a sprawling natural area that features scenic views, rugged terrain, and various recreational facilities. Established in 1913, it is one of the oldest state parks in New York and remains a popular destination for both locals and visitors.

Location

Address: 55 Hessian Drive, Bear Mountain, NY 10911

Distance from NYC: Approximately 50 miles north of Manhattan, about a 1-hour drive.

Getting There

By Car:

Overview: The most convenient way to reach Bear Mountain State Park is by car.

Directions: Take I-87 North (New York State Thruway) to Exit 15A, then follow Route 9W north to the park entrance.

Parking: The park has several parking lots near the main attractions, including the Bear Mountain Inn and trailheads.

By Public Transportation:

Overview: If you prefer public transport, you can take a train or bus, followed by a short taxi or rideshare ride.

Train: Take the Metro-North Hudson Line from Grand Central Terminal to Peekskill or Harriman Station, then take a taxi or rideshare to the park.

Bus: The Short Line Bus provides service from NYC to the park area, but you'll need to check schedules and connections.

Activities and Attractions

1. Hiking and Trails

Overview: Bear Mountain offers over 50 miles of hiking trails with varying levels of difficulty. The trails provide stunning views of the Hudson River and surrounding landscape.

Popular Trails:

Appalachian Trail: A segment of the famous trail passes through Bear Mountain, offering a challenging hike with rewarding views.

Bear Mountain Loop Trail: A moderate trail that circles the mountain and provides scenic overlooks.

Hessian Lake Trail: A shorter, easy trail around the lake that's perfect for a leisurely stroll.

2. Scenic Views and Lookouts

Bear Mountain Summit: The summit offers panoramic views of the Hudson River Valley and the surrounding mountains. It's accessible via several trails and is a popular spot for photos.

The Perkins Memorial Tower: Located at the summit, this stone tower provides an even higher vantage point with spectacular views. It's a great place to take in the landscape.

3. Recreational Facilities

Bear Mountain Inn: The historic inn offers dining options and a visitor center. It's a good place to stop for a meal or learn more about the park's history and wildlife.

Lake and Boating: Hessian Lake provides opportunities for picnicking and boating. While motorboats are not permitted, rowboats and canoes are available for rent.

Playground and Picnic Areas: Several designated areas for picnicking and playgrounds are scattered throughout the park.

4. Wildlife Watching

Overview: Bear Mountain is home to a variety of wildlife, including deer, wild turkeys, and various bird species. Bring binoculars for a chance to observe animals in their natural habitat.

Practical Information

Park Hours: The park is open daily from dawn to dusk. The Bear Mountain Inn and other facilities have varying hours, so check in advance.

Admission Fees: There is a parking fee for visitors. The fee varies by season and can be paid at designated kiosks.

Restrooms: Restrooms are available at the Bear Mountain Inn and several other locations within the park.

Tips for Visiting

Plan Ahead: Review trail maps and park information before your visit. Some trails may be more challenging or have specific entry points.

Wear Appropriate Gear: Bring comfortable hiking shoes, weather-appropriate clothing, and plenty of water. Trails can be rugged and weather conditions can change rapidly.

Check Weather: Weather conditions can affect trail accessibility and overall enjoyment. Check the forecast before heading out.

Stay on Marked Trails: To protect the natural environment and ensure safety, stick to marked trails and follow park guidelines.

Bring Snacks and Meals: While there are dining options available, bringing your own snacks and a packed lunch can enhance your outdoor experience.

Philadelphia

Getting to Philadelphia

By Train:

Overview: The Amtrak Northeast Regional and Acela Express trains provide a convenient and comfortable way to travel from New York City to Philadelphia.

Departure: Trains leave from Penn Station in Manhattan.

Arrival: Trains arrive at Philadelphia's 30th Street Station.

Travel Time: Approximately 1.5 hours.

Tickets: Purchase tickets in advance through the Amtrak website or at the station. Consider booking early for the best prices.

By Bus:

Overview: Several bus services operate routes between NYC and Philadelphia.

Providers: Greyhound, Megabus, and BoltBus are popular choices.

Departure: Buses depart from various locations in Manhattan.

Arrival: Buses typically arrive at locations such as Philadelphia's 30th Street Station or nearby bus terminals.

Travel Time: Approximately 2 hours.

Tickets: Buy tickets online or at the bus terminal. Check for discounts and deals.

By Car:

Overview: Driving gives you flexibility and allows you to explore Philadelphia at your own pace.

Driving Route: Take I-95 South directly to Philadelphia.

Travel Time: Approximately 1.5 hours, depending on traffic.

Parking: Parking can be challenging in the city center. Use parking garages or public lots, and check for street parking restrictions.

Top Attractions in Philadelphia

1. Independence National Historical Park

Overview: This historic area is home to several key American landmarks.

Key Sites:

Independence Hall: The birthplace of the Declaration of Independence and the U.S. Constitution.

Liberty Bell: An iconic symbol of American independence.

Congress Hall: Formerly the seat of the U.S. Congress.

Location: Located in the Old City neighborhood.

Tips: Book tours in advance for Independence Hall and visit early to avoid crowds.

2. Philadelphia Museum of Art

Overview: One of the largest and most renowned art museums in the country.

Highlights:

Rocky Steps: The famous steps featured in the "Rocky" films.

Art Collections: Includes works by Van Gogh, Monet, and Picasso.

Temporary Exhibitions: Frequently changing exhibitions showcase a range of art styles and periods.

Location: 2600 Benjamin Franklin Parkway.

Tips: Visit on the first Sunday of the month for free admission. Check current exhibitions and events on the museum's website.

3. Reading Terminal Market

Overview: A bustling indoor market offering a variety of food and local goods.

Highlights:

Food Stalls: Sample Philly cheesesteaks, Pennsylvania Dutch pretzels, and other local specialties.

Produce and Goods: Fresh produce, baked goods, and artisanal products.

Location: 1136 Arch Street.

Tips: Visit during off-peak hours to avoid crowds. Bring cash, as some vendors may not accept cards.

4. The Franklin Institute

Overview: A hands-on science museum with interactive exhibits for all ages.

Highlights:

Interactive Exhibits: Explore science and technology through engaging displays.

IMAX Theater: Enjoy educational films on a large screen.

Location: 222 N. 20th Street.

Tips: Check the schedule for special exhibits and events. Purchase tickets in advance for popular exhibits.

5. South Street

Overview: A vibrant neighborhood known for its eclectic shops, restaurants, and nightlife.

Highlights:

Shops and Boutiques: Find unique clothing, art, and crafts.

Restaurants: Enjoy a diverse range of cuisines, from American to international.

Nightlife: Bars, live music venues, and entertainment options.

Location: South Street, between 2nd and 8th Streets.

Tips: Explore on foot to fully experience the area. Visit during the evening for a lively atmosphere.

Practical Information

Weather: Philadelphia experiences all four seasons. Check the weather forecast before your trip and dress accordingly.

Safety: Philadelphia is generally safe, but like any major city, be mindful of your surroundings and secure your belongings.

Local Transit: Philadelphia's SEPTA system provides buses, trolleys, and subways. Consider purchasing a day pass for unlimited rides.

Tourist Information: Visit the Philadelphia Visitor Center for maps, brochures, and additional assistance.

Tips for a Successful Visit

Plan Your Itinerary: Decide which attractions interest you most and plan your visit accordingly. Allocate time for each site to ensure you get the most out of your trip.

Wear Comfortable Shoes: Philadelphia is best explored on foot, so comfortable walking shoes are a must.

Stay Hydrated and Eat Well: Carry a water bottle and enjoy local cuisine at various food spots throughout the city.

Check for Events: Philadelphia hosts numerous events and festivals. Check local listings to see if anything special is happening during your visit.

Book in Advance: For popular attractions and tours, book tickets in advance to avoid long lines and ensure availability.

The Ultimate New York City Travel Guide (2025 Edition)

Washington, D.C.

Getting to Washington, D.C.

By Train:

Overview: Amtrak offers frequent and comfortable train services between New York City and Washington, D.C.

Departure: Trains depart from Penn Station in Manhattan.

Arrival: Trains arrive at Washington's Union Station.

Travel Time: Approximately 2.5 to 3 hours.

Tickets: Purchase tickets in advance through the Amtrak website or at the station for better prices.

By Bus:

Overview: Several bus companies provide direct routes between New York City and Washington, D.C.

Providers: Greyhound, Megabus, and BoltBus are popular options.

Departure: Buses leave from various locations in Manhattan.

Arrival: Buses typically arrive at major bus terminals in D.C., such as the Washington D.C. MegaBus stop or near Union Station.

Travel Time: Approximately 4 to 5 hours, depending on traffic.

Tickets: Buy tickets online or at the bus terminal. Look for discounts and promotions.

By Car:

Overview: Driving offers flexibility and the opportunity to explore beyond the city.

Driving Route: Take I-95 South directly to Washington, D.C.

Travel Time: Approximately 4 to 5 hours, depending on traffic.

Parking: Parking in downtown D.C. can be challenging. Consider using parking garages or public lots, and be mindful of parking regulations.

Top Attractions in Washington, D.C.

1. National Mall

Overview: The National Mall is a vast, open area lined with some of the most iconic monuments and museums in the country.

Key Sites:

Washington Monument: An iconic obelisk honoring George Washington.

Lincoln Memorial: The monument dedicated to Abraham Lincoln, offering stunning views of the Reflecting Pool and the National Mall.

Vietnam Veterans Memorial: A poignant tribute to those who served in the Vietnam War.

Location: Centered between the U.S. Capitol and the Lincoln Memorial.

Tips: Wear comfortable walking shoes and plan to spend several hours exploring. The National Mall is best experienced on foot.

2. Smithsonian Museums

Overview: The Smithsonian Institution operates a series of museums and galleries, most of which are free to the public.

Popular Museums:

National Museum of American History: Home to the original Star-Spangled Banner and a vast collection of American artifacts.

National Air and Space Museum: Showcases the history of aviation and space exploration.

National Museum of Natural History: Features exhibits on everything from dinosaurs to gemstones.

Location: Scattered around the National Mall.

Tips: Prioritize the museums you want to visit, as there are many. Check museum hours and plan your visit around special exhibitions or events.

3. U.S. Capitol

Overview: The seat of the United States Congress, the Capitol is an architectural marvel and a symbol of American democracy.

Highlights:

Capitol Tours: Free tours are available, but booking in advance is recommended.

Capitol Visitor Center: Offers exhibits and information about the Capitol's history.

Location: At the eastern end of the National Mall.

Tips: Book Capitol tours in advance. Allow time to explore the surrounding grounds and nearby Congressional offices.

4. The White House

Overview: The official residence and workplace of the President of the United States.

Highlights:

Exterior Viewing: Public tours of the White House are limited and require advance arrangements through a Member of Congress.

Lafayette Park: Offers a good view of the White House's exterior.

Location: 1600 Pennsylvania Avenue NW.

Tips: While interior tours are not usually available to day-trippers, you can enjoy a view of the White House from the exterior and explore nearby landmarks.

5. Georgetown

Overview: A historic neighborhood known for its charming streets, shopping, and dining.

Highlights:

Georgetown University: Visit the beautiful campus and historic buildings.

Waterfront Park: Enjoy views of the Potomac River and various outdoor activities.

M Street and Wisconsin Avenue: Lined with shops, boutiques, and restaurants.

Location: Northwest Washington, D.C.

Tips: Explore on foot and take advantage of the numerous dining options. Georgetown is also known for its historic architecture and vibrant atmosphere.

Practical Information

Weather: Washington, D.C., experiences all four seasons. Check the weather forecast before your trip and dress accordingly.

Safety: Washington, D.C., is generally safe, but remain aware of your surroundings, especially in crowded areas.

Local Transit: The Metro system is a convenient way to get around. Consider purchasing a SmarTrip card for easy travel on buses and trains.

Tourist Information: Visit the Washington D.C. Visitor Center for maps, brochures, and additional assistance.

Tips for a Successful Visit

Plan Your Itinerary: Focus on key attractions you want to visit and plan your day to cover them efficiently.

Wear Comfortable Shoes: The city is best explored on foot, so comfortable walking shoes are essential.

Check for Events: Washington, D.C. frequently hosts special events, festivals, and political activities. Check local listings for any events happening during your visit.

Stay Hydrated and Eat Well: Bring a water bottle and take advantage of the city's diverse dining options for lunch and dinner.

Allow Time for Security: Major attractions like the White House and Capitol may have security checks, so plan accordingly.

Niagara Falls

Getting to Niagara Falls

By Car:

Overview: Driving to Niagara Falls allows flexibility and the opportunity to explore the area at your own pace.

Driving Route: Take I-90 West from New York City towards Buffalo, then follow signs to Niagara Falls.

Travel Time: Approximately 6 to 7 hours, depending on traffic and road conditions.

Parking: There are several parking options near the falls, including paid lots and some free spaces. Look for parking near the attractions to minimize walking.

By Train:

Overview: Amtrak offers train services from New York City to Niagara Falls.

Departure: Trains leave from Penn Station in Manhattan.

Arrival: Trains arrive at Niagara Falls Amtrak Station.

Travel Time: Approximately 9 to 10 hours.

Tickets: Purchase tickets in advance through the Amtrak website or at the station. Note that train travel takes longer than driving or flying.

By Bus:

Overview: Several bus companies provide services between New York City and Niagara Falls.

Providers: Greyhound and Megabus are popular options.

Departure: Buses leave from various locations in Manhattan.

Arrival: Buses typically arrive at Niagara Falls bus terminals.

Travel Time: Approximately 8 to 10 hours.

Tickets: Buy tickets online or at the bus terminal. Look for discounts and promotions.

By Plane:

Overview: Flying is the fastest way to reach Niagara Falls.

Airports: Fly into Buffalo Niagara International Airport (BUF), which is about 30 minutes from Niagara Falls.

Travel Time: Approximately 1.5 hours flight time, plus additional time for airport procedures and transfer to Niagara Falls.

Airlines: Several airlines operate flights between NYC airports (JFK, LGA, EWR) and Buffalo.

Transfer: Shuttle services, rental cars, and taxis are available from Buffalo Airport to Niagara Falls.

The Ultimate New York City Travel Guide (2025 Edition)

Top Attractions at Niagara Falls

1. Maid of the Mist

Overview: A famous boat tour that takes you close to the base of the falls, offering a thrilling and immersive experience.

Highlights:

Boat Ride: Get up close to the roaring waters of the falls and experience the mist firsthand.

Ponchos Provided: Protect yourself from the spray with the provided ponchos.

Location: Tours depart from the dock near the falls.

Tips: The Maid of the Mist operates seasonally, typically from April to November. Check schedules and book tickets in advance during peak seasons.

2. Cave of the Winds

Overview: An exhilarating attraction that lets you walk right next to the Bridal Veil Falls.

Highlights:

Walkways: Navigate through wooden walkways and observation platforms near the falls.

Hurricane Deck: Stand just feet away from the falls and experience the powerful rush of water.

Location: Entrance is located on the American side of the falls.

Tips: Wear water-resistant clothing and footwear. The Cave of the Winds is also a seasonal attraction, open from May to October.

3. Niagara Falls State Park

Overview: America's oldest state park offers panoramic views of the falls and various walking paths.

Highlights:

Observation Points: Enjoy views from several vantage points including Prospect Point and the Observation Tower.

Walking Trails: Explore the park's scenic trails and green spaces.

Location: On the American side of the falls.

Tips: The park is open year-round. Check for seasonal events and activities.

4. Niagara Parks Butterfly Conservatory

Overview: Located on the Canadian side, this indoor tropical rainforest is home to thousands of butterflies.

Highlights:

Butterfly Species: Observe various species of butterflies in a lush, tropical setting.

Educational Displays: Learn about the life cycle and conservation of butterflies.

Location: 2565 Niagara Parkway, Niagara Falls, Ontario.

Tips: Bring a camera and be prepared for warm, humid conditions inside the conservatory.

5. Journey Behind the Falls

Overview: This Canadian attraction offers a unique perspective from behind the Horseshoe Falls.

Highlights:

Observation Platforms: View the falls from tunnels behind the cascading water.

Thunder Alley: Experience the power and sound of the falls from a close vantage point.

Location: 6650 Niagara Parkway, Niagara Falls, Ontario.

Tips: Wear waterproof clothing and sturdy footwear. The attraction operates year-round.

Practical Information

Weather: The weather can vary greatly depending on the season. Summers are warm and crowded, while winters can be cold with potential snow. Check the weather forecast before your visit.

Safety: Niagara Falls is generally safe, but be cautious around wet and slippery areas.

Currency: If visiting the Canadian side, you will need Canadian dollars. Currency exchange services are available at the border and in major areas.

Tourist Information: Visit visitor centers on both sides of the falls for maps, brochures, and additional assistance.

Tips for a Successful Visit

Plan Your Itinerary: Prioritize the attractions you most want to see and plan your visit accordingly. Allocate time for each activity to make the most of your day.

Wear Appropriate Clothing: Prepare for mist and potential rain by wearing waterproof clothing and comfortable shoes.

Check Attraction Hours: Some attractions operate seasonally. Verify opening hours and book tickets in advance when possible.

Stay Hydrated and Eat Well: Bring water and snacks, and take advantage of local dining options for meals.

Be Prepared for Crowds: Niagara Falls is a popular destination, especially during peak tourist seasons. Arrive early to avoid crowds and enjoy the attractions with fewer people.

The Ultimate New York City Travel Guide (2025 Edition)

Chapter 11: Seasonal Events and Festivals in New York

New Year's Eve in Times Square

New Year's Eve in Times Square is renowned for its massive crowds, star-studded performances, and the iconic ball drop that marks the arrival of the new year. The event has been a tradition since 1907 and has become synonymous with celebrating the turn of the year in spectacular fashion.

Location

Times Square, located at the intersection of Broadway and Seventh Avenue in Manhattan, is the epicenter of the New Year's Eve celebrations. The area is transformed into a festive hub filled with people, lights, and energy as the clock counts down to midnight.

History

The tradition of the Times Square ball drop began in 1907. The original ball, a 700-pound iron and wood sphere, was lowered from the flagpole atop One Times Square. The modern version of the ball is a 12-foot, 11,875-pound geodesic sphere covered in thousands of LED lights. Over the years, the event has grown into a global spectacle, attracting millions of viewers both in person and on television.

Event Schedule

Time: Festivities start early in the afternoon and culminate with the ball drop at midnight.

Ball Drop: The ball descends from the flagpole on the roof of One Times Square starting at 11:59 PM and reaches the bottom at midnight, marking the start of the new year.

Top Things to Do

Watch the Ball Drop:

Overview: The highlight of the event is the ball drop itself, accompanied by a countdown from 10 to 1.

Location: The best views are directly in Times Square, though the area gets extremely crowded.

Tips: Arrive early to secure a good viewing spot. Some areas are closed off to new arrivals as the crowd grows.

Enjoy Live Entertainment:

Overview: Times Square hosts live performances by popular musicians, bands, and celebrities.

Stages: Multiple stages are set up throughout Times Square with different acts performing throughout the evening.

Tips: Check the event schedule ahead of time to see which performers will be there.

Participate in the Festivities:

Overview: The celebration includes confetti showers, party hats, and noisemakers.

Atmosphere: The crowd is lively and festive, with thousands of people celebrating together.

Tips: Dress warmly and be prepared for a lot of standing and waiting.

Explore Times Square:

Overview: Take in the dazzling lights, billboards, and the general excitement of the area.

Activities: Many nearby restaurants and shops stay open late to cater to the crowd.

Tips: Be mindful of your belongings and watch for pickpockets in crowded areas.

Practical Information

Transportation:

Public Transit: The subway is the most practical way to reach Times Square, though expect crowded trains and stations.

Roads: Many streets are closed to vehicles on New Year's Eve. Consider taking public transport to avoid traffic and parking issues.

Taxis/Rideshares: Limited access and high demand make taxis and rideshares challenging.

Security:

Overview: Enhanced security measures are in place for the event. Expect to go through security checkpoints.

Tips: Arrive early to allow time for security screening and to find a good spot.

Weather:

Overview: December 31st can be cold, with temperatures often dropping below freezing.

Tips: Dress in layers, wear warm clothing, and bring gloves, a hat, and a scarf.

Food and Drink:

Overview: Food vendors and nearby restaurants will be open, but lines can be long.

Tips: Bring snacks and a water bottle, though there are restrictions on large items and alcohol in the event area.

Tips for Visiting

Plan Ahead: Check event details, transportation options, and weather forecasts before heading out.

Arrive Early: The best spots fill up quickly. Arriving in the afternoon will give you the best chance to secure a good view.

Stay Hydrated and Energized: Bring snacks and drinks to stay comfortable throughout the long wait.

Be Patient: The crowd can be overwhelming, and it may take time to move through security and find a spot.

Grace Bennett

Macy's Thanksgiving Day Parade

The Macy's Thanksgiving Day Parade is a grand celebration that takes place on Thanksgiving Day each year. Featuring elaborate floats, marching bands, giant balloons, and celebrity performances, the parade transforms New York City into a festive spectacle that attracts both locals and tourists.

Location

The parade routes through Manhattan, primarily along Central Park West, down 59th Street, and across to 34th Street, ending at Macy's flagship store on Herald Square.

History

Inception: The parade began in 1924, organized by Macy's department store to celebrate Thanksgiving and the start of the Christmas season.

Initial Parade: Originally, it featured employees dressed in costumes, live animals, and a few floats.

Evolution: Over the decades, the parade has grown to include massive helium balloons, elaborate floats, and performances by famous entertainers.

Event Schedule

Date: The parade is held annually on Thanksgiving Day, the fourth Thursday in November.

Start Time: The parade typically begins at 9:00 AM.

Duration: The parade lasts about 3 hours, concluding around noon.

Top Things to Do

Watch the Parade:

Overview: The main attraction is the parade itself, featuring a dazzling array of floats, balloons, and performances.

Floats and Balloons: Enjoy the giant balloons of popular characters and intricately designed floats.

Performances: Experience live performances by marching bands, musical acts, and Broadway shows.

Location: Prime viewing spots are along the parade route, particularly between 59th Street and 34th Street.

Tips: Arrive early to secure a good viewing spot, as the area gets crowded quickly.

Explore the Surrounding Area:

Overview: Discover the festive atmosphere around the parade route.

Activities: Enjoy holiday decorations, shop for seasonal items, and visit nearby attractions like Central Park and Rockefeller Center.

Tips: Be prepared for large crowds and heavy foot traffic.

The Ultimate New York City Travel Guide (2025 Edition)

Attend a Pre-Parade Event:

Overview: In the days leading up to the parade, you can see some of the parade balloons being inflated.

Location: The balloon inflation takes place at the Museum of Natural History (79th Street and Columbus Avenue).

Tips: Check the schedule for inflation times and arrive early to avoid long lines.

Practical Information

Transportation:

Public Transit: The subway is the most convenient way to reach the parade route. Take the 1, 2, or 3 trains to 59th Street/Columbus Circle or the N, Q, R, or W trains to 34th Street/Herald Square.

Roads: Many streets along the parade route are closed to vehicles, so driving is not recommended. Plan to use public transit or walk.

Security:

Overview: Security is tight during the parade. Expect to go through security checkpoints.

Tips: Carry minimal items and be prepared for bag checks.

Weather:

Overview: November weather in New York City can be cold, often with temperatures ranging from 40°F to 50°F (4°C to 10°C).

Tips: Dress warmly in layers and wear comfortable shoes. Check the weather forecast before heading out.

Food and Drink:

Overview: Food vendors are available along the parade route, but lines can be long.

Tips: Bring snacks and drinks to stay energized throughout the morning.

Tips for Visiting

Arrive Early: To secure a prime viewing spot, arrive early in the morning. The best spots along the route fill up quickly.

Dress Appropriately: Wear layers to stay warm and comfortable, as you'll be standing for long periods.

Stay Hydrated: Bring water and snacks, as food options can be limited and lines may be long.

Be Patient and Polite: The parade attracts large crowds. Be prepared for wait times and be courteous to fellow parade-goers.

Plan Your Route: Familiarize yourself with the parade route and nearby subway stations to make navigation easier.

New York Fashion Week

New York Fashion Week is a major event in the fashion calendar, presenting the spring/summer and fall/winter collections of top designers. The week-long event attracts designers, models, celebrities, and fashion enthusiasts from around the world. It serves as a platform for new trends, innovative designs, and industry networking.

Location

Fashion Week events take place across various venues in Manhattan. Key locations include:

The Shed: Located at Hudson Yards, this cultural space hosts major fashion shows.

Spring Studios: A popular venue for shows, located in Tribeca.

Pier 59 Studios: Known for its high-profile presentations, situated at Chelsea Piers.

Other Venues: Shows can also be held in hotels, galleries, and unique spaces across the city.

History

Origins: New York Fashion Week began in 1943 as "Press Week" by Eleanor Lambert, aiming to promote American designers during World War II.

Growth: It evolved into a major international event over the decades, solidifying its role as a global fashion hub.

Current Status: Today, NYFW is part of the "Big Four" fashion weeks, alongside Paris, Milan, and London.

Event Schedule

Timing: Fashion Week is held twice a year:

Fall/Winter Collections: Typically in February, showcasing collections for the following fall and winter.

Spring/Summer Collections: Usually in September, presenting collections for the upcoming spring and summer.

Duration: Each season lasts about a week, featuring multiple shows and events.

Top Things to Do

Attend Fashion Shows:

Overview: Experience the latest collections from renowned designers and emerging talents.

Tickets: Access to shows is often by invitation or through purchasing tickets, available through official NYFW channels or designer websites.

Tips: Check show schedules in advance and secure tickets early, as popular shows can sell out quickly.

Explore Showrooms:

Overview: Visit showrooms to see collections up close and interact with designers and brands.

Location: Showrooms are typically open to industry professionals, but some may offer public viewing opportunities.

Tips: Reach out to showrooms or designers for access and appointment details.

Attend Industry Events and Parties:

Overview: Fashion Week includes various parties, networking events, and industry gatherings.

Invitations: Many events are invitation-only, but some may be open to the public or require RSVPs.

Tips: Look out for event announcements and social media updates for opportunities to attend.

Shop Pop-Up Stores:

Overview: NYFW often features exclusive pop-up shops and sample sales where you can purchase designer pieces.

Location: Pop-ups are typically set up in fashionable districts like SoHo or the Lower East Side.

Tips: Check NYFW websites and social media for locations and timings of pop-up shops.

Practical Information

Transportation:

Public Transit: The subway and buses are convenient ways to navigate Manhattan. Major venues are well-connected by public transit.

Taxis/Rideshares: Taxis and rideshare services like Uber and Lyft are also options but may be subject to traffic delays.

Walking: Many venues are within walking distance of each other in central Manhattan.

Accommodation:

Overview: Book accommodations well in advance, as hotels near the main venues can fill up quickly.

Tips: Look for hotels in neighborhoods such as Midtown, Chelsea, or SoHo for proximity to Fashion Week events.

Security:

Overview: Security is typically tight at venues. Be prepared for bag checks and follow any instructions from event staff.

Tips: Carry minimal items and arrive early to avoid long lines.

Weather:

Overview: Check the weather forecast for the week, as New York weather can vary significantly.

Tips: Dress in layers and wear comfortable footwear for navigating the city and attending events.

Tips for Visiting

Plan Ahead: Review the schedule, secure tickets, and make accommodation arrangements well in advance.

Stay Updated: Follow NYFW's official website and social media channels for the latest information on shows, events, and updates.

Network: Use Fashion Week as an opportunity to connect with industry professionals, designers, and fellow fashion enthusiasts.

Document the Experience: Bring a camera or smartphone to capture moments from shows and events, but be mindful of venue rules regarding photography.

Pride Week and Parade

Pride Week in New York City is a week-long celebration leading up to the Pride Parade. The festivities include various events such as parties, rallies, educational panels, and performances, culminating in the iconic Pride Parade, which marches through Manhattan and showcases the diverse LGBTQ+ community.

Location

Pride Parade Route: The parade typically runs along Fifth Avenue, starting from 36th Street and ending at Christopher Street, passing through Greenwich Village and ending near Stonewall Inn.

Events: Various Pride Week events are held across Manhattan, with major activities centered around the parade route and key LGBTQ+ neighborhoods like the West Village and Chelsea.

History

Origins: The first Pride Parade in New York City took place on June 28, 1970, marking the one-year anniversary of the Stonewall Riots. The Stonewall Riots, which occurred in 1969, were a series of spontaneous demonstrations by members of the LGBTQ+ community against police raids at the Stonewall Inn, a gay bar in Greenwich Village.

Growth: Over the decades, the parade and associated events have grown significantly, reflecting broader societal changes and increasing support for LGBTQ+ rights.

Current Status: Today, NYC Pride is one of the largest and most prominent Pride celebrations in the world, drawing millions of participants and spectators each year.

Event Schedule

Pride Week: Events typically begin the week before the parade and include a variety of activities such as parties, film screenings, art exhibitions, and educational panels.

Pride Parade:

Date: Held on the last Sunday of June.

Start Time: The parade usually kicks off around noon.

Duration: The parade lasts approximately 4-6 hours.

Top Things to Do

Attend the Pride Parade:

Overview: The parade features colorful floats, performances, and marching groups representing LGBTQ+ organizations, allies, and communities.

Viewing Spots: Prime viewing locations are along Fifth Avenue between 36th Street and Christopher Street. Arrive early to secure a good spot.

Tips: Be prepared for large crowds and consider bringing sun protection, water, and snacks.

Participate in Pride Week Events:

Overview: Join a range of activities including LGBTQ+ themed parties, discussions, and cultural events.

Venues: Events take place at various locations around Manhattan, including bars, clubs, and cultural institutions.

Tips: Check the NYC Pride website and social media for event schedules and ticket information.

Visit Iconic LGBTQ+ Landmarks:

Overview: Explore historical and cultural sites related to LGBTQ+ history.

Key Sites: Stonewall Inn, The LGBT Community Center, and various historical markers throughout Greenwich Village.

Tips: Many of these sites host special events and exhibitions during Pride Week.

Support LGBTQ+ Businesses and Organizations:

Overview: Patronize LGBTQ+-owned businesses and support organizations dedicated to LGBTQ+ advocacy.

Areas: Neighborhoods like the West Village are home to many LGBTQ+-friendly establishments.

Tips: Look for special promotions or events supporting Pride Week.

Practical Information

Transportation:

Public Transit: The subway is a convenient way to reach Pride events. Nearby stations include 34th Street-Herald Square, 23rd Street, and Christopher Street.

Roads: Be aware of road closures and traffic disruptions around the parade route. Plan your travel in advance.

Walking: Many events are within walking distance of each other, particularly in Manhattan neighborhoods.

Accommodation:

Overview: Book accommodations early, as hotels near the parade route and popular areas fill up quickly during Pride Week.

Tips: Consider staying in neighborhoods like the West Village, Chelsea, or Midtown for proximity to events.

Security:

Overview: Expect increased security around parade routes and event venues. Follow instructions from event staff and law enforcement.

Tips: Carry minimal items and be prepared for bag checks.

Weather:

Overview: June weather in New York City can be warm, with temperatures ranging from 70°F to 85°F (21°C to 29°C).

Tips: Dress comfortably, wear sunscreen, and stay hydrated.

Tips for Visiting

Plan Ahead: Review the schedule of events, secure tickets if needed, and make accommodation arrangements well in advance.

Stay Informed: Follow NYC Pride's official website and social media for the latest updates on events and parade details.

Embrace the Spirit: Participate enthusiastically and respectfully in the celebrations, honoring the spirit of Pride and the LGBTQ+ community.

Be Patient: The crowds can be large and the atmosphere festive. Approach the experience with patience and an open mind.

Village Halloween Parade

The Village Halloween Parade is renowned for its creative costumes, diverse participants, and festive atmosphere. Featuring elaborate floats, marching bands, and thousands of costumed revelers, the parade showcases the best of Halloween creativity and community spirit. It attracts locals and visitors alike, offering a one-of-a-kind Halloween experience.

Location

Parade Route: The parade runs up Sixth Avenue, starting at Spring Street and ending at 16th Street, passing through the heart of Greenwich Village.

Viewing Areas: Prime viewing spots are along Sixth Avenue, especially between Spring Street and 16th Street. Major intersections such as Houston Street and 14th Street also provide good vantage points.

History

Origins: The parade was founded in 1974 by artist and parade director Ralph Lee as a small community event. It has since grown into a major annual celebration.

Growth: Over the decades, the parade has expanded significantly, evolving into a major cultural event with hundreds of thousands of participants and spectators.

Current Status: Today, it is recognized as one of the largest and most celebrated Halloween parades in the world, known for its inclusivity and creativity.

Event Schedule

Date: October 31st every year.

Start Time: The parade typically begins at 7:00 PM.

Duration: The parade lasts approximately 2-3 hours.

Top Things to Do

Watch the Parade:

Overview: Experience the parade's stunning floats, creative costumes, and dynamic performances.

Viewing Spots: Arrive early to claim a good spot along the parade route, especially between Spring Street and 16th Street.

Tips: Be prepared for large crowds and street closures. Dress warmly and consider bringing a portable chair or blanket.

Participate in the Parade:

Overview: Join the parade as a participant by registering in advance. Participation is open to individuals and groups with creative costumes and themed outfits.

Registration: Registration details are usually available on the official parade website or through community organizations.

Tips: Plan your costume well in advance and follow parade guidelines for safety and inclusivity.

Explore Greenwich Village:

Overview: Enjoy the festive atmosphere of Greenwich Village, known for its historic charm and lively nightlife.

Activities: Visit local bars, restaurants, and shops that often have Halloween-themed specials and events.

Tips: Make reservations ahead of time if you plan to dine out, as the area can be very busy.

Attend Pre-Parade Events:

Overview: Participate in pre-parade activities such as costume contests, themed parties, and Halloween-themed exhibitions.

Locations: Check local listings and community boards for information on pre-parade events.

Tips: Look for events that offer opportunities for costume showcases and community engagement.

Practical Information

Transportation:

Public Transit: Use the subway to get to the parade. Nearby stations include West 4th Street, 14th Street, and Houston Street.

Roads: Be aware of road closures and detours around the parade route. Plan alternative routes if driving.

Walking: Walking is often the easiest way to navigate around the parade area due to street closures and heavy traffic.

Accommodation:

Overview: Book accommodations early, as hotels in and around Greenwich Village can fill up quickly during Halloween.

Tips: Consider staying in neighborhoods with easy access to public transportation, such as Chelsea or the East Village.

Safety and Security:

Overview: Security is tight around the parade route. Follow instructions from event staff and law enforcement.

Tips: Carry minimal items, avoid bringing large bags, and be aware of your surroundings.

Weather:

Overview: October weather in New York City can be cool, with temperatures ranging from 50°F to 60°F (10°C to 15°C).

Tips: Dress in layers and wear comfortable footwear for walking and standing for extended periods.

Tips for Visiting

Plan Ahead: Review the parade route and schedule, secure accommodation if needed, and check for any updates or changes to the event.

Arrive Early: To get a good viewing spot, arrive early and be prepared for crowds.

Be Creative: If participating, create a unique and imaginative costume that reflects the spirit of Halloween.

Respect the Community: Embrace the diversity and creativity of the parade while being considerate of fellow participants and spectators.

The Ultimate New York City Travel Guide (2025 Edition)

Holiday Markets and Ice Skating Rinks

Holiday Markets

Overview:

New York City's holiday markets are a magical experience, offering unique gifts, festive treats, and a joyful atmosphere. These markets are set up in various locations around the city, providing a charming backdrop for holiday shopping and seasonal festivities.

Top Holiday Markets:

Union Square Holiday Market:

Location: Union Square Park, between 14th and 17th Streets.

Overview: Known for its wide selection of artisanal gifts, crafts, and food vendors.

Opening Hours: Usually open daily from mid-November to Christmas Eve, from 11:00 AM to 8:00 PM.

Bryant Park Winter Village:

Location: Bryant Park, between 40th and 42nd Streets, and 5th and 6th Avenues.

Overview: Features a large market with vendors selling holiday gifts, decorations, and food. It also includes an ice skating rink.

Opening Hours: Typically open from late October to early January, from 11:00 AM to 8:00 PM.

Columbus Circle Holiday Market:

Location: Columbus Circle, at the southwest corner of Central Park.

Overview: A smaller, upscale market with high-quality gifts and gourmet food options.

Opening Hours: Open from mid-November to Christmas Eve, from 10:00 AM to 8:00 PM.

Grand Central Holiday Fair:

Location: Grand Central Terminal, in the historic Vanderbilt Hall.

Overview: Offers a range of gifts and crafts in a stunning historic setting.

Opening Hours: Open from mid-November to Christmas Eve, from 10:00 AM to 8:00 PM.

Holiday Shops at Winter Village:

Location: Bryant Park, but separate from the ice skating rink area.

Overview: Features a European-inspired market with over 170 holiday shops.

Opening Hours: Typically open from mid-October to early January, from 11:00 AM to 8:00 PM.

Tips for Visiting:

Arrive Early: To avoid crowds and get the best selection, visit the markets early in the day.

Dress Warmly: Be prepared for chilly weather, especially if you plan to spend a lot of time outdoors.

Cash and Card: Many vendors accept both cash and card, but it's a good idea to carry some cash for smaller purchases.

Check Hours: Verify opening hours before visiting, as they may vary or change.

Ice Skating Rinks

Overview:

Ice skating is a quintessential winter activity in New York City. The city boasts several iconic rinks, each offering a unique skating experience amidst spectacular settings.

Top Ice Skating Rinks:

Wollman Rink:

Location: Central Park, at 59th Street and 6th Avenue.

Overview: An iconic rink with beautiful views of Central Park. Known for its festive atmosphere and historic charm.

Opening Hours: Generally open from late October to early April, with varying hours depending on the day.

Bryant Park Ice Rink:

Location: Bryant Park, between 40th and 42nd Streets, and 5th and 6th Avenues.

Overview: A large rink with stunning views of the surrounding skyscrapers and a charming holiday market nearby.

Opening Hours: Open from mid-October to early March, from 8:00 AM to 10:00 PM.

Rockefeller Center Ice Rink:

Location: Rockefeller Center, between 49th and 50th Streets, and 5th and 6th Avenues.

Overview: Perhaps the most famous rink, located beneath the giant Christmas tree. Known for its small size and bustling atmosphere.

Opening Hours: Typically open from mid-October to early April, from 8:30 AM to midnight.

Lasker Rink:

Location: Central Park, at 110th Street and Lenox Avenue.

Overview: A smaller, less crowded rink compared to Wollman Rink, offering a more relaxed skating experience.

Opening Hours: Open from late October to early April, with varying hours.

South Street Seaport Ice Rink:

Location: South Street Seaport, near the historic ships.

Overview: A seasonal rink with views of the East River and the Brooklyn Bridge.

Opening Hours: Typically open from mid-November to mid-January.

Tips for Visiting:

Book in Advance: Popular rinks like Rockefeller Center can get crowded, so consider booking tickets or reservations in advance.

Wear Warm Clothes: Ice skating rinks can be cold, so dress in layers and wear warm gloves.

Skate Rentals: Most rinks offer skate rentals, but bring your own if you prefer.

Arrive Early: For a more enjoyable experience with shorter wait times, try to visit early in the day or during off-peak hours.

Chapter 12: Museums and Art Galleries

Metropolitan Museum of Art

The Met is not only one of the largest art museums in the world but also one of the most visited. It houses an extensive collection ranging from ancient Egyptian artifacts to contemporary art, offering something for every visitor. The museum is a treasure trove of history, art, and culture, making it a central hub for artistic exploration in New York City.

Location

The Met Fifth Avenue:

Address: 1000 Fifth Avenue, New York, NY 10028

Overview: The Met's main building, located on the eastern edge of Central Park. It is an architectural marvel and a cultural landmark.

The Met Cloisters:

Address: 99 Margaret Corbin Drive, Fort Tryon Park, New York, NY 10040

Overview: Located in Fort Tryon Park in Upper Manhattan, The Met Cloisters is dedicated to the art and architecture of medieval Europe. It is set in a picturesque location with gardens and views of the Hudson River.

History

Founding: The Met was founded in 1870 by a group of American citizens including businessmen, financiers, and philanthropists who wanted to create a museum that would bring art and culture to the public.

Growth: Over the decades, the museum has expanded its collection through acquisitions, donations, and bequests, establishing itself as a leading institution in the art world.

Current Status: Today, The Met encompasses over 2 million works of art and is a pivotal institution in the global art community.

Opening Hours

The Met Fifth Avenue:

Monday–Thursday: 10:00 AM – 5:00 PM

Friday and Saturday: 10:00 AM – 9:00 PM

Sunday: 10:00 AM – 5:00 PM

The Met Cloisters:

March–October: 10:00 AM – 5:15 PM

November–February: 10:00 AM – 4:45 PM

Closed: January 1, the first Monday in May, and December 25.

Top Things to Do

Explore the Collections:

Overview: Wander through the museum's vast collections, which include works from ancient Egypt, European paintings, American art, and Asian art. Highlights include pieces by artists like Rembrandt, Vermeer, and Van Gogh.

Tip: Pick up a map or use the museum's app to navigate the galleries and locate your areas of interest.

Visit Special Exhibitions:

Overview: The Met frequently hosts special exhibitions that delve into specific themes, artists, or periods. These exhibitions offer a deeper exploration of particular aspects of art and culture.

Tip: Check The Met's website for information on current and upcoming exhibitions and purchase tickets in advance if necessary.

Admire the Architecture:

Overview: The Met Fifth Avenue is a stunning example of Beaux-Arts architecture. Its grand staircase and ornate ceilings are as much a part of the museum's charm as its art collection.

Tip: Take time to explore the museum's architectural features and enjoy the view from the Met's American Wing's balcony.

Explore The Met Cloisters:

Overview: The Met Cloisters offers a unique experience with its medieval European art and architecture set in a tranquil garden setting.

Tip: Allow extra time for a visit to The Met Cloisters, and enjoy the scenic views of the Hudson River.

Attend Public Programs:

Overview: The Met offers a range of educational programs, lectures, and tours designed to enhance your museum experience.

Tip: Check the museum's calendar for scheduled programs and consider attending a guided tour to gain deeper insights into the collections.

Practical Information

Admission:

The Met Fifth Avenue: Suggested admission for adults is $30, seniors $22, and students $17. Members and children under 12 are free. New York State residents and NY, NJ, and CT students can pay what they wish.

The Met Cloisters: Admission is included with The Met Fifth Avenue ticket.

Accessibility:

Overview: The Met is accessible to visitors with disabilities. Wheelchairs are available for use, and accessible entrances are located at several points.

Tip: For specific accessibility needs, consult The Met's website or contact visitor services.

Dining:

Overview: Both The Met Fifth Avenue and The Met Cloisters have dining options, including cafés and casual dining.

Tip: Consider dining at The Met's restaurants or cafés for a convenient meal during your visit.

Shopping:

Overview: The Met's gift shops offer a range of art-inspired gifts, books, and souvenirs.

Tip: Browse the shops for unique items to remember your visit.

Tips for Visiting

Plan Your Visit: With its extensive collections, it's wise to plan which exhibits you want to see in advance.

Use the App: Download The Met's app for maps, exhibit information, and audio guides.

Visit During Off-Peak Hours: For a more relaxed experience, visit early in the morning or later in the afternoon.

Comfortable Shoes: Be prepared to do a lot of walking, so wear comfortable shoes.

Museum of Modern Art (MoMA)

MoMA is one of the most influential art museums globally, celebrated for its extensive collection of modern and contemporary art. The museum's collection includes masterpieces of painting, sculpture, design, film, and performance art, reflecting the evolution of art and culture from the late 19th century to the present.

Location

Address: 11 West 53rd Street, Manhattan, New York, NY 10019

Overview: Situated in Midtown Manhattan, MoMA is centrally located, making it easily accessible from various parts of the city.

History

Founding: MoMA was established in 1929 by a group of philanthropists and art collectors, including Abby Aldrich Rockefeller and Lillie P. Bliss, who sought to create a museum dedicated to modern art.

Growth: Over the decades, MoMA has expanded both its collection and its physical space. It has become a leading institution in promoting modern and contemporary art through acquisitions, exhibitions, and educational programs.

Current Status: Today, MoMA stands as a beacon of modern art, renowned for its influential exhibitions and educational initiatives.

Opening Hours

Monday, Tuesday, Wednesday, Friday, Saturday, and Sunday: 10:30 AM – 5:30 PM

Thursday: 10:30 AM – 8:00 PM

The Ultimate New York City Travel Guide (2025 Edition)

Closed: January 1, the first Monday in May, and December 25.

Top Things to Do

Explore the Collection:

Overview: MoMA's collection includes iconic works by artists such as Vincent van Gogh, Pablo Picasso, Andy Warhol, and Jackson Pollock. Highlights include Van Gogh's *Starry Night*, Picasso's *Les Demoiselles d'Avignon*, and Warhol's *Campbell's Soup Cans*.

Tip: Use MoMA's website or app to explore the collection before your visit and make a list of must-see artworks.

Visit Special Exhibitions:

Overview: MoMA regularly hosts special exhibitions that delve into specific themes, artists, or movements. These exhibitions provide in-depth insights and often include new and emerging artists.

Tip: Check MoMA's website for information on current and upcoming exhibitions and purchase tickets in advance if necessary.

Experience the Sculpture Garden:

Overview: MoMA's Abby Aldrich Rockefeller Sculpture Garden is a tranquil outdoor space featuring sculptures by artists such as Henri Matisse and Alexander Calder.

Tip: Visit the sculpture garden for a peaceful break and to enjoy art in an open-air setting.

Attend Public Programs:

Overview: MoMA offers a range of educational programs, lectures, film screenings, and performances. These programs provide deeper engagement with the museum's exhibitions and collections.

Tip: Check MoMA's calendar for scheduled programs and consider attending a lecture or film screening.

Explore the Design Store:

Overview: MoMA's Design Store offers a curated selection of design objects, books, and gifts inspired by the museum's collections.

Tip: Browse the store for unique and art-inspired gifts and souvenirs.

Practical Information

Admission:

General Admission: $25 for adults, $18 for seniors (65 and older), and $14 for students. Free for members, children (16 and under), and New York City residents on Friday evenings (4:00 PM – 8:00 PM).

Online Tickets: Purchase tickets online to avoid lines and save time.

Accessibility:

Overview: MoMA is accessible to visitors with disabilities. Wheelchairs are available, and accessible entrances and restrooms are provided.

Tip: For specific accessibility needs, consult MoMA's website or contact visitor services in advance.

Dining:

Overview: MoMA has dining options including cafes and a restaurant. These offer a range of meals, snacks, and beverages.

Tip: Consider dining at MoMA's restaurant for a convenient meal or snack during your visit.

Shopping:

Overview: MoMA's Design Store offers a wide range of art-inspired products, including design objects, books, and stationery.

Tip: Explore the store for unique gifts and memorabilia.

Tips for Visiting

Plan Your Visit: With its extensive collection and frequent exhibitions, it's helpful to plan which galleries and artworks you want to see.

Use the App: Download MoMA's app for interactive maps, exhibit information, and audio guides.

Visit During Off-Peak Hours: To avoid crowds, consider visiting early in the morning or later in the afternoon.

Comfortable Shoes: Be prepared to walk extensively, so wear comfortable shoes.

American Museum of Natural History

AMNH is one of the largest and most prestigious natural history museums in the world. Its extensive collection spans a wide range of topics, including paleontology, astronomy, anthropology, and geology. The museum is renowned for its impressive dioramas, fossil displays, and interactive exhibits, which provide a deep understanding of the natural world.

Location

Address: Central Park West at 79th Street, New York, NY 10024

Overview: Situated on the western edge of Central Park, AMNH is easily accessible and centrally located, making it a convenient stop for visitors exploring New York City.

History

Founding: Established in 1869, AMNH was created to advance the study and appreciation of the natural world. Its founding aimed to provide a public space for scientific research and education.

Growth: Over the years, the museum has expanded its collections and facilities, incorporating cutting-edge exhibits and research programs. It has become a leading institution in natural history and scientific research.

Current Status: Today, AMNH stands as a major center for scientific research and public education, attracting millions of visitors annually.

The Ultimate New York City Travel Guide (2025 Edition)

Opening Hours

Daily: 10:00 AM – 5:30 PM

Closed: Thanksgiving Day and December 25.

Top Things to Do

Explore the Fossil Halls:

Overview: The fossil halls showcase some of the most impressive dinosaur skeletons and prehistoric creatures, including the iconic Tyrannosaurus rex and the Brachiosaurus.

Tip: Don't miss the Hall of Saurischian Dinosaurs for a detailed look at the evolution of dinosaurs.

Visit the Hayden Planetarium:

Overview: The Hayden Planetarium, part of the Rose Center for Earth and Space, offers immersive space shows and exhibits about the cosmos.

Tip: Purchase tickets in advance for planetarium shows, which are highly popular and offer a captivating view of the universe.

Explore the Human Origins Exhibit:

Overview: This exhibit delves into the evolution of humans and our ancestors, featuring fossil casts and interactive displays.

Tip: Take your time to explore the detailed reconstructions of early human ancestors.

Discover the Hall of Biodiversity:

Overview: This exhibit highlights the diversity of life on Earth and the importance of preserving ecosystems.

Tip: The Hall of Biodiversity features a stunning diorama of the rainforest that's worth seeing.

Walk Through the Hall of Ocean Life:

Overview: The Hall of Ocean Life features a dramatic diorama of a giant blue whale and exhibits on marine ecosystems.

Tip: Spend time observing the blue whale model and learning about oceanic biodiversity.

Explore the Milstein Hall of Ocean Life:

Overview: Known for its remarkable 94-foot-long blue whale model, this exhibit provides insights into marine life and oceanography.

Tip: The blue whale model is a focal point and offers an awe-inspiring view of marine giants.

Practical Information

Admission:

General Admission: Suggested admission for adults is $23, seniors and students $18, and children (2-12) $13. The museum offers a "pay-what-you-wish" policy for New York State residents and NY, NJ, and CT students.

Special Exhibitions: Tickets for special exhibitions and the Hayden Planetarium are sold separately.

Accessibility:

Overview: AMNH is fully accessible to visitors with disabilities. Wheelchairs are available, and accessible entrances and restrooms are provided.

Tip: For specific accessibility needs, consult AMNH's website or contact visitor services.

Dining:

Overview: The museum has several dining options, including a café and a food court with various meal choices.

Tip: Consider dining at one of the museum's cafés for a convenient meal or snack during your visit.

Shopping:

Overview: The museum's gift shops offer a range of educational toys, books, and souvenirs related to natural history.

Tip: Browse the gift shops for unique items and memorabilia related to your visit.

Tips for Visiting

Plan Your Visit: With its vast array of exhibits, it's helpful to plan which areas you want to explore. Prioritize the exhibits that interest you the most.

Use the Museum App: Download the AMNH app for interactive maps, exhibit information, and audio guides.

Visit Early: To avoid crowds, visit the museum early in the day, especially if you plan to explore popular exhibits.

Comfortable Shoes: Wear comfortable shoes as you'll be doing a lot of walking.

Guggenheim Museum

The Guggenheim Museum is as much an architectural marvel as it is a repository of modern art. Designed by Frank Lloyd Wright, the museum's spiraling design is a testament to innovative architectural concepts. Inside, visitors can explore a diverse collection of modern and contemporary art from the 20th century to today.

Location

Address: 1071 Fifth Avenue, New York, NY 10128

Overview: Situated on Fifth Avenue, the Guggenheim is centrally located on Manhattan's Upper East Side, making it easily accessible from various parts of the city.

History

Founding: The museum was founded in 1937 by Solomon R. Guggenheim, a philanthropist and art collector, with the goal of creating a museum dedicated to modern art.

Architectural Design: Frank Lloyd Wright's design was chosen for its innovative approach, featuring a unique spiral ramp that allows visitors to view artworks in a continuous flow.

Expansion: The Guggenheim has expanded its collection and programming over the years, becoming a key player in the promotion of modern and contemporary art.

Opening Hours

Monday, Wednesday, Thursday, and Sunday: 10:00 AM – 5:30 PM

Friday and Saturday: 10:00 AM – 7:00 PM

Closed: Tuesday and major holidays such as Thanksgiving and December 25.

Top Things to Do

Explore the Spiral Ramp:

Overview: The museum's signature spiral ramp allows visitors to view artworks as they ascend or descend, offering a unique and immersive experience.

Tip: Start at the top of the ramp and work your way down to ensure you don't miss any exhibits.

Visit the Rotunda:

Overview: The central rotunda of the museum is a focal point, often featuring large-scale installations and special exhibitions.

Tip: Check out the current exhibitions and installations in the rotunda for a unique experience.

Explore the Collection:

Overview: The Guggenheim's collection includes works by prominent modern and contemporary artists such as Wassily Kandinsky, Marc Chagall, and Pablo Picasso.

Tip: Use the museum's website or app to get information on current exhibitions and must-see pieces.

Attend Public Programs:

Overview: The Guggenheim offers lectures, film screenings, and performance art as part of its public programming.

Tip: Review the museum's schedule and attend a program that interests you for a deeper engagement with the art.

Visit the Museum Store:

Overview: The museum store offers art-inspired merchandise, books, and gifts.

Tip: Browse the store for unique souvenirs and art-related items.

Practical Information

Admission:

General Admission: $25 for adults, $18 for seniors (65+), and $15 for students. Free for members and children (under 12). Pay-What-You-Wish admission on Saturdays from 5:00 PM – 7:00 PM.

Special Exhibitions: Tickets for special exhibitions are included with general admission unless otherwise specified.

Accessibility:

Overview: The Guggenheim is accessible to visitors with disabilities. Wheelchairs are available, and accessible entrances and restrooms are provided.

Tip: For specific accessibility needs, consult the museum's website or contact visitor services in advance.

Dining:

Overview: The museum offers dining options including a café and a restaurant, providing a range of meals and refreshments.

Tip: Consider dining at the museum's café for a convenient break during your visit.

Shopping:

Overview: The museum store offers a variety of art-inspired gifts, books, and merchandise.

Tip: Visit the store for unique art-related gifts and souvenirs.

Tips for Visiting

Plan Your Visit: The museum's unique layout and rotating exhibitions mean planning ahead can enhance your experience. Check the museum's website for information on current exhibitions and events.

Use the Museum App: Download the Guggenheim app for interactive maps, exhibit information, and audio guides.

Visit Early or Late: To avoid crowds, consider visiting early in the day or later in the afternoon, especially on weekends.

Comfortable Shoes: The museum's spiral ramp means a lot of walking, so wear comfortable shoes.

Whitney Museum of American Art

The Whitney Museum focuses on American art and contemporary works, featuring a diverse collection that highlights various artistic movements and trends. The museum is recognized for its innovative approach to exhibitions and its support of emerging artists.

Location

Address: 99 Gansevoort Street, New York, NY 10014

The Ultimate New York City Travel Guide (2025 Edition)

Overview: Situated in the vibrant Meatpacking District, the Whitney is easily accessible and positioned near other cultural attractions, including the High Line park and Chelsea Market.

History

Founding: Established in 1931 by Gertrude Vanderbilt Whitney, a patron and artist, the museum was created to support and exhibit American art.

Original Location: The Whitney originally opened in a Beaux-Arts building on West 8th Street, before moving to its current location in 2015.

Current Building: Designed by architect Renzo Piano, the museum's new building is a modern architectural marvel with an innovative design that includes terraces and open spaces.

Opening Hours

Monday, Wednesday, Thursday, Friday, and Sunday: 10:30 AM – 6:00 PM

Saturday: 10:30 AM – 10:00 PM

Closed: Tuesday and major holidays such as Thanksgiving and December 25.

Top Things to Do

Explore the Main Galleries:

Overview: The Whitney's main galleries feature a rotating selection of contemporary art from its collection, highlighting both established and emerging artists.

Tip: Check the museum's website for information on current exhibitions and must-see works.

Visit the Fifth Floor Terraces:

Overview: The museum's terraces offer stunning views of the city, including the Hudson River and the Meatpacking District.

Tip: Visit the terraces for a relaxing break and a unique vantage point of the cityscape.

Attend Special Exhibitions:

Overview: The Whitney hosts a variety of special exhibitions, including retrospectives, thematic shows, and solo exhibitions.

Tip: Plan your visit around special exhibitions to experience unique and often thought-provoking art.

Participate in Public Programs:

Overview: The museum offers a range of public programs, including artist talks, panel discussions, and film screenings.

Tip: Review the schedule of public programs on the museum's website and attend events that align with your interests.

Explore the Biennial Exhibition:

Overview: The Whitney Biennial is a major event showcasing contemporary American art and is held every two years.

Tip: The Biennial is a highlight of the museum's programming, offering a comprehensive overview of current trends and emerging artists.

Practical Information

Admission:

General Admission: $25 for adults, $18 for seniors (65+), and $18 for students. Free for members and children (18 and under). Pay-What-You-Wish on Fridays from 7:00 PM – 10:00 PM.

Special Exhibitions: Tickets for special exhibitions are included with general admission unless otherwise specified.

Accessibility:

Overview: The Whitney is fully accessible to visitors with disabilities. Wheelchairs are available, and accessible entrances and restrooms are provided.

Tip: For specific accessibility needs, consult the museum's website or contact visitor services in advance.

Dining:

Overview: The museum offers dining options, including a café and a full-service restaurant, providing a range of meals and refreshments.

Tip: Consider dining at the museum's restaurant for a more leisurely meal with views of the city.

Shopping:

Overview: The museum store offers art-inspired merchandise, books, and gifts related to current exhibitions.

Tip: Browse the store for unique gifts and art-related items to remember your visit.

Tips for Visiting

Plan Your Visit: The museum's dynamic exhibitions and public programs mean there's always something new to see. Check the website for current exhibitions and events before you go.

Use the Museum App: Download the Whitney app for interactive maps, exhibit information, and audio guides.

Visit During Off-Peak Hours: To avoid crowds, consider visiting during weekdays or later in the evening on Saturdays.

Comfortable Shoes: Expect to do a fair amount of walking, so wear comfortable footwear.

The Ultimate New York City Travel Guide (2025 Edition)

The Ultimate New York City Travel Guide (2025 Edition)

Chapter 13: 5 Day New York City Itinerary

Day 1: Iconic Manhattan & Midtown

Morning

Start Your Day:

Breakfast at: Balthazar

Location: 80 Spring Street, New York, NY 10012

Overview: This classic French bistro offers a hearty breakfast to start your day. Try the croissants, eggs Benedict, or a classic French toast.

Price: $20-$40 per person

Opening Hours: 7:30 AM – 11:00 AM

Activities:

Times Square

Location: Manhattan, NY 10036

Overview: Begin your day by immersing yourself in the dazzling lights and energy of Times Square. Explore the billboards, street performers, and shops.

Price: Free

Opening Hours: Open all day

Broadway Theaters

Location: Theater District, Manhattan

Overview: Walk through the Theater District to admire the famous Broadway marquees. If you're interested in catching a show, check ticket availability for matinee performances.

Price: $50-$200+ for show tickets

Opening Hours: Varies by show

Mid-Morning

Activities:

Empire State Building Observation Deck

Location: 350 5th Ave, New York, NY 10118

Overview: Head to the Empire State Building to take in panoramic views of New York City from the 86th-floor observation deck.

Price: $44 for adults, $38 for seniors (62+), $38 for children (6-12)

The Ultimate New York City Travel Guide (2025 Edition)

Opening Hours: 8:00 AM – 2:00 AM (last elevator up at 1:15 AM)

Tip: Buy tickets in advance online to avoid long lines.

Afternoon

Lunch at: **Keen's Steakhouse**

Location: 72 W 36th St, New York, NY 10018

Overview: Enjoy a classic New York steakhouse experience with options like prime rib and famous mutton chop.

Price: $40-$80 per person

Opening Hours: 11:45 AM – 9:00 PM

Activities:

The Museum of Modern Art (MoMA)

Location: 11 W 53rd St, New York, NY 10019

Overview: Explore MoMA's vast collection of modern and contemporary art, including works by Picasso, Van Gogh, and Warhol.

Price: $25 for adults, $18 for seniors (65+), $14 for students

Opening Hours: 10:30 AM – 5:30 PM (Fridays until 9:00 PM)

Tip: Allocate at least 2 hours to fully enjoy the exhibits.

Mid-Afternoon

Activities:

Stroll through Central Park

Location: Central Park, New York, NY

Overview: Take a leisurely walk or rent a bike to explore the park's famous landmarks like Bethesda Terrace, Strawberry Fields, and Bow Bridge.

Price: Free (bike rental varies)

Opening Hours: Open all day

Snack at: **Levain Bakery**

Location: 167 W 74th St, New York, NY 10023

Overview: Grab a famous chocolate chip cookie or a baked good from this beloved bakery.

Price: $5-$10

Opening Hours: 8:00 AM – 7:00 PM

Evening

Dinner at: **Carmine's Italian Restaurant**

Location: 200 W 44th St, New York, NY 10036

Overview: Enjoy a family-style Italian meal with hearty portions of classic dishes like lasagna and veal parmigiana.

Price: $30-$60 per person

Opening Hours: 11:30 AM – 11:00 PM

Activities:

Top of the Rock Observation Deck

Location: 30 Rockefeller Plaza, New York, NY 10112

Overview: Experience stunning nighttime views of the city's skyline, including the Empire State Building lit up.

Price: $43 for adults, $36 for seniors (62+), $36 for children (6-12)

Opening Hours: 9:00 AM – 11:00 PM

Tip: The view at night is spectacular, and the observation deck is less crowded in the evening.

Night

Activities:

Walk through Bryant Park

Location: Between 40th and 42nd Streets & Fifth and Sixth Avenues

Overview: Relax in Bryant Park's open space, enjoy the seasonal outdoor activities, or simply admire the illuminated skyscrapers.

Price: Free

Opening Hours: Open all day

Times Square at Night

Location: Manhattan, NY 10036

Overview: End your day by returning to Times Square to see the dazzling lights and feel the city's vibrant energy after dark.

Price: Free

Opening Hours: Open all day

Getting Around

Subway: The subway system is a quick and efficient way to navigate Manhattan. Use lines like the 1, 2, or 3 for Midtown, or the B, D, F, or M for access to Central Park and MoMA.

Walking: Many attractions in Midtown are within walking distance of each other. Wear comfortable shoes for walking.

Biking: Rent a Citi Bike for exploring Central Park or short trips between attractions.

Taxis/Rideshares: Available throughout the city for convenient travel, especially in the evenings or when distances are longer.

Final Tips

Purchase Tickets in Advance: For popular attractions like the Empire State Building and MoMA, buying tickets ahead of time can save you from long waits.

Use a MetroCard: For subway and bus rides, purchase a MetroCard from a vending machine or store.

Dress Comfortably: Manhattan involves a lot of walking, so wear comfortable clothing and shoes.

Day 2: Central Park, Museums, and Fifth Avenue

Morning

Start Your Day:

Breakfast at: **The Loeb Boathouse Central Park**

Location: E 72nd St, New York, NY 10021

Overview: Enjoy a delightful breakfast with a scenic view of Central Park's waterfront. Popular dishes include the smoked salmon bagel and the French toast.

Price: $20-$40 per person

Opening Hours: 8:00 AM – 10:00 AM

Activities:

Explore Central Park

Location: Central Park, New York, NY

Overview: Start your day with a leisurely stroll or bike ride through Central Park. Highlights include Bethesda Terrace, the Bow Bridge, and the Central Park Zoo.

Price: Free (bike rental varies)

Opening Hours: Open all day

Tip: Consider renting a bike from one of the nearby rental stations to cover more ground.

Mid-Morning

Activities:

Visit The Metropolitan Museum of Art (The Met)

Location: 1000 Fifth Avenue, New York, NY 10028

Overview: Spend your mid-morning exploring The Met's extensive collection of art spanning 5,000 years. Must-see sections include the Egyptian artifacts and European paintings.

Price: $30 for adults, $22 for seniors (65+), $17 for students

Opening Hours: 10:00 AM – 5:30 PM (Friday and Saturday until 9:00 PM)

Tip: Allocate at least 2-3 hours to fully appreciate the museum's highlights.

Afternoon

Lunch at: Café Sabarsky

Location: 1048 Fifth Avenue, New York, NY 10028

Overview: Located inside the Neue Galerie, this charming Viennese café offers a refined lunch menu with options like strudel and schnitzel.

Price: $20-$40 per person

Opening Hours: 11:00 AM – 4:00 PM

Activities:

Explore the American Museum of Natural History

Location: Central Park West & 79th St, New York, NY 10024

Overview: Spend your afternoon discovering the museum's fascinating exhibits, including dinosaur fossils, the Hayden Planetarium, and the dioramas of the Hall of Biodiversity.

Price: $23 for adults, $18 for seniors (60+), $13 for children (2-12)

Opening Hours: 10:00 AM – 5:30 PM

Tip: Don't miss the giant blue whale in the Milstein Hall of Ocean Life.

Mid-Afternoon

Activities:

Walk Down Fifth Avenue

Location: Fifth Avenue, New York, NY

Overview: Enjoy a stroll along Fifth Avenue, known for its high-end shopping and iconic landmarks. Visit landmarks such as St. Patrick's Cathedral and Rockefeller Center.

Price: Free to browse (shopping varies)

Opening Hours: Shops typically open 10:00 AM – 6:00 PM

Tip: Take your time exploring the flagship stores and designer boutiques.

Evening

Dinner at: **The Modern**

Location: 9 W 53rd St, New York, NY 10019

Overview: Located at the Museum of Modern Art, The Modern offers a refined dining experience with contemporary American cuisine. Try the tasting menu for a culinary adventure.

Price: $80-$150 per person

Opening Hours: 5:30 PM – 10:00 PM

Activities:

Visit Rockefeller Center

Location: 45 Rockefeller Plaza, New York, NY 10111

Overview: After dinner, explore Rockefeller Center, famous for its ice skating rink and the iconic tree lighting ceremony during the winter months.

Price: Free to explore (ice skating varies)

Opening Hours: Open all day

Top of the Rock Observation Deck

Location: 30 Rockefeller Plaza, New York, NY 10112

Overview: End your day with a visit to the Top of the Rock for stunning views of the city skyline at night, including the Empire State Building and Central Park.

Price: $43 for adults, $36 for seniors (62+), $36 for children (6-12)

Opening Hours: 9:00 AM – 11:00 PM (last elevator up at 10:15 PM)

Tip: Sunset and nighttime views are especially spectacular.

Night

Activities:

Enjoy a Nightcap at: **The Stinger Cocktail Bar & Kitchen**

Location: 132 W 31st St, New York, NY 10001

Overview: Relax with a signature cocktail or a glass of wine at this stylish bar, located near the Empire State Building.

Price: $15-$25 per drink

Opening Hours: 5:00 PM – 12:00 AM

Getting Around

Subway: Utilize the subway for efficient travel between attractions. The 1, 2, or 3 lines can take you from Central Park to the Met and the American Museum of Natural History.

Walking: Many sites are within walking distance, especially in the Midtown area. Comfortable shoes are recommended.

Biking: Use Citi Bike for a scenic ride through Central Park or between nearby attractions.

Taxis/Rideshares: Available for convenient travel, particularly in the evenings or if you prefer direct routes.

Day 3: Lower Manhattan & Brooklyn

Morning

Start Your Day:

Breakfast at: The Egg Shop

Location: 151 Elizabeth St, New York, NY 10012

Overview: Begin with a hearty breakfast featuring creative egg dishes and fresh, wholesome ingredients.

Price: $15-$25 per person

Opening Hours: 8:00 AM – 3:00 PM

Activities:

Explore the Financial District

Location: Manhattan, NY

Overview: Visit landmarks such as Wall Street, the New York Stock Exchange, and the Charging Bull statue. Stroll around the historic financial district and soak in its rich history.

Price: Free

Opening Hours: Open all day

Tip: Early morning is a great time to avoid crowds and get photos with fewer people.

Visit the 9/11 Memorial & Museum

Location: 180 Greenwich St, New York, NY 10007

Overview: Pay your respects and learn about the events of September 11, 2001, through exhibits and personal stories at the museum.

Price: $26 for adults, $20 for seniors (65+), $15 for youth (7-17)

Opening Hours: 9:00 AM – 8:00 PM

Tip: Allocate 2-3 hours for the museum visit.

Mid-Morning

Activities:

Walk Across the Brooklyn Bridge

Location: Entrance at Park Row, Manhattan, NY

Overview: Enjoy stunning views of the Manhattan skyline and the East River as you walk across this iconic bridge connecting Manhattan and Brooklyn.

Price: Free

Opening Hours: Open all day

Tip: The bridge is best explored in the morning to avoid heavy crowds.

Afternoon

Lunch at: **Juliana's Pizza**

Location: 19 Old Fulton St, Brooklyn, NY 11201

Overview: Savor some of Brooklyn's best pizza at Juliana's, known for its delicious, classic pies and casual atmosphere.

Price: $20-$40 per person

Opening Hours: 11:30 AM – 10:00 PM

Activities:

Explore DUMBO (Down Under the Manhattan Bridge Overpass)

Location: Brooklyn, NY

Overview: Wander through DUMBO, a trendy Brooklyn neighborhood with cobblestone streets, art galleries, boutiques, and great views of Manhattan.

Price: Free

Opening Hours: Open all day

Tip: Check out Brooklyn Bridge Park for waterfront views and photo opportunities.

Visit the Brooklyn Museum

Location: 200 Eastern Pkwy, Brooklyn, NY 11238

Overview: Explore a diverse range of exhibits from ancient Egyptian artifacts to contemporary art in this renowned museum.

Price: $16 for adults, $10 for seniors (65+), $6 for students

Opening Hours: 11:00 AM – 6:00 PM (Thursday and Friday until 10:00 PM)

Tip: The museum has a variety of exhibitions, so check ahead for special exhibits.

Mid-Afternoon

Activities:

Explore Prospect Park

Location: Brooklyn, NY

Overview: Discover the natural beauty of Prospect Park with its expansive greenery, lakes, and recreational activities. Visit the Brooklyn Botanic Garden nearby if time permits.

Price: Free

Opening Hours: Open all day

Tip: Rent a bike to cover more ground and enjoy the park's highlights.

Evening

Dinner at: **The River Café**

Location: 1 Water St, Brooklyn, NY 11201

Overview: Enjoy a romantic dinner with breathtaking views of the Manhattan skyline and the Brooklyn Bridge. The menu features upscale American cuisine with a focus on fresh, local ingredients.

Price: $80-$150 per person

Opening Hours: 5:00 PM – 10:00 PM

Activities:

Brooklyn Heights Promenade

Location: Brooklyn, NY

Overview: After dinner, take a leisurely stroll along the Brooklyn Heights Promenade for stunning views of the Manhattan skyline at night.

Price: Free

Opening Hours: Open all day

Enjoy a Nightcap at: **Clementine Bakery**

Location: 425 Sackett St, Brooklyn, NY 11231

Overview: Wrap up your day with a relaxing drink or dessert at this cozy bakery known for its charming ambiance and delicious treats.

Price: $10-$20 per person

Opening Hours: 7:00 PM – 10:00 PM

Getting Around

Subway: The 4, 5, or 6 lines will take you to the Financial District and Lower Manhattan. From there, use the A or C line to get to Brooklyn.

Walking: Many attractions, especially in DUMBO and Brooklyn Heights, are best explored on foot.

Biking: Rent a bike for easy travel across the Brooklyn Bridge and through Prospect Park.

Taxis/Rideshares: Available for convenient transport between neighborhoods, especially for evening activities.

Day 4: Museums and Neighborhoods

Morning

Start Your Day:

Breakfast at: Balthazar

Location: 80 Spring St, New York, NY 10012

Overview: Begin your day with a classic French breakfast at Balthazar, known for its pastries, croissants, and eggs Benedict.

Price: $20-$40 per person

Opening Hours: 7:00 AM – 11:00 AM

Activities:

Visit the Guggenheim Museum

Location: 1071 Fifth Avenue, New York, NY 10128

Overview: Explore the Guggenheim's iconic spiral architecture and its impressive collection of modern and contemporary art. Highlights include works by Picasso, Kandinsky, and more.

Price: $25 for adults, $18 for seniors (65+), $15 for students

Opening Hours: 11:00 AM – 6:00 PM (Saturday until 8:00 PM)

Tip: Allocate 2 hours to enjoy the museum and its unique architecture.

Mid-Morning

Activities:

Explore the Metropolitan Museum of Art (The Met) - Met Cloisters

Location: 99 Margaret Corbin Drive, Fort Tryon Park, New York, NY 10040

Overview: Visit The Met Cloisters, a branch of The Met dedicated to medieval art and architecture, located in a beautiful setting overlooking the Hudson River.

Price: Included with The Met general admission ticket

Opening Hours: 10:00 AM – 5:15 PM

Tip: Enjoy the peaceful gardens and medieval art collection, including the famous Unicorn Tapestries.

Afternoon

Lunch at: The Spotted Pig

Location: 314 W 11th St, New York, NY 10014

Overview: Enjoy a gastropub lunch in the West Village, known for its creative menu featuring dishes like the signature chargrilled burger and shoestring fries.

Price: $20-$40 per person

Opening Hours: 11:30 AM – 12:00 AM

Activities:

Explore the West Village

Location: Manhattan, NY

Overview: Stroll through the charming, historic streets of the West Village, known for its quaint brownstones, independent shops, and cozy cafes.

Price: Free

Opening Hours: Open all day

Tip: Visit Bleecker Street for boutique shopping and enjoy the neighborhood's artistic atmosphere.

Visit the Whitney Museum of American Art

Location: 99 Gansevoort St, New York, NY 10014

Overview: Discover American art from the 20th century to the present at the Whitney, featuring works by artists such as Edward Hopper and Jeff Koons.

Price: $25 for adults, $18 for seniors (65+), $18 for students

Opening Hours: 10:30 AM – 6:00 PM (Friday and Saturday until 10:00 PM)

Tip: The museum's outdoor terraces offer fantastic views of the city.

Mid-Afternoon

Activities:

Explore Chelsea Market

Location: 75 9th Ave, New York, NY 10011

Overview: Dive into Chelsea Market for a unique shopping and dining experience. Browse through gourmet food vendors, artisanal shops, and enjoy a snack or coffee.

Price: Varies by vendor

Opening Hours: 7:00 AM – 10:00 PM

Tip: Try the famous Lobster Place for a seafood treat or grab a sweet from Doughnuttery.

Walk the High Line

Location: New York, NY

Overview: Enjoy a scenic walk along the High Line, an elevated park built on a former rail line, offering beautiful views, gardens, and art installations.

Price: Free

Opening Hours: 7:00 AM – 10:00 PM

Tip: The High Line is particularly lovely in the afternoon when the light softens, and you can often catch local performances or art installations.

Evening

Dinner at: Estela

Location: 47 E Houston St, New York, NY 10012

Overview: Enjoy a refined dining experience at Estela, which offers a menu of innovative dishes with fresh, seasonal ingredients. Popular choices include the ricotta and honey dish.

Price: $60-$100 per person

Opening Hours: 5:30 PM – 11:00 PM

Activities:

Experience a Night Out in Greenwich Village

Location: Manhattan, NY

Overview: Explore the lively Greenwich Village neighborhood, known for its vibrant nightlife, jazz clubs, and comedy venues.

Price: Varies by venue

Opening Hours: Varies by venue

Tip: Consider catching a show at the Comedy Cellar or a live music performance at the Village Vanguard.

Getting Around

Subway: Use the 1, 2, or 3 lines to reach the West Village and Chelsea. The A, C, or E lines will take you to the High Line.

Walking: Many of the day's attractions are within walking distance of each other, especially in Greenwich Village and Chelsea.

Biking: Consider renting a bike to easily navigate between neighborhoods and along the High Line.

Taxis/Rideshares: Convenient for traveling between the West Village and Chelsea or for evening activities.

Final Tips

Museum Tickets: Buy tickets in advance where possible to avoid long lines.

Comfortable Clothing: Wear comfortable clothes and shoes for a day of exploring and walking.

Local Delights: Be sure to sample local treats and unique finds at Chelsea Market and Greenwich Village.

Day 5: Day Trip or Relax

Option 1: Day Trip

Destination: Long Island – Beaches and Vineyards

Morning:

Breakfast at: Bagel Boss

Location: 1771 1st Ave, New York, NY 10128

Overview: Grab a classic New York bagel with cream cheese or a breakfast sandwich before heading out for the day.

Price: $10-$15 per person

Opening Hours: 7:00 AM – 2:00 PM

Travel to Long Island:

By Train: Take the Long Island Rail Road (LIRR) from Penn Station to Ronkonkoma, which is a gateway to the North Fork and South Fork of Long Island.

Duration: Approximately 1.5 hours

Price: $20-$25 round trip

Mid-Morning:

Explore the Hamptons

Location: South Fork, Long Island

Overview: Visit one of the upscale Hamptons towns like East Hampton or Southampton. Enjoy the picturesque beaches and boutique shopping.

Price: Free to explore, shopping and dining extra

Tip: The Hamptons are known for their beautiful beaches and charming towns.

Lunch:

At: **The Lobster Roll**

Location: 1980 Montauk Hwy, Amagansett, NY 11930

Overview: Enjoy a fresh seafood lunch featuring the famous lobster roll and other seafood dishes.

Price: $20-$40 per person

Opening Hours: 11:30 AM – 8:00 PM

Afternoon:

Visit a Vineyard on the North Fork

Location: North Fork, Long Island

Overview: Spend your afternoon at a local vineyard such as **Wölffer Estate Vineyard** or **Bedell Cellars**, where you can tour the winery and enjoy a wine tasting.

Price: $15-$30 for tastings

Tip: Many vineyards require advance reservations, so book ahead.

Evening:

Return to NYC

By Train: Take the LIRR back to Penn Station.

Duration: Approximately 1.5 hours

Dinner at: **Katz's Delicatessen**

Location: 205 E Houston St, New York, NY 10002

Overview: After your return, enjoy a classic New York meal at Katz's, famous for its pastrami sandwiches.

Price: $20-$40 per person

Opening Hours: 8:00 AM – 10:00 PM

Option 2: Relax in NYC

Morning:

Breakfast at: Dominique Ansel Bakery

Location: 189 Spring St, New York, NY 10012

Overview: Start your day with a sweet treat from Dominique Ansel, known for innovative pastries like the Cronut.

Price: $10-$20 per person

Opening Hours: 8:00 AM – 7:00 PM

Relax in Central Park

Location: Manhattan, NY

Overview: Spend a leisurely morning in Central Park. Enjoy a stroll, rent a rowboat, or simply relax on the Great Lawn.

Price: Free

Opening Hours: Open all day

Tip: Pack a picnic and enjoy it in one of the park's scenic spots.

Mid-Morning:

Visit a Local Café

At: Cafe Regular

Location: 271 E 10th St, New York, NY 10009

Overview: Enjoy a coffee or light snack in this cozy café known for its charming atmosphere.

Price: $5-$15 per person

Opening Hours: 8:00 AM – 7:00 PM

Afternoon:

Visit the New York Public Library

Location: 476 5th Ave, New York, NY 10018

Overview: Explore the historic library and its impressive architecture. The Rose Main Reading Room is a highlight.

Price: Free

Opening Hours: 10:00 AM – 6:00 PM

Tip: Check for any special exhibitions or tours that may be available.

Explore Bryant Park

Location: Between 40th and 42nd Streets and Fifth and Sixth Avenues

Overview: Relax in Bryant Park, which offers a tranquil setting with lush greenery, a reading room, and seasonal events.

Price: Free

Opening Hours: Open all day

Evening:

Dinner at: **Le Bernardin**

Location: 155 W 51st St, New York, NY 10019

Overview: Indulge in a fine dining experience at Le Bernardin, known for its exquisite seafood dishes and elegant atmosphere.

Price: $100-$200 per person

Opening Hours: 5:30 PM – 10:00 PM

Relaxing Evening Stroll:

Location: Walk along the Hudson River Park or through the illuminated streets of Manhattan.

Overview: Enjoy the evening ambiance of NYC and take in the skyline views.

Getting Around

For Day Trip: Use the LIRR for travel to Long Island. Consider renting a car for more flexibility on Long Island or use ride-sharing services.

For Relaxing Day: Use the subway, buses, or walk to explore the city. Taxis and rideshares are convenient for longer distances.

Final Tips

Day Trip: Plan ahead for train schedules and vineyard reservations.

Relaxing Day: Wear comfortable clothing and shoes for a mix of relaxation and light exploration.

Weather Check: Always check the weather forecast to prepare for outdoor activities.

Chapter 14: Practical Travel Information

Language Tips and Useful Phrases

Basic Language Tips

English Is Predominant:

English is the primary language used for all public signs, menus, and interactions. Most New Yorkers are fluent in English, making communication relatively straightforward for English-speaking tourists.

Cultural Sensitivity:

New Yorkers are used to encountering people from all over the world. Being polite and respectful goes a long way. Use "please" and "thank you" in your interactions.

Understanding Accents:

Be aware that New Yorkers may speak with different regional accents or speak quickly. If you don't understand something, don't hesitate to ask for clarification.

Emergency Services:

In case of an emergency, dial 911. Operators will provide assistance in English, and many emergency services are equipped to handle calls in other languages if necessary.

Useful Phrases

Greetings and Basics:

Hello: "Hello" or "Hi"

Goodbye: "Goodbye" or "Bye"

Please: "Please"

Thank you: "Thank you" or "Thanks"

Excuse me: "Excuse me"

Getting Directions:

"Can you help me find [place]?"

Example: "Can you help me find the nearest subway station?"

"How do I get to [place]?"

Example: "How do I get to the Metropolitan Museum of Art?"

"Is this the right way to [place]?"

Example: "Is this the right way to Times Square?"

At Restaurants and Shops:

"Can I see the menu, please?"

"Do you have any recommendations?"

"How much is this?"

"Can I pay with a credit card?"

Making Small Talk:

"How are you?"

"I'm just visiting. Do you have any recommendations for things to do in the city?"

"What's the best way to get around?"

Asking for Help:

"I'm lost. Can you help me?"

"Where is the nearest restroom?"

"Can you call a cab for me?"

Transportation Specifics:

"Which subway line goes to [place]?"

"How do I get a MetroCard?"

"Where can I catch a bus to [place]?"

Additional Language and Communication Tips

Use Technology:

Translation Apps: Use apps like Google Translate for real-time translation if you encounter language barriers.

Maps and Navigation: Utilize navigation apps such as Google Maps or Apple Maps for detailed directions and public transit information.

Learn Basic Local Slang:

"NYC": Abbreviation for New York City.

"The City": Refers to Manhattan specifically.

"Subway": The underground train system.

"Bagels": A popular NYC breakfast item.

Be Clear and Specific:

When asking for directions or information, be specific about your destination or needs to avoid confusion.

Respect Local Customs:

New Yorkers are generally direct in their communication. It's normal to be straightforward, but always maintain politeness.

Health and Safety Tips

Health Tips

Stay Hydrated and Eat Well:

Water: Carry a reusable water bottle and drink plenty of water throughout the day, especially if you're exploring on foot.

Food: NYC has a diverse food scene, so try to balance indulgent meals with healthy options. Look for fresh fruit, vegetables, and whole grains.

Weather Preparedness:

Cold Weather: In winter, dress in layers and wear warm clothing, including a hat, gloves, and scarf. Check weather forecasts to be prepared for snow or icy conditions.

Hot Weather: In summer, wear light clothing, use sunscreen, and take breaks in the shade. Be mindful of heat exhaustion and avoid excessive outdoor activity during peak heat hours.

Medical Needs:

Pharmacies: Pharmacies are widely available for over-the-counter medications and health supplies. Major chains include CVS and Walgreens.

Doctors and Hospitals: In case of a medical emergency, dial 911. For non-emergencies, you can find urgent care centers throughout the city.

Vaccinations and Health Precautions:

Travel Vaccinations: Ensure your routine vaccinations are up to date. Consult your doctor if you have specific health concerns before traveling.

Travel Health Insurance: Consider purchasing travel health insurance to cover any unexpected medical costs during your trip.

COVID-19 Precautions:

Masks: While mask mandates have relaxed, wearing a mask in crowded areas or on public transit can still be a good practice.

Hand Hygiene: Wash your hands frequently with soap and water or use hand sanitizer.

Safety Tips

Be Aware of Your Surroundings:

Personal Safety: Stay alert in busy areas, especially when using your phone or navigating through crowds. Keep your belongings secure and avoid displaying expensive items.

The Ultimate New York City Travel Guide (2025 Edition)

Neighborhood Awareness: Familiarize yourself with the areas you plan to visit. Some neighborhoods are more tourist-friendly than others, so research ahead of time.

Use Reliable Transportation:

Public Transit: The subway and buses are safe and efficient. Be cautious during late-night travel and keep your belongings close.

Taxis and Rideshares: Use official taxi services or reputable rideshare apps like Uber and Lyft. Verify the vehicle and driver details before getting in.

Emergency Contacts:

Emergency Services: Dial 911 for police, fire, or medical emergencies.

Local Authorities: Each neighborhood has its own precinct. Know the nearest police station if needed.

Avoiding Scams:

Street Performers and Solicitors: Be cautious with street performers or people asking for money. Politely decline if you feel uncomfortable.

Tourist Traps: Research attractions and restaurants beforehand to avoid overpriced or low-quality options.

Securing Your Belongings:

Pickpockets: Keep wallets, phones, and other valuables secure and close to your body, especially in crowded areas and on public transit.

Hotel Safety: Use the safe in your hotel room for important documents and valuables.

Local Laws and Regulations:

Drug Laws: Be aware of local drug laws. Marijuana is legal in NYC but be mindful of where you can legally use it.

Alcohol Laws: The legal drinking age is 21. Public consumption of alcohol is generally prohibited unless in designated areas.

Health and Safety Resources

NYC Health Department: Offers resources and information on health-related concerns.

NYC 311: Provides information on city services and non-emergency issues.

Traveler's Assistance: Available through hotel concierges and local tourism centers for help with any issues that arise during your stay.

Emergency Contacts and Services

Emergency Services

Emergency Number:

911: This is the number to dial for any immediate police, fire, or medical emergencies. Operators are available 24/7 and can dispatch appropriate emergency services.

Police:

NYC Police Department (NYPD): For non-emergencies or general inquiries, you can contact the NYPD precinct relevant to your location. Precincts are spread across the five boroughs, and their contact numbers are available online.

Fire Department:

FDNY: The Fire Department of New York handles fires, rescues, and hazardous material incidents. In an emergency, dial 911. For non-emergency inquiries, visit the FDNY website or contact the local precinct.

Medical Emergencies:

Hospitals: NYC has numerous hospitals offering emergency care, including:

NewYork-Presbyterian Hospital: One of the city's largest and most renowned hospitals.

Mount Sinai Health System: Provides comprehensive emergency services.

Lenox Hill Hospital: Known for its emergency care and specialized services.

Urgent Care: For non-life-threatening conditions requiring immediate attention, urgent care centers are available throughout the city.

Poison Control:

New York City Poison Control Center: Call **1-800-222-1222** for assistance with poisoning or exposure to hazardous substances.

Emergency Management:

NYC Office of Emergency Management (OEM): Provides information and updates on emergencies such as natural disasters, severe weather, and other city-wide incidents. Visit their website for alerts and guidance.

General Assistance

NYC 311:

311: This number provides non-emergency city services and information, including assistance with housing, sanitation, and neighborhood services. It's also a resource for reporting issues like street repairs and noise complaints.

The Ultimate New York City Travel Guide (2025 Edition)

Local Tourist Information:

NYC & Company: The city's official tourism organization can offer assistance and information for visitors. Their website provides resources on attractions, accommodations, and local tips.

Legal and Safety Assistance:

Legal Aid Society: Provides legal assistance for various issues, including tenant rights and consumer protection. Visit their website or call for guidance.

Travel and Visitor Assistance:

Concierge Services: Most hotels offer concierge services that can assist with emergency situations or provide information on local services.

Language Assistance:

Language Line Services: Many emergency services and public agencies offer translation services to assist non-English speakers. Indicate your language preference when calling 911 or visiting a service provider.

Tips for Handling Emergencies

Know Your Location: Always be aware of your current location and nearby landmarks to provide accurate information when seeking help.

Keep Important Numbers Handy: Store emergency contact numbers in your phone or write them down for quick access.

Stay Calm: In an emergency, remain as calm as possible to communicate clearly and follow instructions.

Follow Safety Instructions: Adhere to guidance from emergency personnel and public announcements during emergencies.

Have a Plan: Familiarize yourself with emergency exits and procedures at your accommodation and major attractions.

Internet and Connectivity

Wi-Fi Access

Public Wi-Fi:

NYC Wi-Fi: New York City offers free public Wi-Fi in several locations, including parks, plazas, and major transit hubs. Look for the "NYC Free Wi-Fi" network.

Wi-Fi Hotspots: Many cafes, restaurants, and shops offer free Wi-Fi for customers. Look for signage indicating Wi-Fi availability and ask staff for the password if needed.

Municipal Hotspots:

LinkNYC: The city's LinkNYC kiosks provide free Wi-Fi across NYC. These kiosks are located on sidewalks and offer high-speed internet access. No password is needed—just connect to the "LinkNYC" network.

Libraries and Public Spaces:

Public Libraries: Many New York Public Library branches offer free Wi-Fi. You can use the internet while visiting these locations.

Public Spaces: Wi-Fi is often available in public spaces like Bryant Park, Union Square, and parts of Central Park.

Mobile Connectivity

SIM Cards and Data Plans:

Local SIM Cards: Purchase a local SIM card with a data plan from carriers like Verizon, AT&T, or T-Mobile. SIM cards are available at major electronics stores, airport kiosks, and carrier retail locations.

International SIM Cards: If you're visiting from abroad, consider buying an international SIM card that offers coverage in the U.S. These can be ordered online or purchased at major airports.

Mobile Hotspots:

Rent a Hotspot: Portable Wi-Fi hotspots can be rented for the duration of your stay. This option provides a reliable internet connection for multiple devices. Rental services are available online or at major airports.

Roaming Plans:

Check with Your Carrier: Before traveling, check if your home mobile carrier offers international roaming plans for data usage in the U.S. These plans may be more convenient if you prefer not to switch SIM cards.

Internet Cafés and Co-Working Spaces

Internet Cafés:

Locations: Internet cafés are available throughout NYC, particularly in tourist areas and near major transit hubs. These provide computer access and internet connectivity.

Co-Working Spaces:

Day Passes: Co-working spaces like WeWork or Regus offer day passes that include access to high-speed internet and workstations. These spaces are ideal if you need a quiet environment to work.

Tips for Staying Connected

Battery Management:

Charging Stations: Many public areas, including airports and major train stations, have charging stations for phones and devices. Carry a portable charger to ensure you have backup power.

Network Security:

Use VPNs: When using public Wi-Fi, consider using a Virtual Private Network (VPN) to secure your connection and protect your personal information.

Data Usage:

Monitor Usage: Be mindful of your data usage, especially if using a local SIM card or international plan with limited data. Turn off automatic updates and use Wi-Fi whenever available.

Emergency Access:

Offline Maps: Download offline maps and important information before traveling to ensure you have access even if connectivity is limited.

Accessibility in New York City

Transportation Accessibility

Subway System:

Accessible Stations: Not all subway stations are fully accessible, but the MTA (Metropolitan Transportation Authority) is working on improving accessibility. Accessible stations are equipped with elevators, ramps, and wide turnstiles.

Elevator Locations: Use the MTA's website or app to find accessible stations and elevators. Look for the "Accessible Stations" map.

Assistance: MTA staff can provide assistance. Request help at a station if needed, or call the MTA's accessibility hotline.

Buses:

Accessible Buses: All NYC buses are wheelchair accessible and have audio and visual announcements for stops.

Bus Stops: Ensure that the bus stop you are using has a wheelchair-accessible platform.

Taxis and Rideshares:

Accessible Taxis: New York City has a fleet of wheelchair-accessible yellow taxis. You can request one by calling the dispatch center or using ride-hailing apps like Uber and Lyft, which offer options for accessible vehicles.

Rideshare Services: Uber and Lyft have options for wheelchair-accessible vehicles. Select the appropriate option in the app to request an accessible ride.

Ferries:

Accessible Ferries: NYC ferries are equipped with accessible features, including ramps and designated seating. Check schedules and accessibility information on the NYC Ferry website.

Attractions and Landmarks

Central Park:

Accessible Routes: Central Park has accessible paths and entrances. Some attractions within the park, like the Central Park Zoo and certain playgrounds, are also accessible.

Wheelchair Rentals: Wheelchairs are available for rent at certain locations within the park.

Museums and Cultural Institutions:

Accessibility Features: Major museums, including The Met, MoMA, and the American Museum of Natural History, offer accessibility features such as ramps, elevators, and wheelchairs. Many also provide guided tours and sensory accommodations.

Assistive Devices: Museums often offer assistive listening devices and braille materials. Check their websites or contact them in advance for specific needs.

Broadway Theaters:

Accessible Seating: Many Broadway theaters offer accessible seating options and services. It's best to book tickets in advance and notify the box office of any special requirements.

Public Buildings and Attractions:

Accessibility: Most public buildings, including city halls and tourist information centers, are accessible. Look for accessible entrances and restrooms.

Accommodation Accessibility

Hotels:

Accessible Rooms: Many hotels in NYC offer accessible rooms with features like roll-in showers, grab bars, and wider doorways. Contact the hotel directly to ensure they can meet your specific needs.

Reservation: When booking a room, specify any accessibility requirements to ensure the hotel can accommodate your needs.

Rental Apartments:

Accessibility: Platforms like Airbnb offer filters to find accessible rental options. Look for properties with features like ramps, elevators, and accessible bathrooms.

Accessibility Resources

NYC Disability Resources:

NYC Mayor's Office for People with Disabilities: Provides information and resources related to accessibility in NYC. Visit their website or contact them for assistance.

Accessible NYC App: This app provides information on accessible locations and services across the city.

Travel Guides:

Accessible Travel Guides: Various online resources and guides focus on accessible travel in NYC. They provide detailed information about accessible attractions, transportation, and services.

Local Assistance:

Visitor Centers: NYC visitor centers can provide information on accessibility features and assistance during your stay.

General Tips

Plan Ahead: Research and plan your itinerary with accessibility needs in mind. Contact venues and transportation providers in advance to confirm accessibility features.

Use Technology: Leverage accessibility apps and online resources to find and navigate accessible locations.

Communicate Needs: Clearly communicate your accessibility needs to service providers, including hotels, restaurants, and attractions, to ensure they can accommodate you.

Chapter 15: Travel Tips and Final Thoughts

Frequently Asked Questions

1. What's the best way to get around New York City?

Subway: The subway is efficient, relatively affordable, and covers most areas of the city. It operates 24/7.

Buses: Buses are a good option for traveling above ground and can be useful for short distances.

Taxis and Rideshares: Cabs and rideshare services like Uber and Lyft are convenient but can be expensive and affected by traffic.

Walking: Many neighborhoods are best explored on foot. It's often quicker to walk than to drive or take a cab.

Biking: Citi Bike offers a bike-sharing service that's perfect for short trips and exploring the city.

Ferries: Ferries offer scenic routes and access to areas like Staten Island and Brooklyn.

2. What's the best time to visit New York City?

Spring (April to June): Pleasant weather and fewer crowds. Ideal for outdoor activities and sightseeing.

Fall (September to November): Mild weather and beautiful fall foliage. Great for walking tours and exploring neighborhoods.

Summer (July to August): Warm weather and many outdoor events. However, it can be crowded and hot.

Winter (December to February): Cold weather but festive holiday events and decorations. Perfect for experiencing New York's winter charm.

3. How much should I budget for a trip to New York City?

Accommodation: Expect to pay $200-$500 per night for mid-range to luxury hotels. Budget accommodations and hostels can range from $50-$150 per night.

Food: Dining costs vary widely. Budget around $10-$20 per meal for casual dining and $50-$100 for a mid-range restaurant.

Attractions: Many attractions have entrance fees ranging from $25-$50. Some museums and sites offer free or reduced admission on certain days.

Transportation: Subway rides cost $2.90 each. Taxis start at $2.50 plus $0.50 per 1/5 mile or minute in traffic. Rideshares can be more variable.

4. Is New York City safe for tourists?

Generally Safe: New York City is generally safe, but like any large city, it's important to stay aware of your surroundings and take basic safety precautions.

Stay Alert: Be cautious of pickpockets, especially in crowded areas and tourist spots. Avoid displaying expensive items and keep your belongings secure.

5. What should I pack for a trip to New York City?

Comfortable Shoes: You'll be doing a lot of walking, so comfortable, sturdy shoes are essential.

Weather-Appropriate Clothing: Pack layers for spring and fall, lightweight clothing for summer, and warm clothing for winter. Include a rain jacket or umbrella.

Essential Items: Don't forget your phone charger, camera, and any medications you may need.

6. Can I use my cell phone in New York City?

Cell Service: Most international and U.S. cell phones work in NYC. Consider purchasing a local SIM card or activating an international plan for data and calls.

Wi-Fi: Free Wi-Fi is available in many public spaces and businesses. Use a VPN for secure browsing on public networks.

7. What are some must-see attractions in New York City?

Statue of Liberty and Ellis Island

Central Park

Times Square

Empire State Building

Broadway Shows

Metropolitan Museum of Art

Brooklyn Bridge

8. How do I get tickets for popular attractions?

Advance Purchase: Many attractions offer online ticket sales. It's best to buy tickets in advance to avoid long lines and ensure availability.

City Passes: Consider purchasing a New York City Pass or Explorer Pass, which offers discounted admission to multiple attractions.

9. Are there any free activities in New York City?

Central Park: Enjoy the park's many trails, open spaces, and landmarks.

Museums: Some museums offer free or pay-what-you-wish admission on specific days.

Public Events: Check out free events and festivals happening around the city.

10. How do I handle emergencies while in New York City?

Emergency Numbers: Call 911 for police, fire, or medical emergencies.

Medical Services: New York City has numerous hospitals and urgent care centers. Know the location of the nearest hospital or urgent care facility.

Lost Items: Report lost items to the local police precinct or the Lost and Found department of the relevant public transport service.

Tips for First-Time Visitors

1. Plan Ahead

Research and Itinerary: Before your trip, research the attractions you want to see and create a rough itinerary. Prioritize must-see sights and plan your days to make the most of your time.

Tickets and Reservations: Book tickets for popular attractions and Broadway shows in advance to avoid long lines and secure your spot.

2. Use Public Transportation

Subway System: The subway is the most efficient way to get around. Purchase a MetroCard and familiarize yourself with subway lines and stops. Use a subway map or navigation app to help you find your way.

Buses and Ferries: Buses are a good option for traveling above ground. Ferries offer a scenic route and can take you to places like Staten Island or Brooklyn.

3. Wear Comfortable Shoes

Walking City: New York City is best explored on foot. Wear comfortable, sturdy shoes as you'll be walking a lot throughout the day.

4. Stay Hydrated and Snack Smart

Stay Hydrated: Carry a reusable water bottle and refill it at public water fountains. Staying hydrated will help you keep up with the city's fast pace.

Healthy Snacks: Pack snacks for when you're on the go, especially if you plan to explore for long stretches without stopping for a meal.

5. Be Aware of Your Surroundings

Safety First: Keep your belongings secure and be mindful of your surroundings. Avoid displaying expensive items and stay alert, especially in crowded areas.

Personal Space: Respect personal space and be aware of local customs regarding behavior in public places.

6. Embrace the City's Pace

Fast-Paced Environment: New York City is known for its fast-paced lifestyle. Don't be discouraged if you feel rushed or if people seem in a hurry. Keep up with the flow and enjoy the energy of the city.

7. Learn Basic Local Etiquette

Tipping: Familiarize yourself with tipping practices in New York. Tips are expected in restaurants, taxis, and for other services.

Queueing: Respect lines and wait your turn. Queueing is a standard practice and is expected in most places.

8. Explore Different Neighborhoods

Neighborhoods: Each neighborhood in NYC has its own unique character. Explore areas like SoHo, Greenwich Village, and Williamsburg to get a feel for the city's diversity.

Local Eats: Try local favorites and explore different cuisines. New York is known for its diverse food scene, from street food to fine dining.

9. Keep an Eye on the Weather

Weather Preparedness: Check the weather forecast before heading out each day and dress accordingly. NYC weather can change quickly, so it's good to be prepared for any conditions.

10. Use a Navigation App

Apps: Use apps like Google Maps or Citymapper to navigate the subway system and find your way around the city. These apps can provide real-time directions and updates.

11. Respect the City's Rules and Regulations

Local Laws: Follow local laws and regulations, such as restrictions on smoking and alcohol consumption. Be aware of regulations specific to public spaces and transportation.

12. Take Time to Relax

Downtime: NYC is a bustling city, but it's important to take breaks and enjoy some downtime. Relax in a park, sit in a café, or take a leisurely walk to recharge.

13. Interact with Locals

Local Tips: Don't be afraid to ask locals for recommendations or directions. New Yorkers are generally helpful and can provide valuable insights into the best places to visit and eat.

Tips for Solo Travelers

1. Stay Connected

Local SIM Card or Roaming Plan: Ensure you have a reliable way to stay connected. Consider getting a local SIM card or activating an international roaming plan for data and calls.

Useful Apps: Download essential apps such as Google Maps, Citymapper, Uber/Lyft, and any apps for public transportation to help you navigate the city efficiently.

2. Choose Accommodation Wisely

Safe and Central Locations: Select accommodation in safe, well-lit neighborhoods that are centrally located. Areas like Midtown, the Upper West Side, and Downtown are popular among tourists.

Hostels and Shared Spaces: If you're staying in a hostel or shared accommodation, it can be a great way to meet other travelers and share tips and experiences.

3. Plan Your Itinerary

Flexible Schedule: While it's good to have a plan, leave room for spontaneity. NYC has a lot to offer, and some of the best experiences come from unplanned discoveries.

Prioritize Must-Sees: List the top attractions you want to visit and plan your days around them. This ensures you don't miss out on key experiences.

4. Stay Safe

Personal Safety: Keep your belongings secure and be cautious of your surroundings, especially in crowded areas and late at night. Avoid displaying expensive items like jewelry and large amounts of cash.

Emergency Contacts: Familiarize yourself with local emergency numbers and know the locations of nearby police stations and hospitals.

5. Use Public Transportation

Subway and Buses: The subway system is efficient and safe, but be cautious during late hours. Buses are also a good option for exploring above ground. Always check schedules and routes before heading out.

Avoid Late-Night Travel: If you're traveling late at night, consider using rideshare services or taxis rather than the subway.

6. Engage with Locals

Ask for Recommendations: New Yorkers are generally friendly and can offer great advice on places to eat, visit, and explore. Don't hesitate to ask for recommendations or directions.

Participate in Tours: Joining group tours or walking tours can be a great way to meet other travelers and get insider tips on the city.

7. Embrace Solo Dining

Solo Dining: Don't be afraid to dine alone. NYC has a vibrant food scene, and many restaurants are welcoming to solo diners. Consider sitting at the bar or café counters where interactions are more casual.

Food Tours: Participate in food tours or cooking classes to explore local cuisine and meet fellow food enthusiasts.

8. Be Mindful of Your Health

Stay Hydrated and Eat Well: Make sure to drink plenty of water and eat balanced meals to keep your energy levels up while exploring the city.

Rest Periods: Take breaks when needed. NYC is a bustling city, and it's important to rest and recharge to fully enjoy your trip.

9. Explore at Your Own Pace

Solo Exploration: Enjoy the freedom of exploring the city at your own pace. Visit museums, parks, and neighborhoods that interest you without the need to accommodate others' schedules.

Self-Care: Take time to relax and engage in activities you enjoy, whether it's reading in a park, enjoying a spa day, or taking a leisurely stroll.

10. Document Your Journey

Travel Journal: Keep a travel journal or blog to document your experiences and reflections. It's a great way to remember your solo adventure and share it with friends and family.

Photography: Capture memories with photos, but be mindful of your surroundings when taking pictures, especially in crowded or sensitive areas.

11. Trust Your Instincts

Stay Alert: Trust your instincts and avoid situations or areas that make you uncomfortable. If something doesn't feel right, it's best to remove yourself from the situation.

Know When to Seek Help: If you're lost or need assistance, don't hesitate to seek help from local authorities or trusted individuals.

Grace Bennett

How to Avoid Tourist Traps

1. Research Before You Go

Read Reviews: Look up reviews and ratings on sites like TripAdvisor, Yelp, and Google Reviews to gauge the quality of attractions and restaurants.

Seek Local Recommendations: Use forums like Reddit, or local blogs, and ask New Yorkers for advice on where to go and where to avoid.

2. Avoid Peak Tourist Areas During Peak Times

Popular Spots: Iconic places like Times Square, the Empire State Building, and Broadway shows are often crowded, especially during peak hours. Visit early in the morning or late in the evening to avoid the crowds.

Timing: Plan your visits to major attractions during off-peak times, such as weekdays or early mornings.

3. Be Wary of High Prices

Restaurants: Tourist-heavy restaurants, especially those near major landmarks, often have inflated prices. Look for dining options a few blocks away from tourist attractions for better prices and authentic cuisine.

Souvenirs: Souvenir shops in high-traffic areas tend to be overpriced. Consider shopping in local neighborhoods or markets for more reasonably priced and unique items.

4. Look for Free or Low-Cost Alternatives

Free Attractions: NYC offers many free or low-cost attractions. Explore Central Park, visit public museums on their free admission days, or attend free events and festivals.

Walking Tours: Consider free walking tours or self-guided tours to explore neighborhoods and landmarks without the high cost of commercial tours.

5. Avoid Generic Chain Restaurants

Local Dining: Instead of dining at generic chain restaurants, seek out local eateries and food trucks. Use apps like Yelp or Google Maps to find highly-rated, lesser-known places.

Neighborhoods: Explore diverse neighborhoods like the Lower East Side, Brooklyn, and Queens for unique dining experiences that offer a taste of the city's culinary diversity.

6. Check for Hidden Fees

Attraction Fees: Some attractions have hidden fees or mandatory charges. Read the fine print on tickets and be aware of additional costs such as service fees or booking charges.

Tours: Be cautious of tours that promise more than they deliver or those that have unexpected additional costs. Check reviews and what's included before booking.

7. Beware of Overly Aggressive Vendors

Street Vendors: In tourist-heavy areas, be cautious of vendors who aggressively promote their products or services. It's better to avoid these interactions and seek out recommendations from trusted sources.

Times Square: Watch out for people dressed as characters or performers who may ask for tips or charge for photos. Enjoy the spectacle but be mindful of any financial expectations.

8. Use Public Transportation Wisely

Avoid Cabs in Traffic: During rush hours, taxis can be stuck in traffic and cost more. Opt for the subway or buses for quicker and more cost-effective travel.

Know Your Route: Familiarize yourself with the subway and bus routes to avoid getting lost or taking longer routes than necessary.

9. Explore Beyond Manhattan

Other Boroughs: Manhattan is packed with tourist spots, but exploring other boroughs like Brooklyn, Queens, and the Bronx can provide a more authentic and diverse experience.

Local Neighborhoods: Discover neighborhoods like Williamsburg, Astoria, and the Upper West Side for a taste of local life and culture.

10. Be Prepared for Marketing Gimmicks

Timeshare Sales: Be wary of offers for free tickets or discounted tours that require a time-consuming sales pitch. These can often be high-pressure tactics to sell timeshares or other services.

Street Performers: Enjoy street performances but be prepared for the expectation of tips. Always have some cash on hand if you want to support performers.

What to Do in Case of Emergencies

1. Medical Emergencies

Emergency Services: Call 911 immediately for medical emergencies. This will connect you to police, fire, and medical services. Operators can provide instructions and dispatch help.

Emergency Rooms: If you need urgent medical care but it's not life-threatening, you can visit an emergency room (ER) or urgent care center. Major hospitals like NewYork-Presbyterian and Mount Sinai have ERs that are open 24/7.

Pharmacies: For non-urgent medical needs, such as prescriptions or over-the-counter medicine, visit a pharmacy like CVS or Walgreens, which are widely available throughout the city.

2. Lost or Stolen Items

Report Theft: If your belongings are lost or stolen, report it to the local police precinct. You can find the nearest precinct on the NYPD website or by asking locals.

Credit Cards: Contact your bank or credit card company immediately to report stolen cards and prevent unauthorized transactions. They can cancel the card and issue a replacement.

3. Lost Passports or Identification

Contact Your Embassy: If your passport or ID is lost or stolen, contact your country's embassy or consulate in New York City. They can assist with emergency travel documents and provide guidance on next steps.

NYPD Report: File a report with the NYPD, which may be required for obtaining new documents.

4. Natural Disasters

Weather Alerts: Monitor local news and weather apps for updates on severe weather, such as hurricanes, snowstorms, or floods. The NYC Office of Emergency Management provides real-time alerts and safety information.

Evacuation Plans: Follow instructions from local authorities regarding evacuation routes and shelters. Familiarize yourself with emergency evacuation procedures for your accommodation.

5. Fire Emergencies

Fire Safety: If you encounter a fire, use the nearest exit and avoid using elevators. If trapped, signal for help from a window and stay low to avoid smoke inhalation.

Fire Department: Call 911 to report a fire or if you see smoke. The FDNY (Fire Department of New York) responds to fire emergencies.

6. Crime and Safety Concerns

Report Crime: If you witness or are involved in a crime, contact the police immediately by calling 911. For non-urgent crime reports, you can visit a local precinct or use the NYPD's online reporting system.

Personal Safety: If you feel unsafe or threatened, seek help from nearby businesses or public spaces, and contact local authorities.

7. Transportation Issues

Subway Disruptions: If the subway or bus system is disrupted, check the MTA website or app for real-time updates and alternative routes.

Lost Property: For lost items on public transportation, contact the MTA Lost and Found department. Items left on subways, buses, or trains can often be retrieved through their system.

8. Financial Issues

Emergency Funds: In case of financial emergencies, such as losing access to funds, visit a local bank branch for assistance. Some banks offer emergency services for travelers.

Travel Insurance: If you have travel insurance, contact your provider for assistance with emergencies, including medical issues, trip cancellations, or lost items.

9. Language Barriers

Interpreter Services: If you have difficulty communicating due to a language barrier, ask for assistance at hospitals, police stations, or emergency services. Many locations have multilingual staff or access to interpreter services.

10. General Safety Tips

Stay Informed: Keep up-to-date with local news and alerts through apps and news websites. Follow guidance from local authorities and the U.S. State Department if needed.

Emergency Contacts: Have a list of important contacts, including local emergency services, your embassy, and family or friends back home.

Useful Travel Apps

1. Navigation and Maps

Google Maps: Offers detailed maps, real-time navigation, and public transportation routes. Useful for finding directions, nearby attractions, and local businesses.

Citymapper: Provides comprehensive transit information, including subway, bus, and bike routes. Great for planning your journeys and understanding the best travel options.

MTA Subway Map: An official app from the Metropolitan Transportation Authority (MTA) that provides subway maps, real-time updates, and service alerts.

2. Public Transportation

Transit: A handy app for real-time transit information, including bus and subway schedules, route planning, and alerts. It covers multiple transit systems and provides accurate arrival times.

Uber/Lyft: Rideshare apps for convenient car services throughout the city. Useful for getting a ride quickly and tracking your driver.

3. Dining and Food

Yelp: Offers reviews, ratings, and photos of restaurants, cafes, and bars. Helps you find highly recommended dining spots and avoid tourist traps.

OpenTable: Allows you to make restaurant reservations and discover new places to eat. Great for planning ahead and securing a table at popular spots.

Grubhub: For food delivery and takeout from a wide range of restaurants. Perfect for ordering food to your accommodation or while on the go.

4. Attractions and Activities

TripAdvisor: Provides reviews, ratings, and information on attractions, tours, and activities. Useful for planning your itinerary and finding popular destinations.

Eventbrite: Lists local events, concerts, and activities happening in the city. Helps you find things to do based on your interests and schedule.

5. Accommodation

Booking.com: Offers a wide range of accommodation options, from luxury hotels to budget stays. Includes reviews, photos, and easy booking features.

Airbnb: For booking unique stays, such as apartments or rooms in local homes. Useful for finding more personalized lodging options.

6. Currency and Budgeting

XE Currency: Provides real-time currency conversion rates. Useful for managing your budget and understanding costs in your home currency.

Mint: Helps track your expenses and manage your budget. Ideal for keeping an eye on your spending while traveling.

7. Safety and Emergency

Smart Traveler: Offers travel advisories and safety information from the U.S. State Department. Useful for staying informed about safety conditions and emergency procedures.

Red Cross First Aid: Provides first aid instructions and emergency guidance. Helpful for basic medical advice and knowing what to do in emergencies.

8. Language and Communication

Google Translate: Useful for translating text and speech in different languages. Handy for overcoming language barriers and communicating with locals.

iTranslate: Offers translation and dictionary services for multiple languages. Helps with understanding signs, menus, and conversations.

9. Connectivity

WiFi Finder: Helps you locate free and public WiFi hotspots in the city. Ideal for staying connected without using your mobile data.

T-Mobile WiFi: If you're a T-Mobile customer, this app provides access to millions of WiFi hotspots around the city.

10. Local Experiences

Guides by Lonely Planet: Provides detailed guides and tips for exploring New York City. Includes recommendations for sights, dining, and local experiences.

Culture Trip: Offers curated recommendations for local attractions, restaurants, and cultural experiences. Helps you discover unique aspects of the city.

THE END!!!

Printed in Great Britain
by Amazon